Windows 10 for Seniors for the Beginning Computer User

Studio Visual Steps

Windows 10
for Seniors
for the Beginning
Computer User

Get started with Windows 10

www.visualsteps.com

This book has been written using the Visual Steps™ method.
Cover design by Studio Willemien Haagsma bNO

© 2015 Visual Steps
Author: Studio Visual Steps

First printing: August 2015
ISBN 978 90 5905 461 5

Resources used: Some of the computer terms and definitions seen here in this book have been taken from descriptions found online at the Windows Help and Support website.

Do you have questions or suggestions?
Email: info@visualsteps.com

Would you like more information?
www.visualsteps.com

Website for this book:
www.visualsteps.com/windows10senior

Table of Contents

Foreword

We wrote this book in order to introduce seniors to the computer. We will show you the basics of the operating system *Windows 10*, step by step. Use this book right next to your computer or laptop as you work through each chapter at your own pace. You will be amazed how easy it is to learn this way.

After completing this book, you will be able to startup a program or an app, write a letter, surf the Internet and send an email, view pictures and much more.

This book makes use of the Visual Steps™ method specifically developed for adult learners by Addo Stuur. You do not need any prior computing experience to use this book.

We hope you will enjoy reading this book!

The Studio Visual Steps authors

P.S.
When you have completed this book, you will know how to send an email. Your comments and suggestions are most welcome. Our email address is:
mail@visualsteps.com

Visual Steps Newsletter

All Visual Steps books follow the same methodology: clear and concise step-by-step instructions with screen shots to demonstrate each task.
A complete list of all our books can be found on our website **www.visualsteps.com**

You can also sign up to receive our **free Visual Steps Newsletter**.
In this Newsletter you will receive periodic information by email regarding:
- the latest titles and previously released books;
- special offers, supplemental chapters, tips and free informative booklets.
Also, our Newsletter subscribers may download any of the documents listed on the web page **www.visualsteps.com/info_downloads**

When you subscribe to our Newsletter you can be assured that we will never use your email address for any purpose other than sending you the information as previously described. We will not share this address with any third-party. Each Newsletter also contains a one-click link to unsubscribe.

Introduction to Visual Steps™

The Visual Steps handbooks and manuals are the best instructional materials available for learning how to work with the computer. Nowhere else can you find better support for getting to know your *Windows* computer or *Mac*, your iPad or iPhone, Samsung Galaxy Tab, the Internet and a variety of computer applications.

Properties of the Visual Steps books:
- **Comprehensible contents**
  Addresses the needs of the beginner or intermediate user for a manual written in simple, straight-forward English.
- **Clear structure**
  Precise, easy to follow instructions. The material is broken down into small enough segments to allow for easy absorption.
- **Screen shots of every step**
  Quickly compare what you see on your screen with the screen shots in the book. Pointers and tips guide you when new windows or alert boxes are opened so you always know what to do next.
- **Get started right away**
  All you have to do is turn on your computer or laptop and have your book at hand. Perform each operation as indicated on your own device.
- **Layout**
  The text is printed in a large size font and is clearly legible.

In short, I believe these manuals will be excellent guides for you.

dr. H. van der Meij
Faculty of Applied Education, Department of Instructional Technology, University of Twente, the Netherlands

What You Will Need

To be able to work through this book, you will need a number of things:

The primary requirement for working with this book is having the US or English version of *Windows 10* installed on your computer or laptop. *Windows* comes equipped with all the programs you need to work with this book. This book is not suitable for tablets.

Please note: The screen shots shown in this book have been made using a local user account. It is also possible to login with a *Microsoft* account. Since this is a book for beginning computer users, we have chosen to not to use this type of account.

If you are working with a *Microsoft* account, you will sometimes see different windows and other options.

It's also important to work with an up-to-date computer. You will learn how to update in *section 9.5 Windows Update*.

 A functioning Internet connection.

You also need:

 A computer mouse. To perform the actions and exercises shown in this book, it is necessary to have a mouse installed.

Do you have a laptop without a mouse? You can buy one in a computer store or other retail outlet. A salesperson can show you how to connect the mouse to a laptop, so that you can get started right away at home.
Learning how to work with a mouse is useful for later on when you want to work on a new or different computer.

 Would you also like to learn to work with the touchpad of your laptop? The *Bonus Chapter Working with a Touchpad* explains step by step how to use a touchpad.
You can read how to open this chapter in *Appendix D Opening the Bonus Online Chapters*.

 Do you have a touchscreen? It is still advisable learn to work with the mouse first. In *Bonus Chapter Working with a touchscreen* you will read how to operate *Windows* with a touchscreen. You can read how to open this chapter in *Appendix D Opening the Bonus Online Chapters*.

The following things are useful. But it is not a problem if you do not have them. You can read through the sections where these items are used.

 A USB stick (also called a USB memory stick or memory stick). You will use this to save files when you work with *Chapter 5 Files and Folders*. A USB stick with a storage capacity of 2 GB is more than enough.

 A printer is required for some of the exercises. If you do not have a printer, you can skip these exercises.

 A music CD are needed for *Chapter 8 Introduction to Photos, Video and Music*.

You will need a digital camera to practice transferring photos from the camera to the computer.

Prior Computer Experience

You do not need any prior computing experience in order to use this book. This book is intended for seniors who have seldom or never used a computer or laptop. Topics like working with a mouse and keyboard and starting up programs are all presented in an easy, step by step manner.

How To Use This Book

This book has been written using the Visual Steps™ method. The method is simple: just place the book next to your computer or laptop and execute all the tasks step by step, directly on your own device. With the clear instructions and the multitude of screen shots, you will always know exactly what to do. This is the quickest way to become familiar with *Windows 10* and use the various programs and services it offers.

In this Visual Steps™ book, you will see various icons. This is what they mean:

Techniques
These icons indicate an action to be carried out:

The mouse icon means you need to do something with the mouse.

The keyboard icon means you should type something on your keyboard.

The hand icon means you should do something else, for example, turn on the computer or carry out a task previously learned.

In addition to these icons, in some areas of this book extra assistance is provided to help you successfully work through each chapter.

Help
These icons indicate that extra help is available:

The arrow icon warns you about something.

The bandage icon will help you if something has gone wrong.

Have you forgotten how to do something? The number next to the footsteps tells you where to look it up at the end of the book in the appendix *How Do I Do That Again?*

In this book you will also find a lot of general information, and tips. This information is displayed in separate boxes.

Extra information
Information boxes are denoted by these icons:

 The book icon gives you extra background information that you can read at your convenience. This extra information is not necessary for working through the book.

 The light bulb icon indicates an extra tip for using a program or service.

The Website Accompanying This Book

On the website that accompanies this book, you will find additional information about this book along with the Bonus Online Chapters and instructional videos. Please, take a look at the website from time to time. The website is **www.visualsteps.com/windows10senior**

Instructional Videos

On the website that accompanies this book you will find instructional videos that illustrate some of the key concepts explained in the book. Each video refers to a specific section in the book. You will recognize a video to ▥.
You can read how to view this videos in *Appendix E Opening the Instructional Videos.*

Test Your Knowledge

After you have worked through this book, you can test your knowledge online, on the **www.ccforseniors.com** website. By answering a number of multiple choice questions you will be able to test your knowledge. After you have finished the test, you will receive a *Computer Certificate.*
Participating in the test is **free of charge**. The computer certificate website is a free service from Visual Steps.

For Teachers

This book is designed as a self-study guide. It is also well suited for use in a group or a classroom setting. For this purpose, we offer a free teacher's manual containing information about how to prepare for the course (including didactic teaching methods) and testing materials. You can download the teacher's manual (PDF file) from the website which accompanies this book: **www.visualsteps.com/windows10senior**

The Screen Shots

The screen shots used in this book indicate which button, folder, file or hyperlink you need to click on your computer screen. In the instruction text (in **bold** letters) you will see a small image of the item you need to click. The line will point you to the right place on your screen.
The small screen shots that are printed in this book are not meant to be completely legible all the time. This is not necessary, as you will see these images on your own computer screen in real size and fully legible.

Here you see an example of an instruction text and a screen shot. The line indicates where to find this item on your own computer screen:

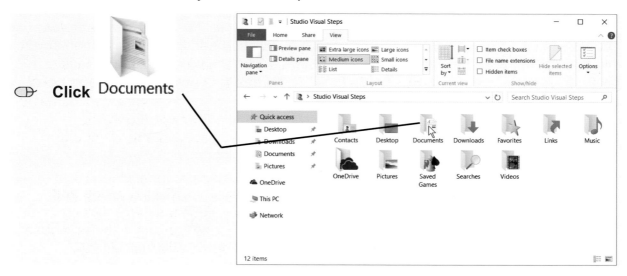

Sometimes the screen shot shows only a portion of a window. Here is an example:

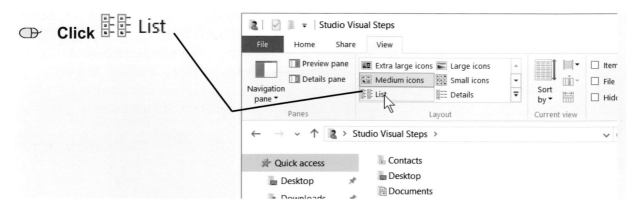

It really will **not be necessary** for you to read all the information in the screen shots in this book. Always use the screen shots in combination with the image you see on your own computer screen.

1. Starting Windows 10

You are all set and ready to go. You have this book on hand, set close to your computer, so you can get started right away with the exercises in this book. Working like this is the fastest way to learn how to work with a computer. At the beginning of each chapter you will find a brief explanatory text such as this one, which will provide you with background information. Also, a brief overview will give you an idea of the topics covered and what you can expect to learn.

The computer on your desk is also called a PC. PC stands for *personal computer*. About 30 years ago, computers were mostly used in business. Nowadays, nearly everyone has a computer at home. And lots of people have a tablet too. This is a kind of computer that is operated by using your fingers to touch the screen. In order to operate a computer you need an operating system. The operating system installed on your computer is called *Windows 10*. *Windows 10* is manufactured by the American *Microsoft* company. You will undoubtedly have heard of this company before.

Windows lets you perform various tasks on your computer, such as opening and closing a computer program, for instance. You carry out these tasks by clicking something with a computer mouse. You will need to practice clicking with the mouse first, if you want to become adept at it. This is what you are going to do in this chapter.

This book is aimed at aspiring computer users who have not worked with a computer before. This means we will explain how to turn a computer on, how to hold the mouse and move it around, and all other sorts of things that are new to you. Take all the time you need to practice. For example, it is very normal that you feel a bit uneasy when you use a computer mouse for the first time.
You will notice that this will improve gradually step by step. Do not hesitate to repeat the exercises in a chapter, if you want to get some additional practice.

After you have read this first chapter, you will understand why this operating system is called *Windows*. You will see that many elements on your screen are displayed in 'windows'.

In this chapter you will learn how to:

- start and stop *Windows 10*;
- point and click the mouse;

- use the desktop;
- open and close programs and apps;
- minimize and maximize a window;
- use the taskbar.

1.1 Desktop Computer or Laptop

Computers come in different sizes and shapes. Desktop computers are designed for use on a desk or table. Desktop computers consist of separate components.

This is a desktop computer:

Monitor:

Computer case or housing:

Keyboard:

Mouse:

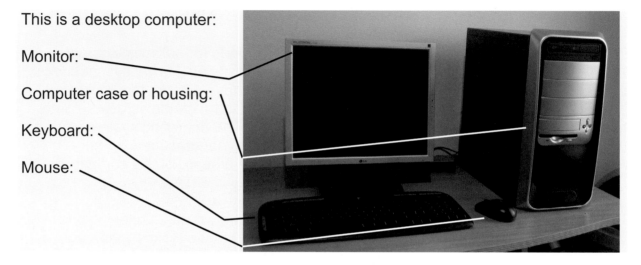

Laptop computers are lightweight portable PCs. They are often called *notebook computers* because of their small size. Laptops can operate on batteries, so you can take them anywhere, even if you do not have a power outlet. Of course, you can also use a laptop computer on your desk. The screen folds down onto the keyboard when not in use. Laptops combine all computer components in a single case.

This is a laptop computer:

Screen:

Keyboard:

Touchpad:

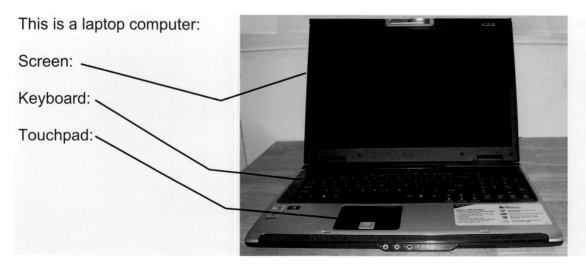

Operating *Windows 10* on either type of computer is the same. It does not matter whether you use a desktop or a laptop.

In order to use your computer, you first need to turn it on. You will learn how to do this in the next section.

1.2 Turning on Your Desktop Computer or Laptop

You turn on your computer by pressing the power button found on the case. Turn on your monitor by pressing its power button. You will see this symbol 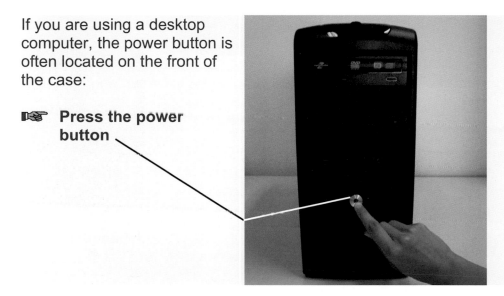 on or near this button.

If you are using a desktop computer, the power button is often located on the front of the case:

☞ **Press the power button**

With some desktop computers you need to turn on the monitor separately. If you do not see anything happening on your monitor after a few moments then your monitor most likely has not yet been turned on:

☞ **Press the monitor's power button**

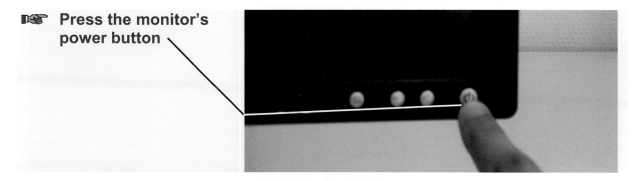

Your computer is now turned on.

On a laptop, the power button is most likely found on the keyboard. You can easily identify this button by this symbol: ⏻.

The laptop in this example has a power button that looks like this:

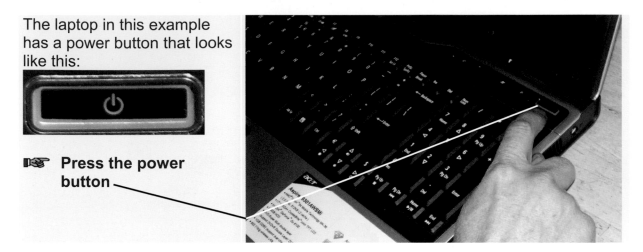

☞ **Press the power button**

Now the laptop is turned on. The laptop screen does not need to be turned on separately.

🩹 HELP! I cannot find the power button.

If you are unable to locate the power button, consult your computer's instruction manual. Usually this will tell you where the power button is.

1.3 Starting Windows 10

Windows 10 will automatically start as soon as you turn on your computer.

After a short while you will see a screen that looks like this:

This is called the *lock screen*.

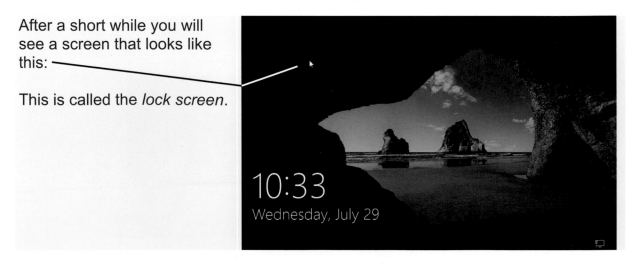

➥ Please note:

The images of the *Windows* screens and windows in this book may differ from what you see on your own screen. That is because every computer user can determine how his or her *Windows* screen or window will look. Some computer manufacturers will also adapt the screens sometimes, so they will look different.
But this will not affect the operation of *Windows* at all. You can just keep on working, even if your screen looks a bit different.

On the screen below you see an image:

Somewhere on your screen

you will see a white arrow.

In this example, the arrow is on the left-hand side:

This arrow may be shown on a different area of your own screen.

This arrow is called the pointer, mouse pointer, or mouse arrow. We will use the term *pointer* in this book.

You can move this pointer across the screen by moving the computer mouse over the table top or desktop. In this chapter you will learn how to do this.

1.4 Mouse, Touchpad or Touchscreen

The pointer can be used as if it were your fingertip. You use it to 'point' to things on the screen such as the icons on the screen. You can move the pointer in any direction on your computer screen. Then you can 'click' the items to perform various actions. This is done with a computer mouse, often referred as simply 'mouse'.

A desktop computer will usually be supplied with a computer mouse:

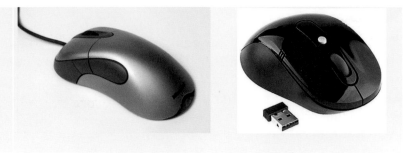

There are many types of designs and options available. They come with a cable or are wireless.

If you are working with a laptop, you can choose whether to operate it with a computer mouse or use the built in touchpad. The touchpad is a sensitive square which reacts when you move your fingertip across it. The movement of your finger on the touchpad is transferred to the computer and this makes the pointer move across your screen.

Here you see the touchpad for this laptop:

A different brand of laptop can have a touchpad that looks slightly different.

The most recent development in screen technology is the *touchscreen*, a screen that is sensitive to the touch of your fingers. A touchscreen looks the same as a regular screen. More and more laptops and desktop computers are equipped with a touchscreen.

If you have a touchscreen you can operate the computer by touching the screen with specific *gestures*. These touchscreen gestures consist of moving one or two fingers across the screen. You could say your fingers act like a mouse. Airline ticket kiosks and ATMs work with touchscreens too, nowadays.

If you are using a laptop for the first time it is good idea to purchase a mouse to go along with it. In this book you will learn how to use a mouse. The advantage is you will be able to use other computers later on.

➥ Please note:

In this book you will learn how to use a computer mouse. If you do not yet have a mouse you can purchase one at your local computer or electronics store.

♀ Tip
Buy a mouse
When you buy a computer mouse at the computer store, ask the sales representative if he can show you how to connect your new mouse to a laptop. Then when you get home you can get started right away.

Here you see a laptop with a computer mouse attached with a cable:

On the back or side of the laptop is a slot in which you can fit the mouse cable's jack.

You can also buy a wireless computer mouse. Instead of the cable connection, a wireless mouse uses a small transmitter that is inserted into the computer, often in one of the USB slots.

♀ Tip
Learn how to use a touchpad or touchscreen
Do you want to learn how to work with a touchpad or touchscreen? Download the *Bonus chapters Working With a Touchpad* and *Working With a Touchscreen* from the website accompanying this book, **www.visualsteps.com/windows10senior**, to learn how to do so. In *Appendix D Opening the Bonus Online Chapters* you can read how to open these bonus chapters on your computer. We advise you to do this only after you have learned how to use the Internet. Or ask someone who is already proficient in using the computer and the Internet to download and print the bonus chapters for you.

1.5 The Computer Mouse

A computer mouse is usually just called a mouse. The mouse sits on your desk or table. The mouse is designed to fit comfortably in the palm of your hand.

Place your mouse beside your keyboard on a clean, smooth surface.

This may be the surface of a table or desk, or a special mousepad.

Hold the mouse gently with your index finger resting on the left button and your thumb resting on the side.

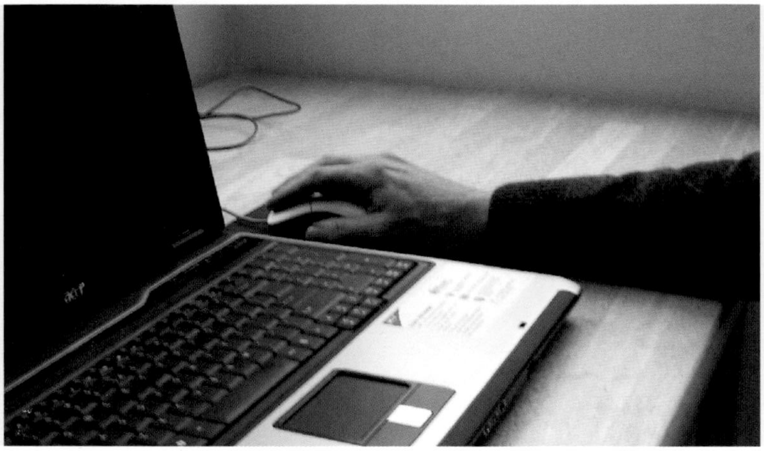

A mousepad is a smooth, square surface for enhancing the movement of a computer mouse. It is not absolutely necessary. You can also use your mouse on a smooth, clean surface such as the table or desk where your computer is located.

Tip

What is the best way to hold the mouse?

Not like this:

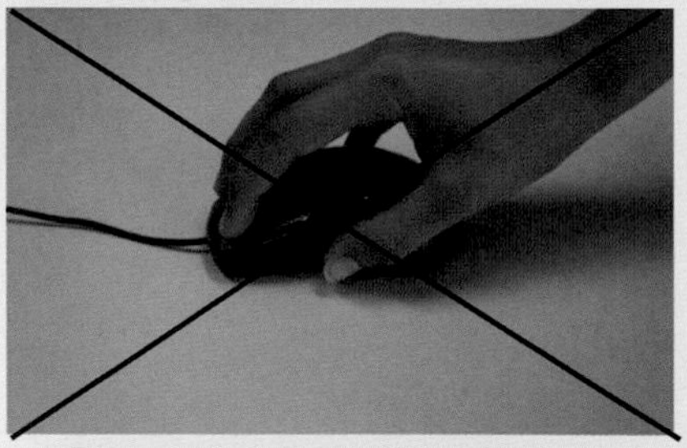

- Do not grasp it between two fingers with the other fingers in the air.
- Do not lift your wrist from the tabletop.
- Do not squeeze or grip your mouse tightly.
- Do not lift the mouse.

But like this:

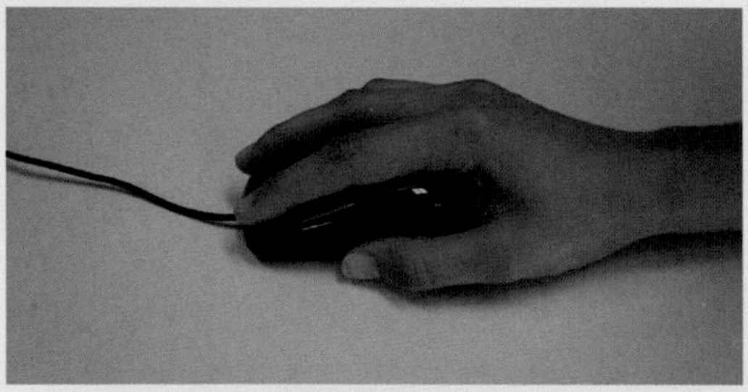

- Hold the mouse gently.
- Hold the palm of your hand lightly on the mouse.
- Your hand follows the shape of the mouse.
- Allow your index finger to gently rest on the left mouse button and keep the other fingers relaxed on top of the mouse and to the side.
- Rest your thumb on the left side of the mouse.
- Rest your wrist and lower arm on the table.
- The mouse buttons are aimed away from you.

- Continue on the next page -

It is important to teach yourself the proper way to hold the mouse from the very beginning. You will only have sufficient control of the mouse and be able to move it precisely if you keep it in the palm of your hand.

1.6 Moving the Mouse

You can operate the computer almost entirely with the mouse alone. This can feel a bit awkward in the beginning as you practice using the mouse, but the more you use it, the more skillful you will become.

In order to move the pointer on the screen, you need to move the mouse. You can do this by moving the mouse gently to the left or right across the table. Just try it:

Somewhere on your screen

you will see the pointer:

☞ **Move the mouse over the table**

The pointer will move along.

If the mouse slides off the mouse pad, or if you do not have enough space to move the mouse any further, you can simply lift the mouse a bit and put it back down somewhere else. Then you can continue moving it. Remember to let your hand rest lightly on the mouse. Your index finger rests on the left mouse button. Your thumb rests against the left side the mouse. You will not need to press any buttons, we will leave this for later.

Somewhere on your screen

you will see the pointer:

Keep watching it.

☞ **Move the mouse to the left or right across the table**

The pointer will move along:

Notice that when you move the mouse, the pointer on the screen moves in the same direction.

➥ Please note:

Move the mouse by moving your forearm from the elbow onwards. Avoid rotating your wrist. By moving the mouse as described above in a relaxed fashion, you may be able to prevent RSI complaints. RSI can develop by repetitive movements of your joints over prolonged periods of time.

HELP! I see a different screen.

You may have accidentally pressed one of the mouse buttons. You will now see a different screen, but you can still perform the operations in this section on that screen as well.

Move the mouse gently back and forth across the table

The pointer on your screen moves along in the same direction:

Slowly move the mouse to the right

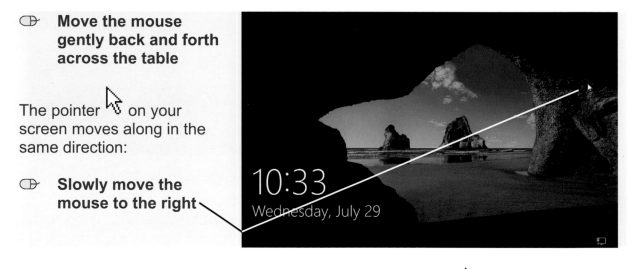

When you move the mouse in a different direction, the pointer will also move

along in the same direction. Keep watching the pointer on the screen as you move the mouse around.

- **Slowly move the mouse towards the computer screen**

- **Slowly move the mouse away from the computer screen**

The pointer on the screen moves along in the same direction:

10:33
Wednesday, July 29

Please note:

If the mouse slides off the mouse pad or bumps into something, you can just lift it a bit and put it back in another spot. Then you can continue moving the mouse.

- **Slowly move the mouse around in a circle**

Just try making small and large circles.

- **Move the mouse around in the shape of a triangle**

First, create small triangles, and then bigger ones.
Keep watching the pointer on the screen as you move the mouse.

10:33
Wednesday, July 29

It is a good idea to keep repeating these movements until you have sufficient control of handling the mouse. Then you can continue with the next sections.

Please note:

Gently rest your hand on the mouse. Watch the position of your index finger and thumb. Rest your forearm and wrist on the table.

1.7 The Four Mouse Operations

You can use your mouse to interact with objects on your computer screen. Most mouse actions combine pointing with pressing one of the mouse buttons. Pointing to an object on the screen means that you move your mouse until the pointer ▷ touches that object. Then you can use one of the mouse buttons to perform a certain command.

There are four types of actions that can be done with the mouse buttons that will allow you to perform specific tasks:

- click (single-click);
- double-click;
- right-click;
- drag.

You can move objects, select them, open them, edit them, close them, or even remove them by using one of these mouse actions. You can instruct your computer to perform different tasks by using these actions. In the following section, for example, you will learn how to point and click with your mouse.

1.8 The Mouse Buttons

A computer mouse comes in various shapes, types and models. The thing they all have in common is that they are equipped with at least two mouse buttons.

The main button is the *left mouse button*:

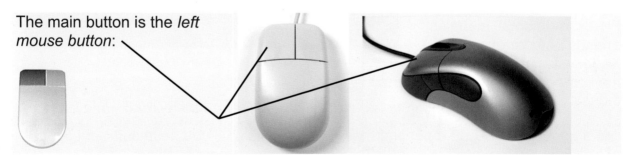

Mouse buttons are made to be pressed and released. This is called *clicking*. You can hear a clicking sound when you press one of the buttons.

1.9 Clicking

Clicking is the mouse action you will use the most. You can read here a little more about clicking. You do not have to do any clicking yet. Clicking is done like this:

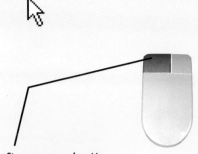

- Position the mouse pointer on the object.
- Hold the mouse gently, with your index finger resting on the left button
- Then briefly press the *left mouse button* and immediately release it.

Left mouse button

Now try this yourself:

☞ **Press the left mouse button briefly, just once**

When you press the mouse you will hear a clicking sound.

Once you have clicked, the screen will change. You will see a window, such as the next picture. This will not be the same window on every computer.

1.10 Pointing

Now you can practice pointing to an *icon* (small picture) on the screen. Pointing to something means moving the mouse across the screen until the pointer is positioned on top of a specific object such as an icon.

You will see small pictures on the screen on the next page. These pictures are called icons. You may see multiple icons on your screen, or perhaps just one. The icons may also look a little different and have different names. The color of your screen can also be different, but none of these things will hinder you in any way as you simply practice pointing with your mouse.

You will see the login screen:

Your name may already appear here: ─────

Or you may not see your name. In both cases you can follow the instructions below.

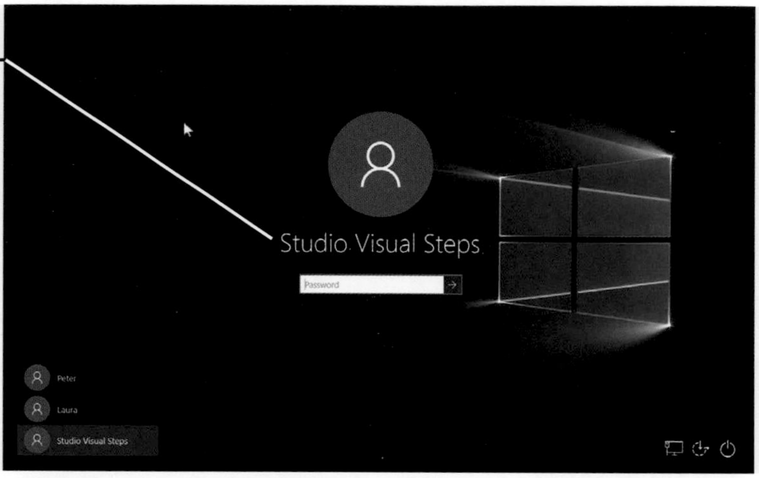

☞ **Slowly move the pointer 🖰 to the  icon with your name**

☞ **Stop moving when the pointer is on top of the icon** ─────

Now the pointer 🖰 is on top of the icon.

Notice that the background of the icon changes a bit.

Now the pointer is on top of the icon. If you did not succeed right away, just try again.

Make sure your hand is gently holding the mouse as your index finger rests above the left mouse button or when pressing the button. At the same time, your thumb is gently holding the left side of the mouse and your forearm rests on the table. When the pointer is on top of the icon, you can click it.

✚ HELP! I do not see these icons.

In this example you also see two small icons in the lower left corner of your screen. This means that multiple user accounts have been set up on this computer. A user account provides access to the computer.

If you do not see any icons in the lower left corner of your screen, you can skip this step and continue on page 34.

HELP! I see the screen of the previous page again.

You may see the lock screen again after a while. To display the login screen again:

☞ **Press the left mouse button gently just once**

☞ **Slowly move the pointer** ↖ **towards the icon** 👤 **with your name**

Loosely hold the mouse and rest your index finger on the left mouse button. At this point you should not move the mouse anymore. Now you are going to click the left mouse button:

☞ **If necessary, move the pointer** ↖ **towards the icon** 👤 **with your name**

☞ **Press the left mouse button briefly, just once**

You will hear a clicking sound when you press the mouse button.

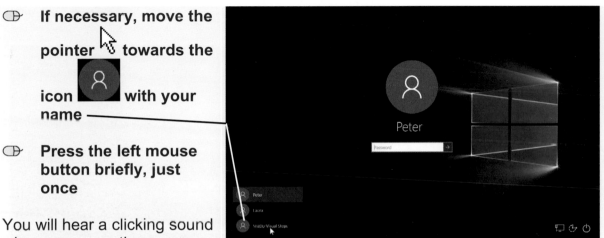

 HELP! The pointer moves away when I press the mouse button.

If the pointer on the screen moves away when you click, you may have accidentally moved the mouse. Try to keep your hand still when you click.

Please note these things:
- Loosely rest your hand on the mouse.
- Rest your index finger on the left mouse button.
- Place your thumb gently against the left side of the mouse.
- Rest your wrist and forearm on the table.

In this way you have the best control over your movements.

☞ **Try it again**

You need a password in order to continue.

The password needs to be typed in the white box:

Use the keyboard of your computer to type the password. Of course, you will need to know the right password. If you do not know the password, ask the owner of the computer.

⌨ **Type the password**

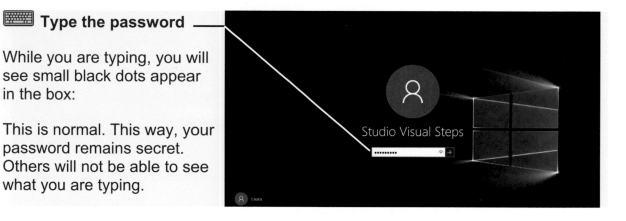

While you are typing, you will see small black dots appear in the box:

This is normal. This way, your password remains secret. Others will not be able to see what you are typing.

Once you have typed the password you can continue:

☞ **Place the pointer on**

→

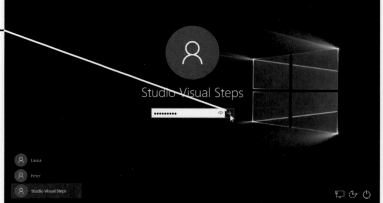

Click the mouse again:

☞ **Press the left mouse button briefly, just once**

You will hear the clicking sound again.

Once you have clicked, the screen will change.
Was it difficult to click the right spot at once? Then try again.

Try to keep your hand relaxed around the mouse as you hold your index finger on the left mouse button. Your thumb rests gently against the left side of the mouse and your forearm rests on the table. In this way you can maintain the best control over the mouse.

1.11 The Desktop

You will see a screen that is similar to the screen in this example. This screen is called the *desktop*.

The desktop shows a solid color in this example. You may see a landscape picture or something else on your own screen.

We use a simple, green desktop color in this book. This makes the screenshots clear and easy to view.

You can change the appearance of the desktop. Perhaps a previous user of this computer has already made changes to the desktop. This will not affect any of the following actions you need to perform.

At the bottom of the desktop you see a horizontal bar across the full width of the screen: ⎯⎯⎯⎯⎯

This bar is called the *taskbar*.

In the left corner of the taskbar you see the ⊞ icon. This is the Start button:

Next to the Home button you see a search function [icon] :

In this example there are four more buttons on the taskbar next to the search function: ——

The taskbar in this example is black, but it may be a different color on your own screen.

You can compare this desktop to an actual desktop. The desktop is the underlying base for everything you do on the computer. For example, if you open a program window, the window appears on top of the desktop.

1.12 Where Do I Place the Pointer?

If you place the pointer on an item, you will often see a small white box or label containing text. Just give it a try:

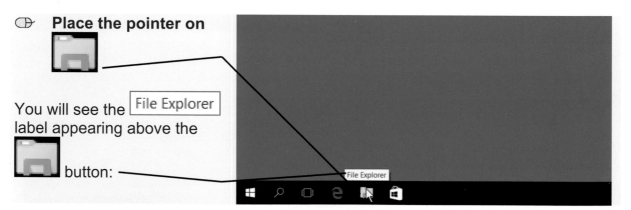

👆 **Place the pointer on** [icon]

You will see the ⎡File Explorer⎤ label appearing above the [icon] button: ——

These labels are used to explain the function of the button that goes with it. If you would click the *File Explorer* icon, for example, you would be able to view all the items on your computer and see which devices are connected. In *Chapter 5 Files and Folders* you will learn how to use the *File Explorer*.

1.13 Opening a Program or an App

Almost everything you do on a computer requires the use of a computer program. A computer program is usually just called a program, or an app. A computer program is a set of commands or instructions that tells the computer what to do in order to carry out certain tasks. There are many different kinds of programs and apps.

Windows 10 comes with a number of standard programs and apps that are built-in and already installed on your computer. In this book you will learn to use some of these programs and apps.

In this book you will come across two different names for a computer program: program and app. *App* is short for *application*, which actually means program. So an app is just another name for a program.

Sometimes, there is a distinction between a program and an app. Originally, an app was a program designed for use on a tablet or a smartphone. But in *Windows 10* you can also use apps on the computer. One of the main differences between the two, is that an app is often less extensive than a program, but not always. In this book you will be working with programs and apps.

As an example, you can take a look at the *Calculator* program. You will need to open it first. Here is how you do that:

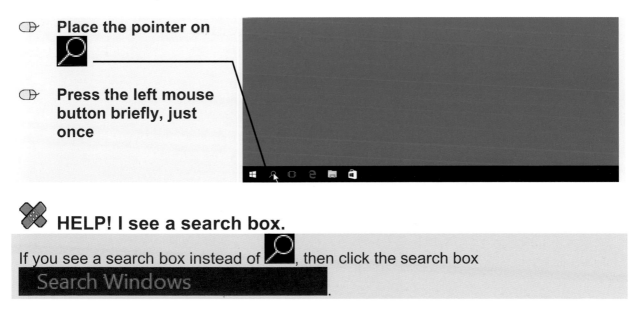

☞ **Place the pointer on**

☞ **Press the left mouse button briefly, just once**

✖ **HELP! I see a search box.**

If you see a search box instead of 🔍, then click the search box

Search Windows

Now you will be able to type letters. In the next image you can see where to find the three letters that you need on the keyboard:

You just need to briefly press the **C**, **A**, and **L** keys, one after the other:

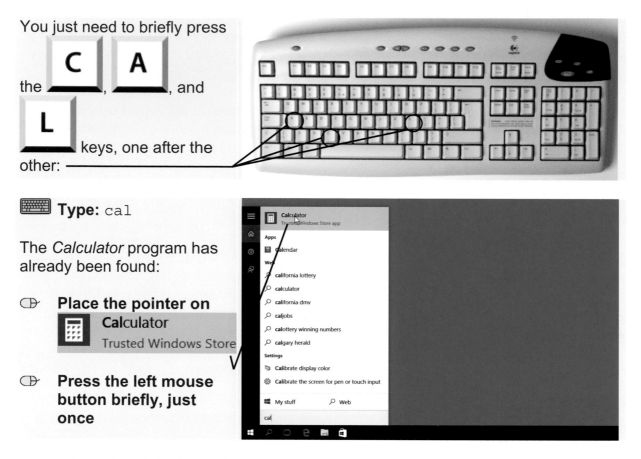

⌨ **Type:** cal

The *Calculator* program has already been found:

☞ **Place the pointer on** Calculator **Trusted Windows Store**

☞ **Press the left mouse button briefly, just once**

You will see the *Calculator* window appear on your desktop:

This is the *Calculator* window:

On the taskbar you will now

see this button ▦ :

This button is called a *taskbar button*.

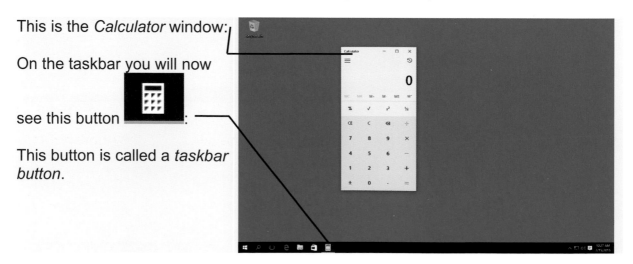

Later on in this chapter you will learn what you can do with this button.

HELP! I have opened the wrong program.

Have you accidentally clicked another program? Then you can close the window containing the program:

☞ **Place the pointer on the ✖ button in the upper right corner of the window**

☞ **Press the left mouse button just once**

Now the window of this accidentally opened program will be closed.

☞ **Follow the steps on this page once more, in order to open the *Calculator* program**

You have instructed the computer to open the *Calculator* program:

Here you see the window of the *Calculator* up close:

At the top of the window you see the *title bar*: ———

This bar contains the name of the Calculator program:

In the upper right corner of the window you see three buttons

— ▢ ✖:

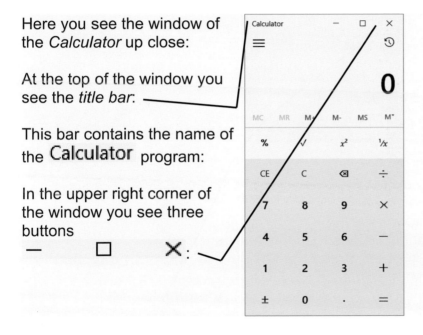

All the programs and apps you open will be displayed in a window on your desktop and all have the same — ▢ ✖ buttons on the title bar in the upper right corner.

1.14 A Menu

Programs will often contain a set of options or several sets of options that can be clicked. You click one of these options (commands) to carry out a certain task. The various options are usually found in menus. A menu is simply a list of the options available. It is visible only when you click a button or icon and hidden otherwise. You can see how this works in the *Calculator* program:

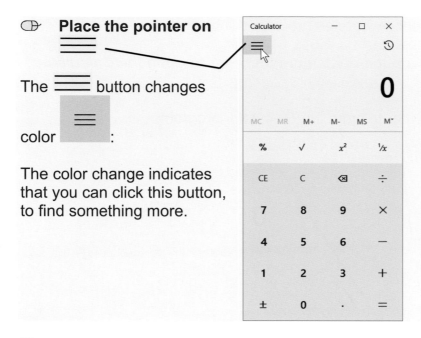

☞ **Place the pointer on** ≡

The ≡ button changes

color ≡ :

The color change indicates that you can click this button, to find something more.

🠖 **Please note:**

From now on, the tasks you need to perform in this book such as
☞ **Place the pointer on ...** plus ☞ **Press the left mouse button briefly, just once** will be replaced by the shorter version ☞ **Click**
This is easier to read, and by now you know what to do. An example:
An action for clicking something
☞ **Click** ≡
is exactly the same as

☞ **Place the pointer on** ≡
☞ **Press the left mouse button briefly, just once**

Practice carrying out the task as written in the shorter version:

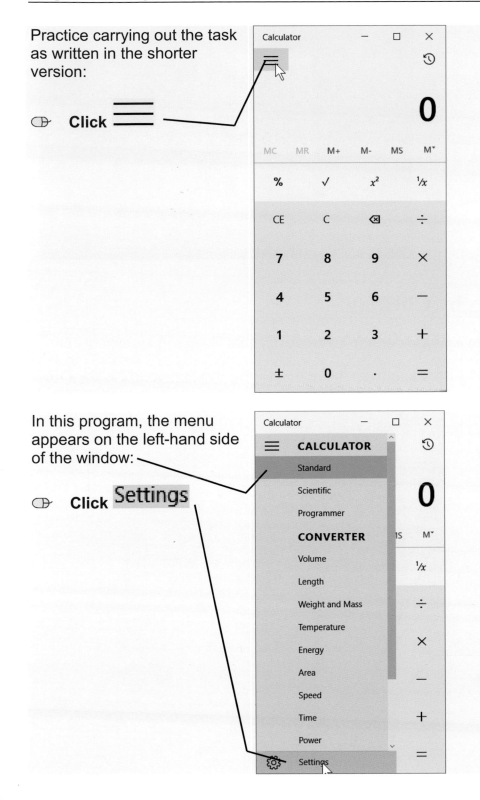

☞ **Click** ≡

In this program, the menu appears on the left-hand side of the window:

☞ **Click** Settings

The left side of the window changes:

You will see information about the program:

You can close this window:

☞ **Click an empty section of the desktop**

1.15 Calculating by Clicking

The *Calculator* program lets you perform calculations, just like a regular calculator.

You can press the *Calculator* buttons on the computer by clicking them. Give it a try.

➥ **Please note:**

The action
☞ **Click ...**
is exactly the same as:
☞ **Place the pointer on ...**
☞ **Press the left mouse button briefly, just once**

☞ **Click 8**

☞ **Click +**

☞ **Click 5**

☞ **Click =**

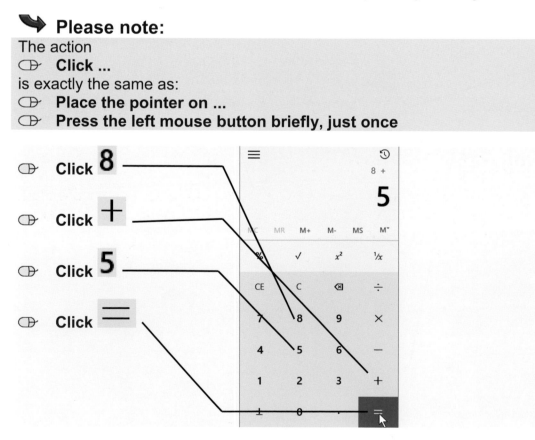

You will see the result of this sum:

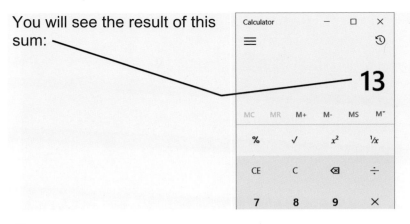

Tip

Do you find it hard to click the right spot?

If the pointer on the screen moves away when you click, you have accidentally moved the mouse. Try to keep your hand still when you click.

Please note these things:

- Loosely rest your hand on the mouse.
- Rest your index finger on the left mouse button.
- Place your thumb gently against the left side of the mouse.
- Rest your wrist and forearm on the table.

This gives you the most control over your movements.

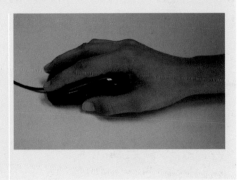

1.16 Minimizing a Window

Minimizing a window means making this window disappear from your desktop without actually closing the program. This can be useful if you want to use another program and need some extra space on your desktop.

In order to minimize a window, you use the — button:

Click —

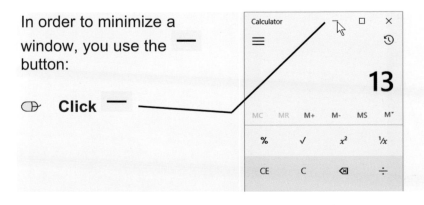

Now the window has been minimized. You will no longer see it on the desktop.

On the taskbar you will still see the taskbar button for the

Calculator 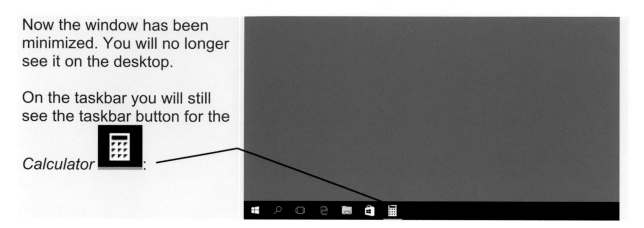 :

This tells you that the *Calculator* is still open. You just cannot see it on the desktop.

1.17 Opening a Second Program or App

You can open multiple programs or apps at once in *Windows 10*. You can search for an app or program and then open it:

In the lower left corner of the screen:

☞ **Click**

You can search using the search function. Type the keyword. In this case, you want to open the *Weather* app:

⌨ **Type:** weather

The search results appear:

☞ **Click**
    Weather
    Trusted Windows Store

The app will be opened on the desktop. You have seen that the *Weather* app is opened in the same way as a program.

Now you will see the *Weather* window:

You can also see that a new taskbar button appears on the taskbar:

Now you see two of these taskbar buttons

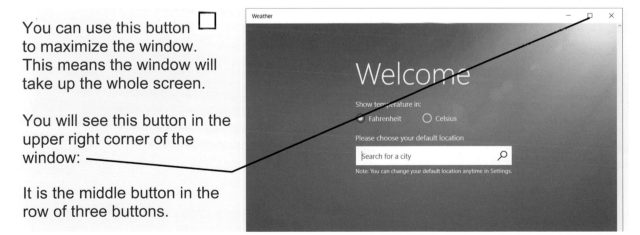

1.18 Maximizing and Minimizing

The window of *Weather* can fill the whole screen, or just a part of it. You can determine this for yourself. There is a special button for changing the size of a window.

You can use this button to maximize the window. This means the window will take up the whole screen.

You will see this button in the upper right corner of the window:

It is the middle button in the row of three buttons.

Click ☐

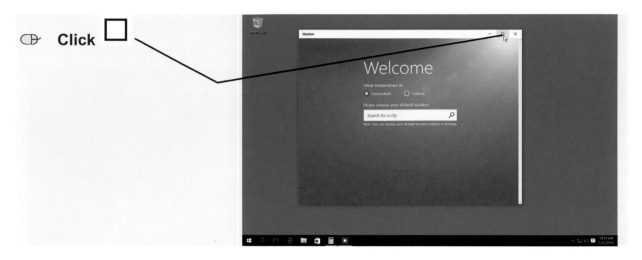

The window changes in size. Now it fills the entire screen; the window has been *maximized*. You can also *minimize* the window, just like you did with the *Calculator* window.

To minimize the window, you use the left button ▬ from the row of three buttons in the upper right corner of the window:

Click ▬

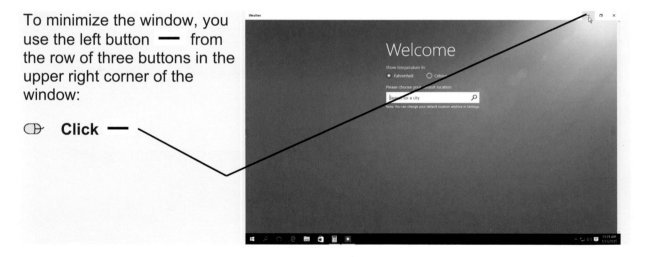

Now you have a programs and an app open: *Calculator* and *Weather*. Both windows have been minimized. This means you will not see the program and app windows. But they have not been closed.

You can tell this by the two taskbar buttons

on the taskbar:

The line under the taskbar button indicates that the program is still opened.

Remember that you can always see which programs and apps are opened on the desktop, by looking at the taskbar buttons.

1.19 Restoring a Window with the Taskbar Button

You can restore the minimized window to its previous size on the desktop with the taskbar button. Another handy feature is that you can view a thumbnail version of the window, to make sure you use the right taskbar button. Just give it a try:

☞ **Place the pointer on**

You will see the thumbnail of the *Calculator*:

☞ **Click**

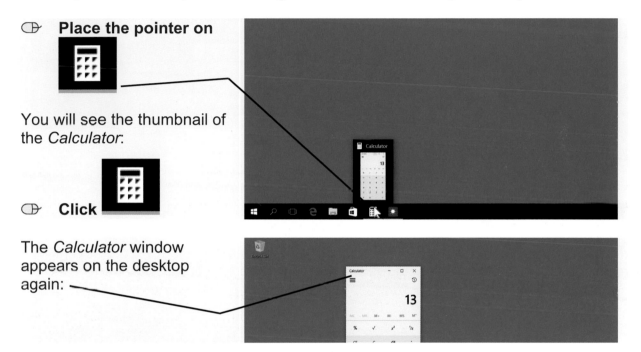

The *Calculator* window appears on the desktop again:

1.20 Closing a Program or App

You can also permanently close a window. When you do this, the program or app will be closed as well. To close a window on the desktop, you use the ✗ button.

You can find this button in the upper right corner of the window:

☞ **Click** ✗

The window is closed. The taskbar button for this program has disappeared from the taskbar. Now the *Calculator* program has been completely closed.

You can now work with the other window again:

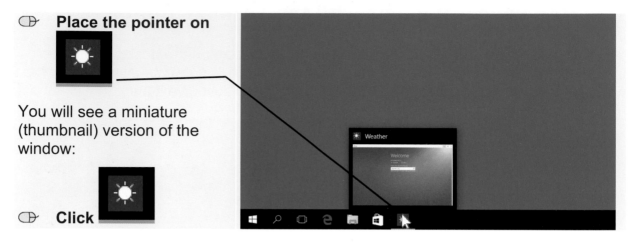

☞ **Place the pointer on**

You will see a miniature (thumbnail) version of the window:

☞ **Click**

Now the *Weather* window will appear in the same size before you minimized it.

1.21 Reducing a Maximized Window

A few steps back in this chapter you maximized the *Weather* window. You can also reduce a maximized window and restore it to the size it had before you maximized it.

For this you use the ⧉ button.

The ⧉ is the middle button from the three buttons in the upper right corner of the window — ⧉ ✕ :

This button will appear instead of the ☐ button, if you have used that button to maximize a window.

☞ **Click** ⧉

Now the window is reduced and restored to its previous size, that is, the size of the window before you maximized it.

You can close this window as well:

⏺ **Click** ✕

The *Weather* window is closed. The accompanying taskbar button has disappeared too. Now the app is closed.

1.22 Turning off Your Computer

When you stop working on your computer, you can turn it off. This will save energy. This is how you do that:

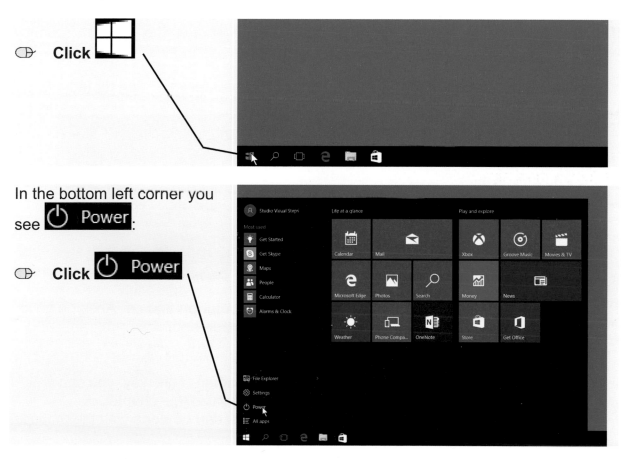

⏺ **Click** ⊞

In the bottom left corner you see ⏻ **Power**.

⏺ **Click** ⏻ **Power**

Now you will see a menu with three options: *Sleep*, *Shut down* and *Restart*. If you select **Shut down**, the computer will be turned off. If you have any programs or apps open, *Windows 10* will ask you whether you want to save your work. Then the computer will be turned off.

The whole process takes just a few seconds. Just try it:

☞   **Click** **Shut down**

Your screen will turn dark. Your computer has been turned off.

💡 Tip

Do not turn off
If you would rather keep on working, just click an empty spot on the desktop. You will be able to continue working right away.

Your screen has immediately turned dark. Now the computer has been turned off.

In order to turn on your computer again, you press the on/off or power switch of your computer:

In this chapter you have learned how to turn your computer on and off. And you have also learned how to work with the mouse, and how to open and close programs and apps.

In the following exercise you can repeat these actions again. This way, you can check whether you have sufficiently mastered the material in this chapter.
In the next chapter you will learn some new actions that can be done with the mouse.

💡 Tip

Practice some more
Would you like to practice a bit more? Just work through this chapter once more starting from the beginning. The more you practice, the better it will go.

1.23 Exercises

The following exercises will help you master what you have just learned. Have you forgotten how to do something? Use the number beside the footsteps 🐾 to look it up in the appendix *How Do I Do That Again?* at the end of this book.

Exercise 1: Opening and Closing

☞ Turn on your computer (and monitor) again and click the lock screen.

☞ If necessary, click your user account and log on with your password. 🐾^{1}

☞ Open the *Calculator*. 🐾^{2}

☞ Minimize the *Calculator* window. 🐾^{3}

☞ Open *Weather*. 🐾^{2}

☞ Maximize the *Weather* window. 🐾^{4}

☞ Minimize the *Weather* window. 🐾^{3}

☞ Display the *Calculator* window on the desktop again by using the taskbar button 🐾^{5} and close the *Calculator*. 🐾^{6}

☞ Display the *Weather* window on the desktop again by using the taskbar button. 🐾^{5}

☞ Minimize the *Weather* window, reduce it to its former size 🐾^{7} and close *Weather*. 🐾^{6}

☞ Turn off your computer. 🐾^{8}

When you have practiced enough, you can continue to read the *Background Information* and *Tips* on the next few pages.
If you would rather keep working with your computer, you can also go on to *Chapter 2 More Use of the Mouse in Windows*. You can read the *Background Information* and *Tips* at your leisure.

1.24 Background Information

Dictionary

App	Short for *application*, which means a program. Originally, an app was a program designed for use on a tablet or a smartphone. But in *Windows 10* you can also use apps on the pc.
Desktop	The work area on a computer screen, comparable to an actual desktop. When you open a program or app, it will appear on the desktop.
File Explorer	The program that is used to open files, among other things.
Icon	A small picture that indicates a file, folder, or program.
Lock screen	The first screen you see when you turn on the computer. When you click this screen, you will go to the login screen.
Log in	By logging in (or on) to something, you can get access to a service or program such as *Windows*, for example. You usually need a username and password in order to log in.
Login screen	The screen that you use to log in with *Windows*. In this screen you can see all the user accounts on the computer.
Menu	A menu contains a list of program or app options. In order to keep the screen less cluttered, menus are often hidden until you click a specific button.
Mouse actions	Most mouse actions consist of a combination of pointing and pressing a mouse button. There are four basic mouse actions: click, double-click, right-click, and drag.
Operating system	This system controls the computer, its programs, and devices such as the mouse and keyboard. *Windows 10* is an operating system.
PC	Short for *personal computer*. Your computer.
Pointer	The arrow you see on your screen. Also called mouse, mouse pointer, or mouse arrow.

- Continue on the next page -

Program	A series of commands or coded instructions used by a computer to perform a certain task.
Screen	Your computer's screen.
Screensaver	An animated image or pattern that appears on the screen when the computer is left idle for a while.
Start menu	The Start menu is a gateway to the programs, apps, folders and settings on your computer.
Taskbar	The taskbar is the horizontal bar at the bottom of the desktop.
Taskbar button	A button on the taskbar that indicates an open program, app or folder. You can use it to switch between windows.
Title bar	The horizontal bar at the top of a window that contains the name of the window. A title bar also contains buttons for closing the window and for changing its size.
Touchpad	An input device with which you can operate a computer, usually a laptop or notebook. By touching the sensitive area with your finger you can move the pointer around on the screen. In this case, your finger works the same way as a mouse.
Touchscreen	A screen that can be operated with your fingers.
User account	A collection of data that tells *Windows* which files and folders you are allowed to access, which computer settings you can change, and what your personal preferences are, for instance your desktop background.
Window	A rectangular area on a computer screen, in which programs and other content are displayed.
(Window) buttons — ☐ X	Buttons on the title bar of a window, used for changing the size of the window, or for closing the window.
Windows 10	The computer program that manages all the other programs on the computer. The operating system saves files, enables the use of programs, and lets you use other devices, such as the keyboard, mouse and printer.

Source: Windows Help, Wikipedia

Circle

Has your pointer turned into a rotating five-point circle ?
This means your computer is busy performing a task, such as saving a file.

☞ **Wait until the circle has disappeared**

Then you can continue working.

The desktop components
The desktop is the work area on a computer screen, comparable to an actual desktop. When you open a program or app, it will appear on the desktop.

Icon:
A small picture that indicates a file, folder, program or app. For example, the *Recycle Bin* icon.

Window:
The framed visual container in which programs, apps and other content are displayed.

Search function:
You can use the search function to find programs, apps and files on your computer and on the Internet.

Taskbar:
Horizontal bar at the bottom of the desktop. Here you can see which programs and apps are running, and you can also switch between the opened windows.

Start button
You can open the Start menu with the Start button. The Start menu provides access to programs, apps, folders, and settings (see the next chapter).

Taskbar button:
A button appears on the taskbar for each program or app that is opened.

The components of a window

Programs and apps are displayed on the desktop in a framed visual area in the shape of a window. Most windows consist of the same basic components:

Title bar: Displays the program or app name.

Menu button: List with commands. Other programs or apps have a menu at the top of the window in the shape of a ribbon, or a row of buttons (for example, see the *WordPad* program that is discussed in *Chapter 3 Working with Text*).

Borders and corners: You can drag these in order to change the size of a window (see *Chapter 2 More Use of the Mouse in Windows*).

Calculator

0

MC	MR	M+	M-	MS	M˅
%	√	x^2	$1/x$		
CE	C	⌫	÷		
7	8	9	×		
4	5	6	—		
1	2	3	+		
±	0	.	=		

Window buttons: Are used to hide, enlarge, or close the window.

— Minimize button. You can use this button to hide a window. This means it will disappear from the desktop. You will see the taskbar button for this window on the taskbar.

▢ Maximize button. You can use this button to enlarge the window to a full screen size.

⧉ Previous size button. You can use this button to restore a maximized window to its previous size. This button appears instead of the *Maximize* button.

✕ Close button. You can use this button to close the window and the program or app. Then the taskbar button will disappear.

1.25 Tips

 Tip

Properly position the mouse
The mouse will sometimes be too far
away from the keyboard or screen, or is
positioned on the edge of the mouse pad.

If this happens, you will not be able to use the mouse properly. You will need to lift
the mouse and set it back in its proper place on the table, or in the middle of the
mouse pad. You do that like this:

☞ **First you place the pointer** ⬉ **in
the center of your screen**

☞ **Lift the mouse**

☞ **Place the mouse on the right spot**

Now you can continue working.

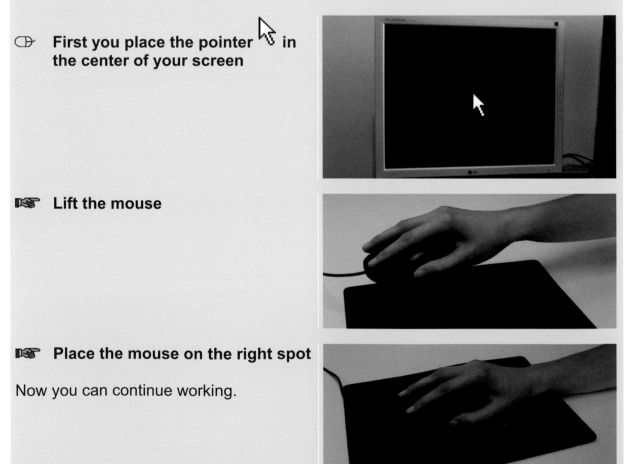

💡 **Tip**

Turning off

After clicking ⊞ you have seen the ⏻ Power button:

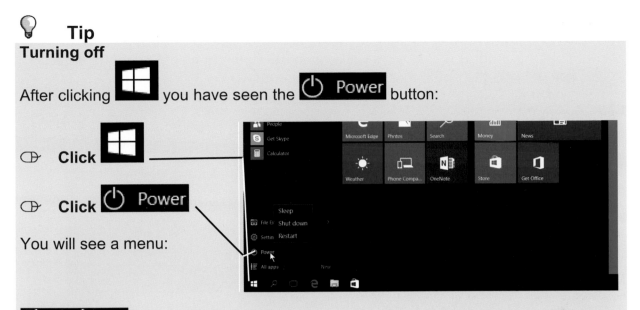

▭ **Click** ⊞

▭ **Click** ⏻ Power

You will see a menu:

Shut down: if you click this option, your computer or laptop will be turned off. In order to turn your computer back on again, you will need to press the on/off switch on the computer case.

Restart: restart your computer. If you click this button, your computer will be turned off and then started up automatically.

Sleep: if you click this button, your computer will go into sleep mode. Each computer has its own way of waking up from sleep mode. Usually you will need to press the on/off switch on the computer case.

You also have an option with which you can just log off. In this case, you log off with your own user account. Then a different user can log in with their account, if needed. All open programs and apps will be closed when you log off.

You can also access the log off options as follows:

▭ **Click** ⊞

▭ **Click your user name**

In order to log off, click **Sign out**.

- Continue on the next page -

You can also lock your user account. This is useful in case you need to step away from your computer for a while, and if you do not want others to work with your user account. All the programs and apps will remain open. If you want to see the desktop again, you will need to enter your password once more.

💡 Tip

Screen saver
Do you suddenly see a completely different image on your screen?

For example, an animated image such as this one: .
This means a *screen saver* has been activated on your computer.

You can stop the screen saver from running by simply pressing any key on the keyboard, or by moving the mouse just a little bit. Then you can continue working as before. You may need to log in again.

You can adjust a screensaver according to your own preferences in *Windows 10*. For example, you can set the amount of screen inactivity time before the screen saver begins to run. You can also disable the screen saver.
You can read more on this subject in *Chapter 9 Useful Settings*.

💡 Tip

Close a window directly from the taskbar
You can close minimized windows from the taskbar without actually opening them first. You do that like this:

☞ **Place the pointer on the thumbnail**

In the upper right corner of the thumbnail you will see ✖:

☞ **Click** ✖

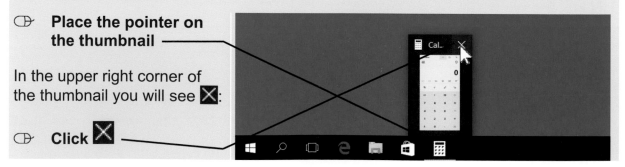

2. More Use of the Mouse in Windows

The mouse has become an essential tool for working with a computer. The first computers were operated by entering a series of complicated commands on a keyboard. This was mainly done by computer technicians.

With more and more people wanting to use computers, it was quickly evident that operating a PC had to become easier. Modern operating systems have implemented a graphical user interface with lots of buttons and icons that is much more user-friendly. You can interact with the computer using a mouse to point and click on these objects rather than entering a lot of complicated text. These actions tell the computer what to do, for example, open a program or show a menu.

Since the emergence of touchscreens and tablet computers, operating systems have been adapted to touch input. *Windows 10* is a good example of this. If you own a touchscreen, you can work in *Windows 10* by touching the objects on your screen.

Since most beginning computer users will not have a touchscreen, this book assumes that you will be using a computer with a mouse. In this chapter you will learn how to use the mouse more fully to accomplish a wide variety of tasks.

If you are curious about working with the touchpad on a laptop computer or with a touchscreen, you can read more about that in a Bonus Online Chapter. See more information in the *Tip* on page 25.

In this chapter you will learn how to:

- use the Start menu;
- drag with the mouse and drag a scroll box;
- use the scroll wheel on the mouse;
- enlarge and reduce a window;
- navigate through a program;
- double-click the mouse;
- right-click the mouse;
- change the size of icons;
- use a program or app.

2.1 Getting Ready

Before you can begin, you need to turn on your computer. In *Chapter 1 Starting with Windows 10* you have learned how to do this.

☞ **Turn on the computer (and the monitor) and click the lock screen**

⬤ **If necessary, click your user account and log in with your password**

2.2 Opening a Program or App through the Start Menu

The following operations require the use of the *Calculator* program. You learned how to open this program in the previous chapter by using the search function. In this section you will learn how to open it from the Start menu. Among other things, the Start menu provides access to the programs and apps on your computer. In order to open the Start menu, you use the Start button:

In the lower left corner of your screen:

⬤ **Click the Start button**

After you have clicked the Start button, you will see a new window:

This window is called the Start menu:

Just like the menu in a restaurant, this menu shows a list of options:

The Start menu on your own computer may look a bit different, but this will not inhibit you from performing the next few steps.

Here you can see a close up of the Start menu:

You see a list on the left with some of the most frequently used programs and apps:

On the right you will see square and rectangular icons. These are called *tiles*. By clicking these tiles you can also open programs and apps:

Open the *Calculator* from the list of frequently used programs and apps:

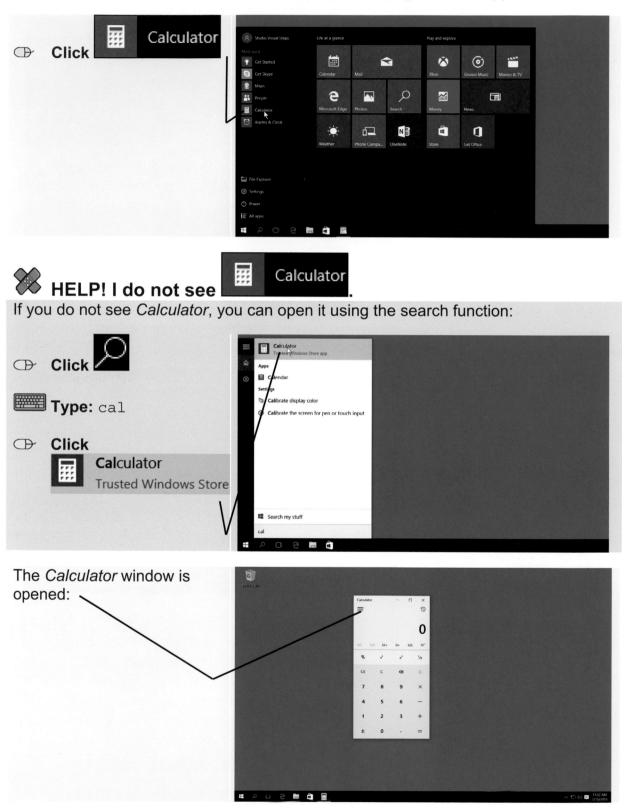

Click [Calculator]

HELP! I do not see [Calculator].

If you do not see *Calculator*, you can open it using the search function:

Click [search icon]

Type: cal

Click
Calculator
Trusted Windows Store

The *Calculator* window is opened:

2.3 The Next Three Mouse Actions

In the previous chapter you have seen that there are four different mouse actions:

- clicking
- dragging
- double-clicking
- right-clicking

You have already practiced clicking in the previous chapter (press the left mouse button briefly, just once). In this chapter you will begin to use the other three mouse actions.

2.4 Dragging

Dragging is used to move windows and icons around on your desktop.
Dragging is done like this:

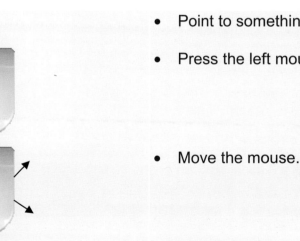

- Point to something with the pointer.

- Press the left mouse button and *hold it down*.

- Move the mouse.

- Release the mouse button when you are done.

For example, you can move the *Calculator* window by dragging it. To do this you need to place the pointer on the window's title bar. Just give it a try:

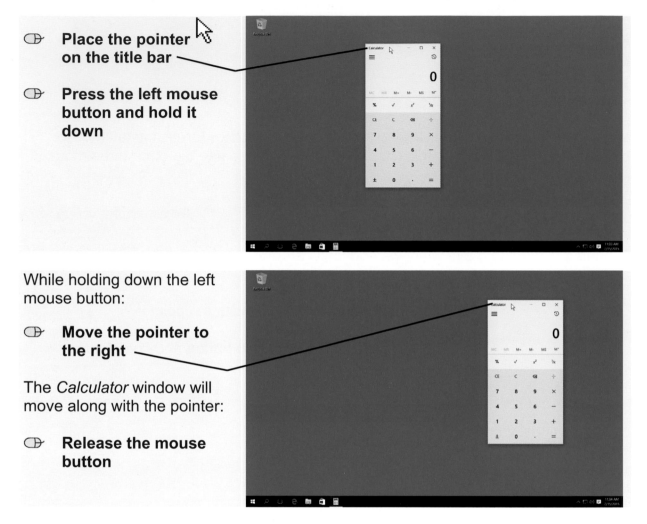

⊕ **Place the pointer on the title bar**

⊕ **Press the left mouse button and hold it down**

While holding down the left mouse button:

⊕ **Move the pointer to the right**

The *Calculator* window will move along with the pointer:

⊕ **Release the mouse button**

You have now *dragged* the window a little to the right. At the end of this chapter you will find some exercises that let you repeat this dragging action.

Close the *Calculator*:

☞ Close the *Calculator* window 🦶[6]

Have you forgotten exactly how to close a window? You can look up this action and many others as well, at the end of this book in the appendix *How Do I Do That Again?* You will see a brief explanation by footstep number 6 🦶[6].

2.5 Dragging a Scroll Box

There are all sorts of situations in *Windows* in which you need to drag some item or other. It often occurs that the information on the screen does not fit in a menu or window. You will then need to move the vertical or horizontal scroll box by dragging it. You can practice this in the Start menu and the *News* window.

➥ Please note:

In order to work through this section, you will need to have an active Internet connection. We assume that this connection has already been set up. If this is not the case, you need to get in touch with your Internet provider, computer supplier, or an experienced computer user.

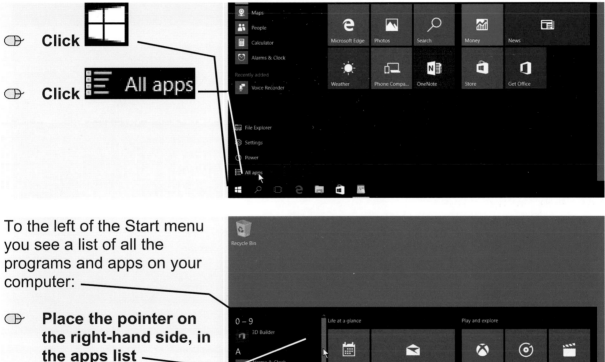

☞ **Click**

☞ **Click** All apps

To the left of the Start menu you see a list of all the programs and apps on your computer:

☞ **Place the pointer on the right-hand side, in the apps list**

You will see a vertical bar. On this bar is a scroll box: ▮.
You can drag this scroll box.

☞ **Place the pointer on the scroll box**

Press the left mouse button and hold it down

Move the pointer downwards

The scroll box will move along.

Release the mouse button when you see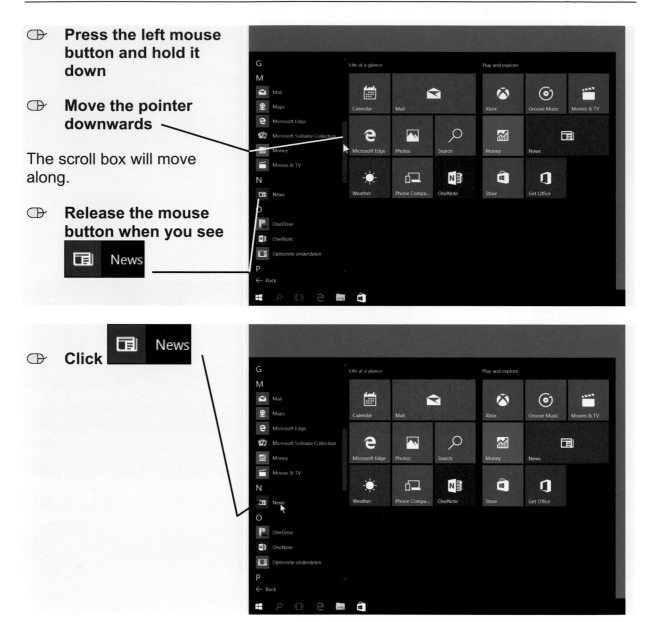

Click

You will see the *News* window: ⎯⎯⎯⎯⎯⎯⎯

This window will look different on your own screen, since the news changes every day, of course.

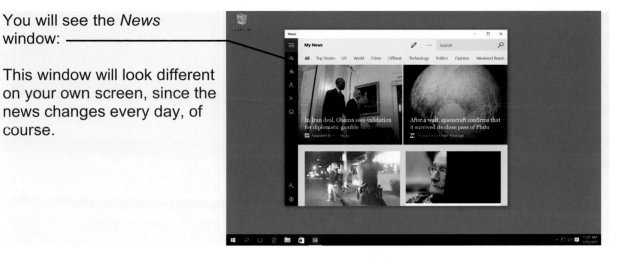

You will see a number of news messages. You can open one of these messages:

👆 **Click a news message**

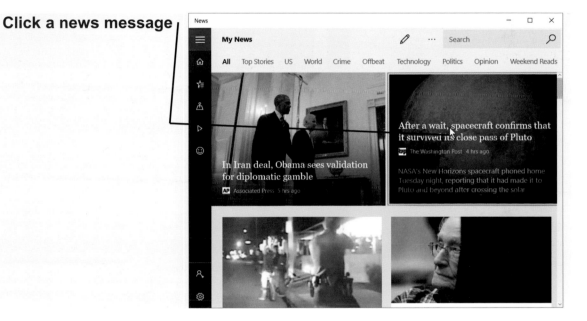

You will see a news article.

If the information in a window does not exactly fit in the window, you will use a scroll box again:

☞ **Place the pointer on the right-hand side of the window**

You will see a vertical bar to the right again. On this bar

you see the scroll box: ▮.

☞ **Place the pointer on the scroll box**

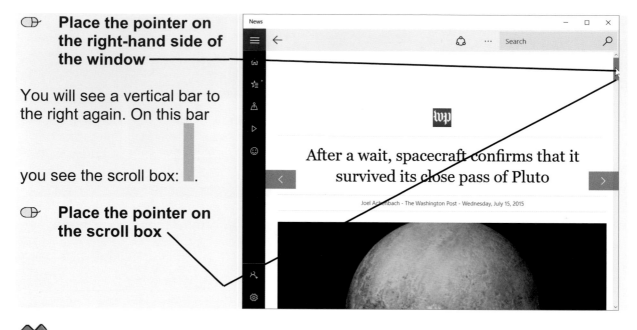

HELP! I do not see a scroll box.

If you do not see a scroll box, you may have opened a news message with only a small amount of text. In that case, this is what you do:

☞ **Click** ←
☞ **Click another news message**

☞ **Press the left mouse button and hold it down**

☞ **Move the pointer downwards**

The scroll box will move along.

☞ **Release the mouse button**

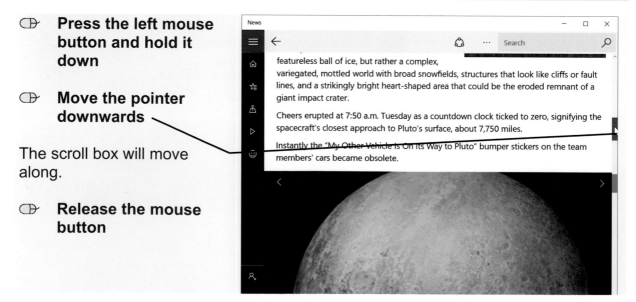

As you move a scroll box up and down more or less of the content can be seen.

2.6 Using the Scroll Wheel on a Mouse

A computer mouse may also be equipped with a scroll wheel. The scroll wheel is located between the left and right mouse buttons:

You can use the scroll wheel to move the scroll box, among other things. You can roll the scroll wheel backwards and forwards with your index or third finger. If you have a mouse with a scroll wheel, you can try it out:

➥ Please note:

Try not to press the scroll wheel down however, as other actions may be carried out if you do. For now you only need to practice rolling the wheel.

To move the scroll box downwards:

☞ **Roll the wheel towards you**

To move the scroll box upwards:

☞ **Roll the wheel away from you**

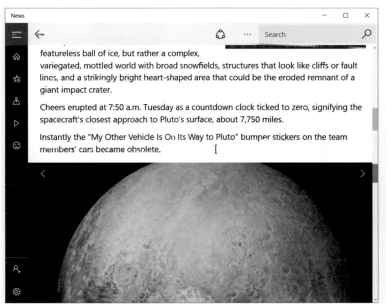

You will see the scroll box and the text move upwards and downwards. You can use the scroll wheel whenever you see a scroll box in a window, or if you see that the text does not completely fit a window. Sometimes you need to click an empty spot in the window first.

2.7 Enlarging and Reducing a Window

If a window is not maximized (full screen view), you can resize the window by dragging its border with the mouse. Just try it:

☞ **Place the pointer on the right edge of the window**

The pointer turns into a double arrow ←→:

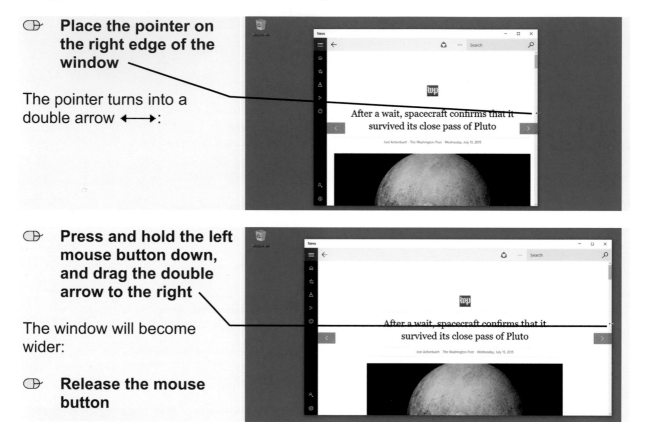

☞ **Press and hold the left mouse button down, and drag the double arrow to the right**

The window will become wider:

☞ **Release the mouse button**

In the same way you can change the height of the window. Remember that this is only possible as long as the window has not been maximized (taking up the full screen).

☞ **Place the pointer on the bottom edge of the window**

The pointer turns into a

double arrow again ↕:

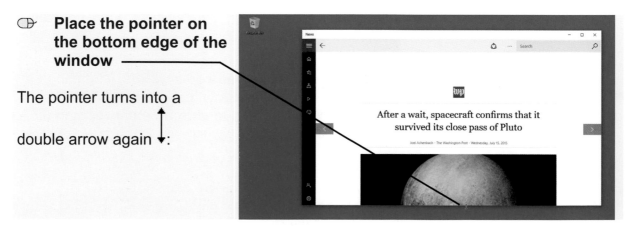

☞ **Press and hold the left mouse button down, and drag the double arrow upwards**

Now the window becomes smaller:

☞ **Release the mouse button**

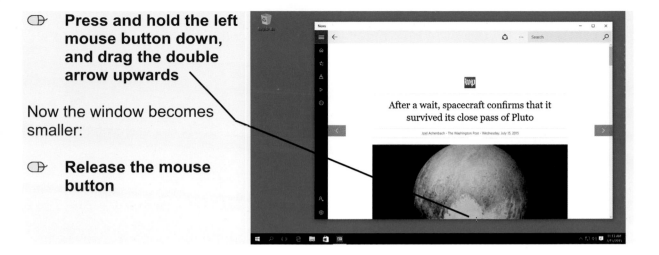

2.8 Back to Where You Started

Now you can take a closer look at the *News* app. Previously, you had clicked the window once in order to display a new page. You can also go back to the first page you saw. You do this using the Back ← button:

In the upper left corner of the window you see the ← button:

☞ **Click** ←

You will see the Home page of the *News* app:

The Home page is the first page you see when you open a app.

Now the ← button has disappeared:

You will see that *Windows 10* has lots of windows that contain the ← button. You will learn more about this further on in the book.

You can close *News* window:

☞ **Close the *News* window** ⬳⁶

2.9 Double-Clicking

Up till now, you have clicked a word, a command, or a button just once. However, in *Windows* you sometimes need to *double-click* things. Double-clicking is often necessary when you want to open an item on the desktop.
For example, you can double-click the *Recycle Bin* icon shown in the top left area of your desktop.

First, read how double-clicking works:

- Place the pointer on an icon.

- Press the left mouse button *twice in rapid succession*.

  Make sure you *do not move the mouse* in between the two clicks.

By double-clicking you can quickly open a window. Give it a try:

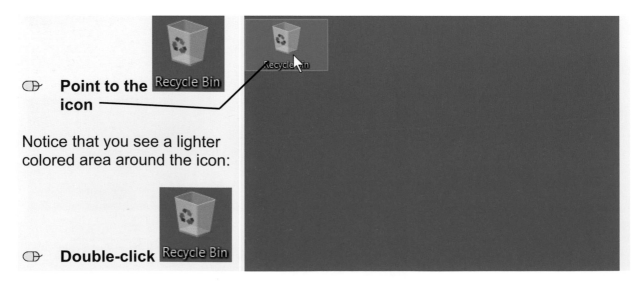

☞ **Point to the** Recycle Bin **icon**

Notice that you see a lighter colored area around the icon:

☞ **Double-click** Recycle Bin

The *Recycle Bin* window is opened:

➥ Please note:

When you double-click, it is important that you *do not move the mouse* between the two clicks. When you do, *Windows* interprets this as two single clicks on two different spots. Also, you need to click the left mouse button *twice in rapid succession*. You may need to try double-clicking a few times before it works for you.

You can also practice beforehand, by double-clicking an empty area on the desktop. When you have mastered the right clicking speed, you can double-click the *Recycle Bin*.

✖ HELP! Double-clicking will not work.

If double-clicking does not work, you can use the following trick:

➪ **Click Recycle Bin once**

The icon is now highlighted by a different background color. This means the icon is

selected:  .

⌨ **Press Enter ⏎ on your keyboard**

Now the *Recycle Bin* window will be opened.

☞ **Close the *Recycle Bin* window** ⏱⁶

Try it once more:

⊕ **Double-click the *Recycle Bin* icon**

You will again see the
Recycle Bin window:

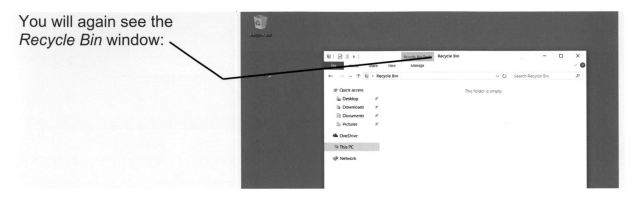

From the *Recycle Bin* window, you can easily go to the window with all the computer components. You will be doing this in the next section.

To the left of the window:

⊕ **Click ☐ This PC**

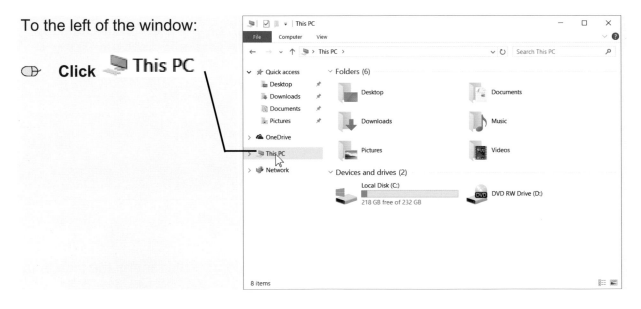

2.10 Right-Clicking

The last mouse action we will discuss is the *right-clicking*. After all, there is a reason why a mouse has two buttons.

Right-clicking is done like this:

- Point to something with the pointer.

- Press the *right mouse button* once and immediately release it.

This is the same action as a regular click but you use the right mouse button instead of the left. The right mouse button has an entirely different function, as you will see.

Use the *left mouse button* first, to select something:

☞ **Using the left mouse button, click**

Documents

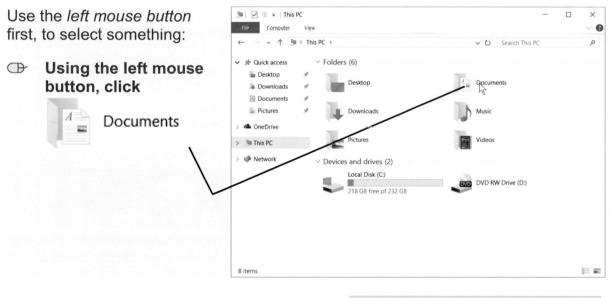

The icon is surrounded by a light blue rectangle

Documents

.
This tells you the icon has been selected.

Now you can practice using the right mouse button:

Right-click

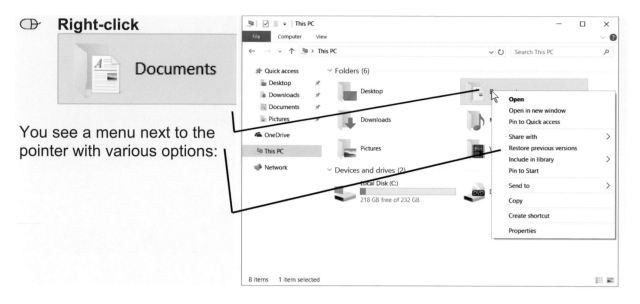

You see a menu next to the pointer with various options:

You can also make this menu disappear. You need to use the left mouse button to do this:

Using the left mouse button, click an empty area somewhere on the window

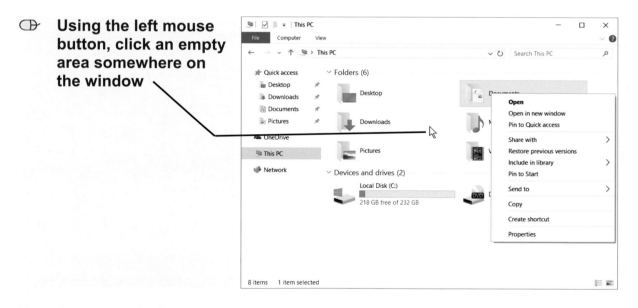

Now the menu will disappear.

☞ **Close the window**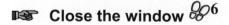

You will see the desktop again.

You can right-click icons, folders and many other items in *Windows.* This will always make a menu appear. These menus can be used to carry out commonly performed tasks related to the item you clicked. You can right-click the desktop, for example:

☞ **Right-click somewhere on the desktop**

Now you see a menu next to the pointer, with a list of various commands:

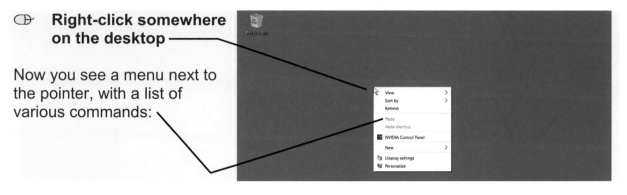

If you want to select a command from a menu of this type, you must use the <u>left</u> mouse button again.

☞ **Click** View

☞ **Click** Large icons

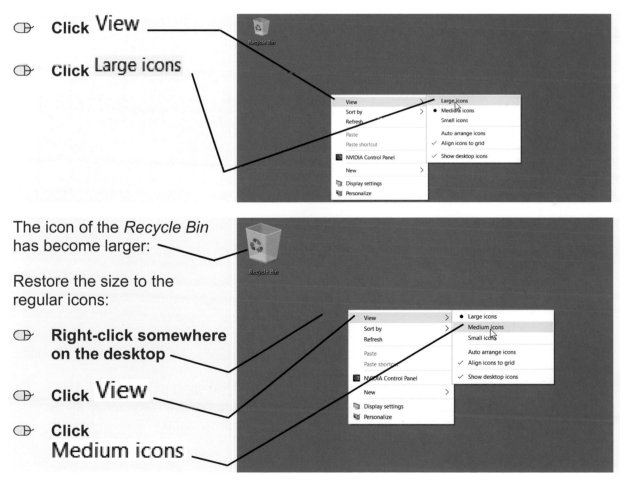

The icon of the *Recycle Bin* has become larger:

Restore the size to the regular icons:

☞ **Right-click somewhere on the desktop**

☞ **Click** View

☞ **Click Medium icons**

Right-clicking an item usually displays a menu. In order to select an item from the menu you need to use the left mouse button.

2.11 Launching a Program or an App from the Tiles

By now you have become acquainted with the four different mouse actions, and you have practiced using them. When you are working with programs and apps, the clicking and dragging actions can be particularly handy. You can practice using these actions a little more with the *Weather* app.

In this section, you will learn how to launch the app from the tiles in the Start menu. Tiles may contain so-called 'live' content, for example, the current weather forecast, as is the case here in the *Weather* app. You will often only see it after you have used it once.

Cloudy

65° 69°
     63°

Boston

➥ **Please note:**

In order to work through this section you need to have an active Internet connection, and we assume your Internet connection has already been set up. If necessary, contact your Internet provider or computer supplier for further information.

Open the *Weather* app:

☞ **Click** ⊞ ───────

In this example you will already see 'live' content by some of the tiles, such as *Sport* and *News*.

☞ **Click the tile**

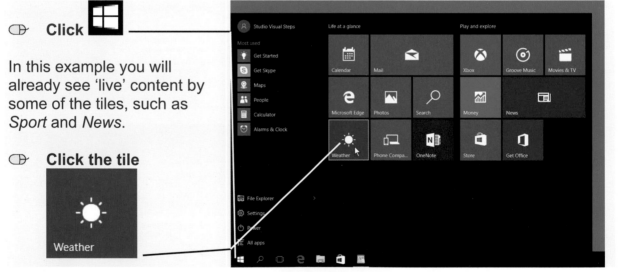

It is possible that the text and image on the tile keeps changing all the time. The *Weather* app will present summaries of the weather conditions in big cities, all over the world. In the *Tips* at the end of *Chapter 9 Useful settings* you will read how to make settings for this.

The *Weather* app is opened.

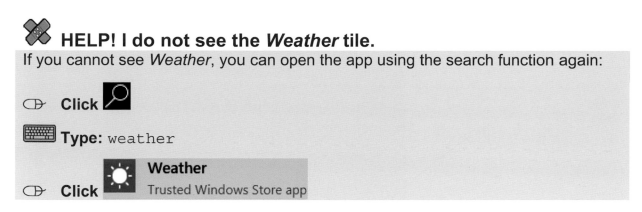

HELP! I do not see the *Weather* tile.

If you cannot see *Weather*, you can open the app using the search function again:

☞ **Click**

⌨ **Type:** weather

☞ **Click**   **Weather**
              Trusted Windows Store app

2.12 Using an App

Weather will be opened. In this app you can display the weather in your own home town:

You may already see your location:

If you do not see your own location, you can add it, like this:

☞ **Click the box**

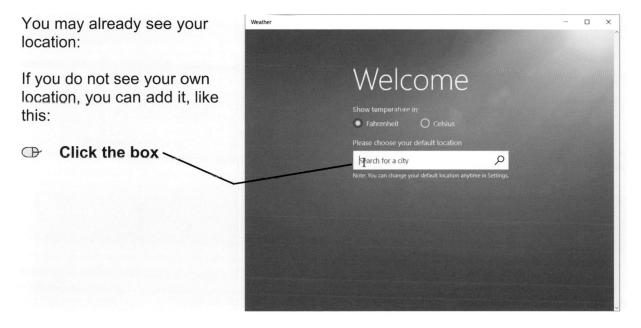

Type the name of your location ――――

In this example we have used Boston.

☞ **Click the location**

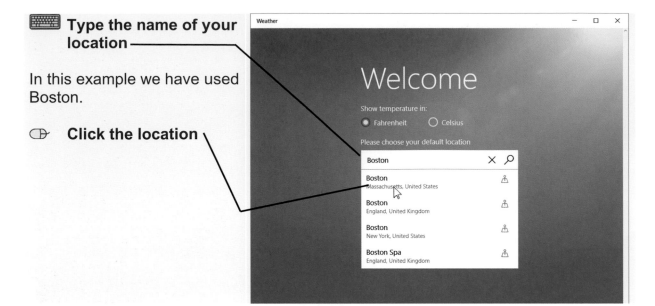

You will see the current weather condition and the forecast for your own home town:

There is more data available:

On the right-hand side of the window:

☞ **Drag the scroll box downwards** ――――

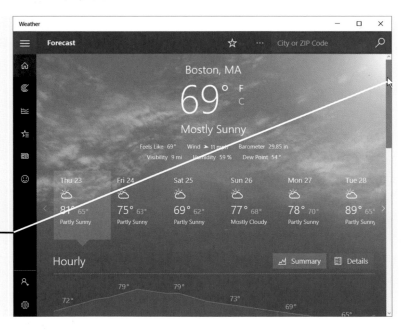

💡 **Tip**

View predictions further ahead
By default, you will see the prediction for the current day and the next couple of

days. If you click the ▶ button (to the right of the window) you can display the predictions for the next five days.

☞ **Drag the scroll box
  upwards again** ————

You will see more data, for
example about the historical
weather:

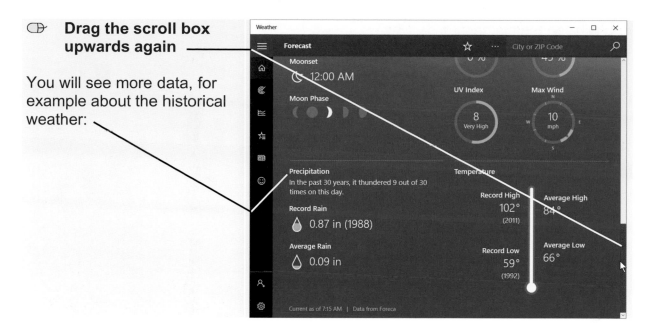

You can also view more historical data regarding the weather in your home town:

On the left-hand side of the
window:

☞ **Click** ▨

You will see the historical average temperatures: ————

Click the ⬤ button to view the historical rainfall: ——

This is how you go back to the weather forecast for your own location: —

⊕ **Click** ⬅

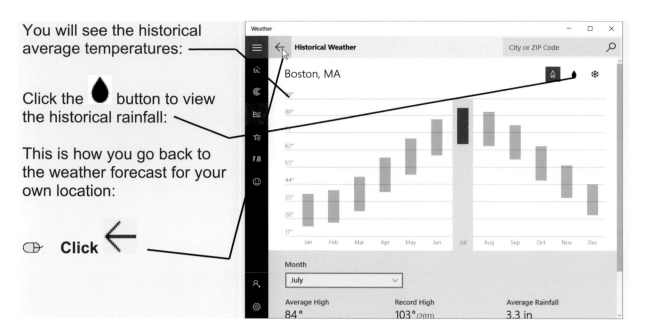

You will see the prediction for your own location again.

☞ **Close** *Weather* ⸙⁶

Are you having problems with clicking and dragging? Then try practicing a few more times with the *Weather* app. Repeat the steps in this section until you feel more comfortable using the mouse.

You can also use the exercises to repeat the actions described in this chapter.

💡 **Tip**

Dragging in Solitaire
A good way to practice dragging, is by playing the popular card game *Solitaire* on your computer. It is the perfect, handy way to learn to use the mouse.

This *Solitaire* program comes with *Windows 10* and it has probably already been installed on your computer.

In *Appendix A. Clicking and Dragging in Solitaire* at the back of this book you can read how to start this program and play the game.

2.13 Exercises

🐾

The following exercises will help you master what you have just learned. Have you forgotten how to do something? Use the number beside the footsteps 🐾 to look it up in the appendix *How Do I Do That Again?* at the end of this book.

Exercise 1: Dragging a Window

☞ Open the *Calculator*. 🐾^{2}

☞ Drag the *Calculator* window to the middle of the desktop. 🐾^{9}

☞ Drag the *Calculator* window to the bottom right. 🐾^{9}

☞ Drag the *Calculator* window to the top left. 🐾^{9}

☞ Close the *Calculator* window. 🐾^{6}

Exercise 2: Clicking, Double-Clicking and Dragging

☞ Open the *Recycle Bin*. 🐾^{10}

☞ Drag the *Recycle Bin* window to the top left of the screen. 🐾^{9}

☞ Close the *Recycle Bin* window. 🐾^{6}

☞ Open *Weather*. 🐾^{2}

☞ Maximize the *Weather* window. 🐾^{4}

☞ Restore the *Weather* to its previous size. 🐾^{7}

☞ Close the *Weather* window. 🐾^{6}

Exercise 3: Clicking and Right-Clicking

Please note: Clicking is done with the left mouse button. Right-clicking is something you do with the right mouse button.

☞ Right-click an empty spot on the desktop.

☞ In the menu, click View .

☞ In the menu, click Medium icons .

☞ Right-click Recycle Bin .

☞ In the menu, click Open .

☞ Close the window of the *Recycle Bin*. $\mathscr{C\!C}^6$

Exercise 4: Open, View, and Close an App

☞ Open *News*. $\mathscr{C\!C}^2$

☞ Click a news message.

☞ View the news message.

☞ If necessary, drag the scroll box downwards. $\mathscr{C\!C}^{11}$

☞ Go back to the *News* home page. $\mathscr{C\!C}^{12}$

☞ Close *News*. $\mathscr{C\!C}^6$

2.14 Background Information

Dictionary

Back button ←	A button that is used to display pages you have previously viewed.
Clicking	Briefly pressing the left mouse button * once. By clicking something you select the item, or you tell the computer to carry out a certain task, by clicking one of the options shown.
Double-clicking	Pressing the left mouse button * twice, in rapid succession. When you double-click an icon, such as the *Recycle Bin*, you open the window.
Drag	Moving something on the screen by selecting it, pressing and holding the mouse button down while moving the item over your screen. You can move a window to another spot on the desktop, for instance, by dragging the title bar of the window.
Right-clicking	Briefly pressing the right mouse button *. When you click something with the right mouse button, you will usually see a menu.
Scroll box	Horizontal or vertical box that appears if the information no longer fits the window. You can drag the scroll box up and down to see more information on the page.
Scroll wheel	Little wheel between the two mouse buttons. If your mouse is equipped with a scroll wheel, you can us this wheel to scroll through the pages. Scroll downwards by rolling the wheel towards you. Scroll upwards by rolling the wheel away from you.
Tile	Tiles let you start a program or app from the Start menu.

If the left and right mouse button functions have been switched, (for lefthanders, - see section 9.9 Setting Up the Mouse), the clicking is done with the right mouse button, and the right-clicking is done with the left mouse button.

Source: Windows Help, Wikipedia

The parts of the computer

The large cabinet that holds the computer itself is called the *computer case* or *housing*:

The case holds the computer's memory and the *processor chip* that makes everything work.
This computer case also holds the CD drive and/or DVD drive and one or more slots for a USB stick.
There may also be other slots available for different types of memory cards for a digital camera, video camera or other mobile devices.

Computer case

Every computer has a monitor. The size of the computer screen is expressed in *inches*. The minimum size of a computer screen these days is 22 inches. Larger screens have become very popular. Other hardware elements are the keyboard, the mouse, the speakers and the printer.

Monitor

A portable computer or laptop is a complete system. The case, the keyboard, the touchpad (the substitute for the mouse), and the display are integrated into a single unit.
The flat display is flipped up when the laptop is being used.
You can connect several devices to a laptop, such as a mouse, a printer, a scanner, and even a separate keyboard.

Laptop

Hardware and software

In the computer world, the terms *hardware* and *software* are often used. Actually, hardware is everything on a computer you can hold on to, and open up, if necessary. *Software* is not tangible; it can be a computer program, an app, a data file, or a computer game. You cannot grab the software itself, but you can hold on to the medium on which the software is stored, such as a USB stick, CD ROM, or a DVD. Software is distributed through a network that is 'elusive' too, such as the Internet.

The components of the Start menu

The Start menu is an important portal for the programs, apps, folders, and settings on your computer. It is called a menu because it provides a list with options, just like a menu in a restaurant. It is the place where you start or open items.

In order to open the Start menu, you click the Start button ⊞ in the bottom left corner of the screen.

On the right-hand side of the screen you will see tiles. You can use these tiles to open programs and apps.

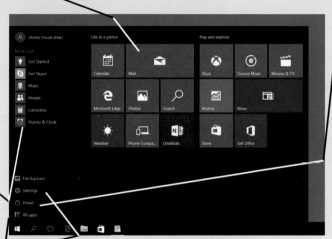

The pane on the left contains a list of programs and apps. This list can change, since *Windows* places the most frequently used programs and apps here. This way, you can quickly find them.

You can use ⏻ Power to turn off the computer, restart, or switch to sleep mode.

If you click 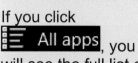, you will see the full list of programs and apps.

You will also find 🗔 File Explorer and ⚙ Settings in the Start menu. These menu options provide access to the folder and files window and your computer's settings. You will learn more about this further on in this book.

2.15 Tips

💡 Tip

Adding multiple locations to Weather
You can set up multiple locations in *Weather*. This can be useful, if you want to check the weather in the place where you are going on vacation, or to see what the weather is like in the country where your relatives live.

☞ **Open** *Weather* 𝄞²

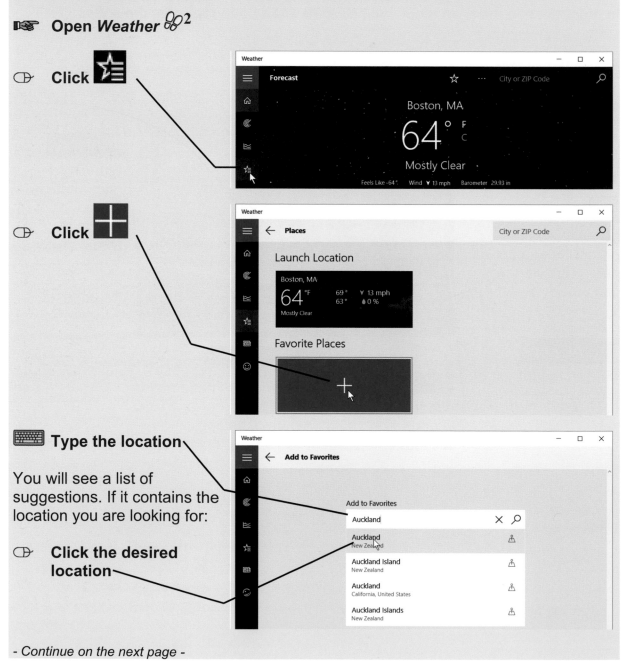

☞ **Click** 📑

☞ **Click** ➕

⌨ **Type the location**

You will see a list of suggestions. If it contains the location you are looking for:

☞ **Click the desired location**

- Continue on the next page -

The location has been added to the favorite locations:

⏻ **Click**

You will see the current weather condition and the forecast for this location:

This is how you go back to the weather in your home town:

⏻ **Click** ←

⏻ **Click your home town**

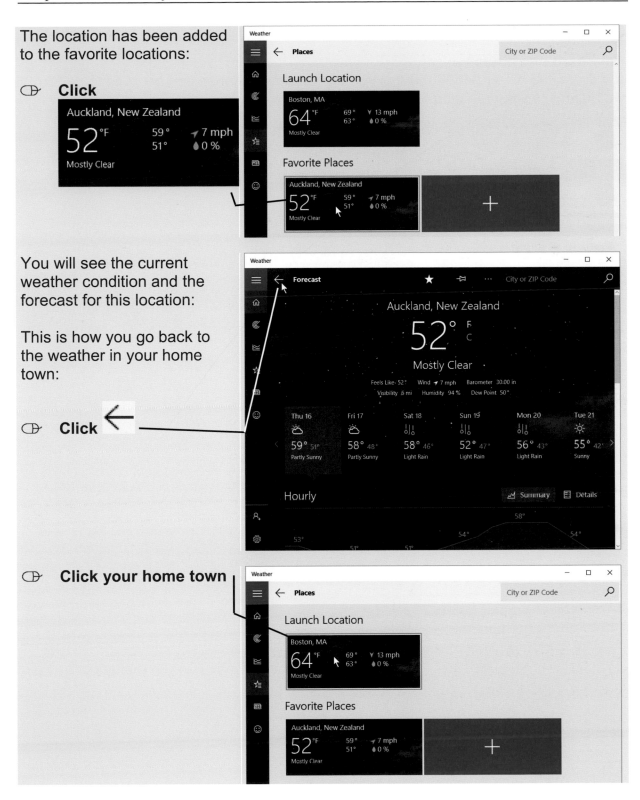

☿ Tip

Keyboard shortcuts

Windows has a number of shortcuts on the keyboard. These can be used to perform various tasks without using the mouse:

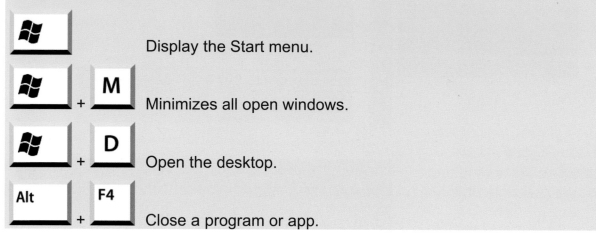

Display the Start menu.

+ M   Minimizes all open windows.

+ D   Open the desktop.

Alt + F4   Close a program or app.

3. Working with Text

Word processing is the application that made the Personal Computer (PC) so popular. It is also the most widely-used application, also on devices such as mobile phones and tablets. The typewriter era is long gone, thanks in part to how easy computers have made it to write and produce texts.

As a computer user, it is useful to have good keyboard and word processing skills. These skills are not only needed for writing letters or email messages, for example, but also for various other things. A certain degree of keyboard skill is also necessary, because not everything can be done with the mouse.

Windows 10 has a simple word-processing program that you can use to practice typing. The program is called *WordPad* and was installed on your computer together with *Windows*.

In this chapter you will learn how to:

- open *WordPad*;
- type using the keyboard;
- correct a typing error;
- type capital letters;
- begin a new paragraph;
- type various special characters;
- move the cursor;
- use a larger or different font;
- open a new document;
- save, open or print a document;
- close *WordPad*.

3.1 Opening WordPad

WordPad is a basic word-processing program that you can use to create and edit documents. You can open it using the search function:

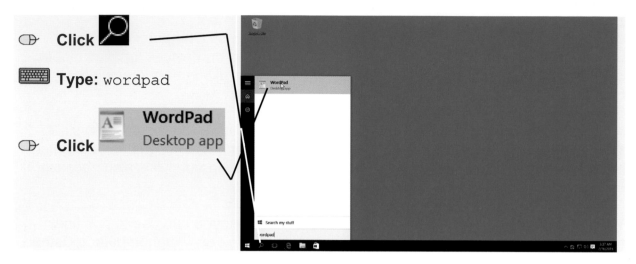

☞ **Click** 🔍

⌨ **Type:** wordpad

☞ **Click** **WordPad** Desktop app

Now you see the empty *WordPad* window:

The text you type will appear in the big white box.

This box is like a blank sheet of paper.

At the top left, you will see a short blinking vertical line. This is called the *cursor*.

In the upper part of the screen you see the *ribbon*. A wide assortment of commands for completing specific tasks can be accessed through the ribbon. You will learn more about this later on.

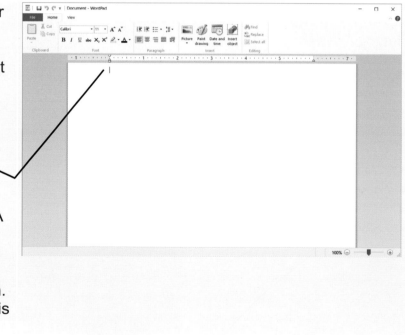

3.2 The Keyboard

A computer keyboard has over one hundred keys. That is much more than the old-fashioned typewriter. When you look at the keyboard, you will see keys for letters and numbers, as well as various other keys. You will learn how to use these keys in this book.

The position of the letters and punctuation marks is still the same as on a typewriter:

The keyboard of a laptop is almost the same:

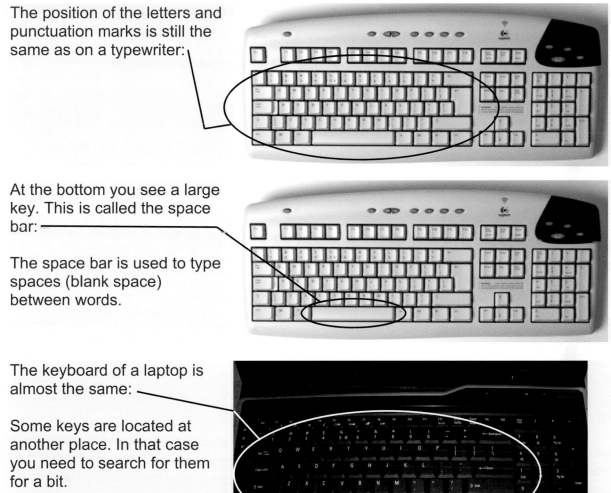

At the bottom you see a large key. This is called the space bar:

The space bar is used to type spaces (blank space) between words.

Some keys are located at another place. In that case you need to search for them for a bit.

Sometimes there are fewer keys on the right-hand side of the keyboard. This does not matter as these keys will not be used while working with this book.

Now you can start typing. The letters will appear where the cursor is positioned:

Type: this is a first line

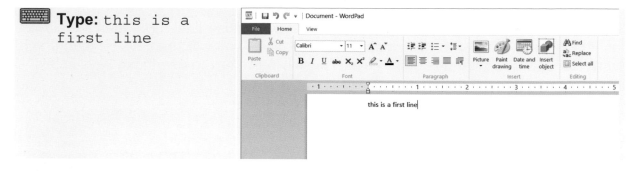

3.3 Repeat Keys

The keys on a computer keyboard are repeat keys. This means that if you keep pressing a key, you will automatically see multiple letters appear on the screen. Try it:

Press the key for the letter 'o' 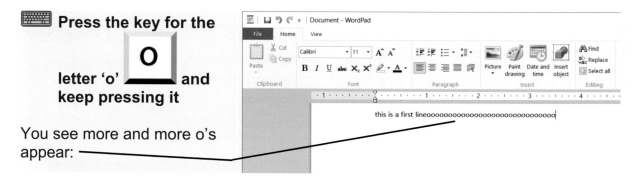 **and keep pressing it**

You see more and more o's appear:

Luckily, it is easy to remove letters you do not need.

3.4 A Typing Error

In this case, you typed the wrong letters 'o' on purpose. But in the future you may press a wrong key by accident. You can remove wrong letters by pressing the Backspace key.

That is a big key, with the left-pointed arrow, sometimes also with the word 'Backspace'.

The Backspace key is usually located at the top right of the keyboard:

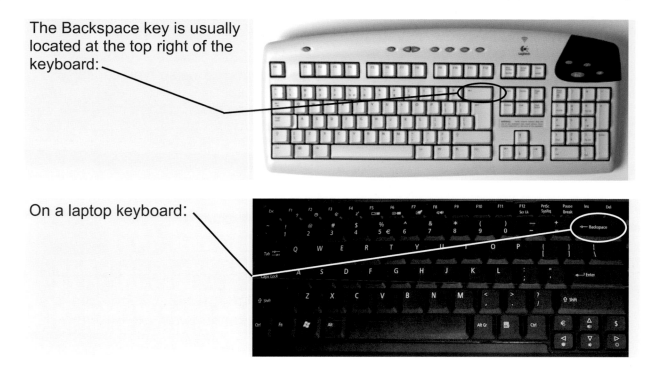

On a laptop keyboard:

The Backspace key is used to remove the letter to the left of the cursor. You can use it to remove the letters 'o' that you do not need, for example:

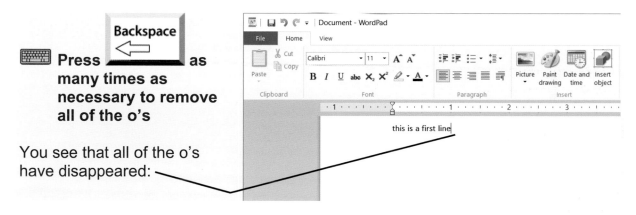

Press **Backspace** **as many times as necessary to remove all of the o's**

You see that all of the o's have disappeared:

Please note:

The Backspace key itself is also a repeat key. Do not press it too long or you will have to retype the text.

3.5 Capital Letters

Until now, you have only typed lower-case letters. But you can also type capital letters.

To do so, you use the large key that says 'Shift':

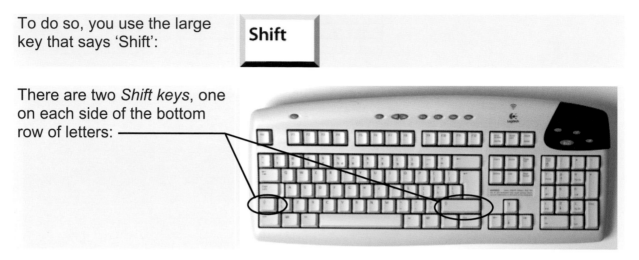

There are two *Shift keys*, one on each side of the bottom row of letters:

The Shift key is always used in combination with a letter, a number or a punctuation mark.

This is how to type a capital letter:

- press the Shift key and keep it depressed;
- type the letter;
- release the Shift key.

Type a space

Type: `This line is about Amsterdam, the capital of Holland.`

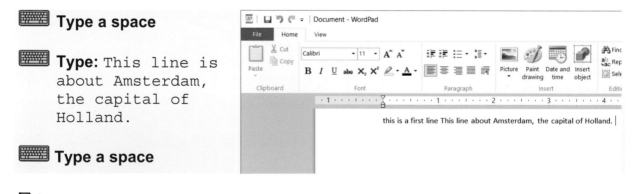

Type a space

➥ Please note:

It is customary to type a blank space after a punctuation mark, such as a full stop, a comma, an exclamation mark, a question mark, a colon, and a semicolon.

3.6 Words on the Next Line

In word processing programs, the program itself distributes the text over the page. If you type multiple sentences in a row, the text will automatically continue on the next line. Take a look:

 Type: Each year, a large number of tourists from all over the world visit Amsterdam.

You see the text continuing on the next line:

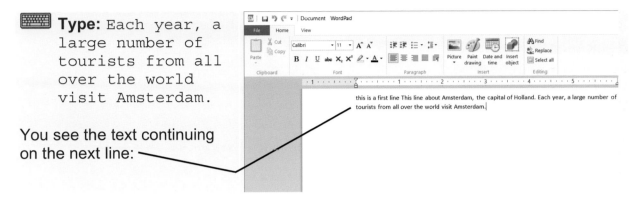

The computer always makes sure that sentences of equal length will fit nicely on the page. This is done automatically.

3.7 Beginning a New Paragraph

A series of sentences that are grouped together is called a paragraph. A new paragraph starts on a new line.

A new line is made using the *Enter key*:

The Enter key is located on the right side of the keyboard:

If you press the Enter key, the cursor (the little blinking line) will move down one line.

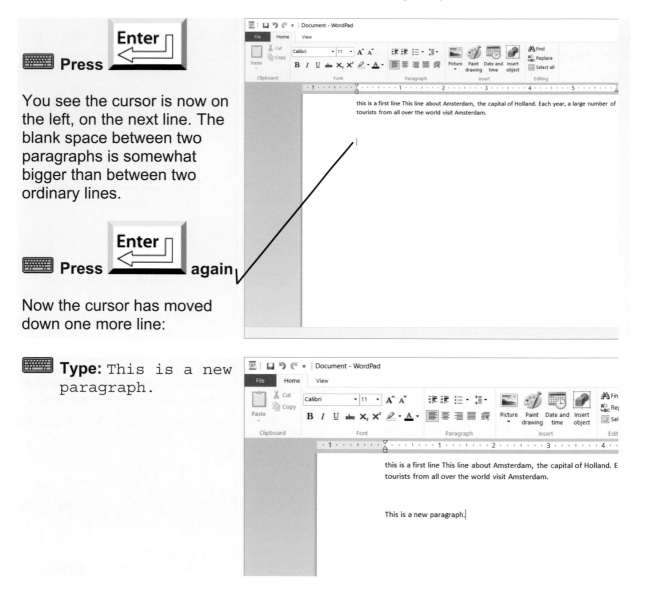

Press You see the cursor is now on the left, on the next line. The blank space between two paragraphs is somewhat bigger than between two ordinary lines.

Press again

Now the cursor has moved down one more line:

Type: This is a new paragraph.

3.8 Colon or @?

The Shift key is also used to type various other characters.

Examples are: : ? @ * % $ + | } < ! ~ & ^

Many of these characters are located at the top of a key:

The character at the top of these keys is typed using the Shift key, just as you do for capital letters.

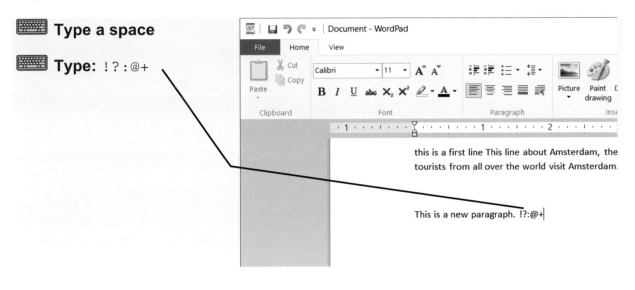

⌨ **Type a space**

⌨ **Type:** ! ? : @+

3.9 The Cursor Keys

Everyone makes a typing error now and then. You often do not notice until later, after you have typed more text. To remove the error with the Backspace key, you would have to remove all of the other text as well. Naturally, that is not very convenient. It is better to move the cursor to the place where the error is.

You can move the cursor using the four special cursor keys. These are the keys with the arrows. They are grouped together:

The *cursor keys* are located on the right side of the keyboard:

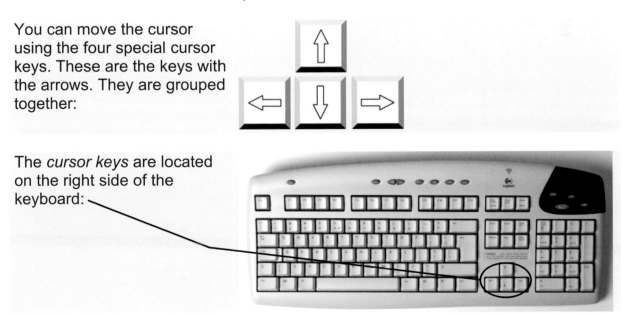

You can use these keys to move the cursor to the left or right, or up and down, through the text.

The cursor is blinking next to the +:

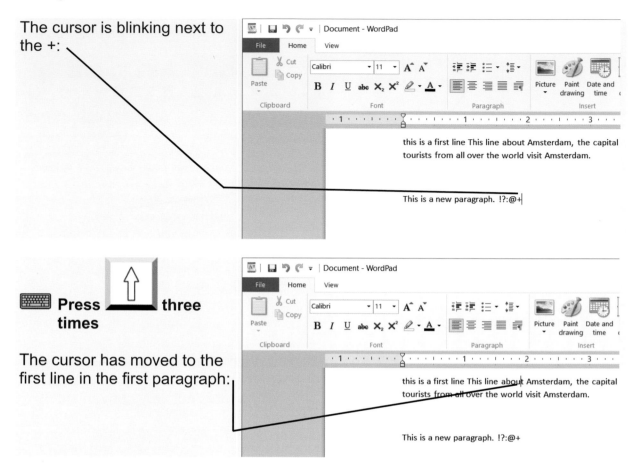

Press ⬆ three times

The cursor has moved to the first line in the first paragraph:

If you move to the left or right, the cursor follows through the text:

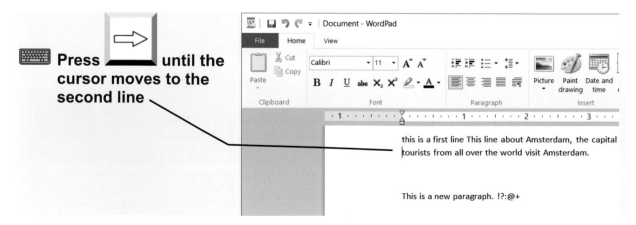

Press ⮕ until the cursor moves to the second line

You see the cursor move to the right, through the text, until it jumps to the next line.

3.10 The Beginning and End of the Text

You can use the cursor keys to move the cursor to any position in the text that you want. But you cannot move the cursor over the entire sheet of paper. The text has a beginning and an end. Try it:

Press ⬅ **until the cursor is at the beginning of the first paragraph**

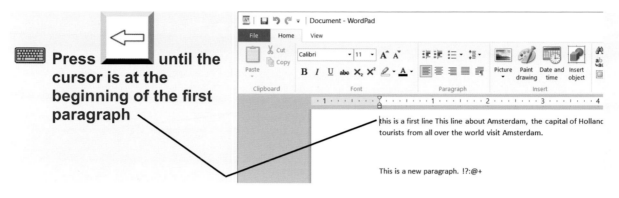

The cursor will not move any further than the beginning of the text. On some computers, the program may even sound a warning signal.

Press ⬇ **until the cursor is at the beginning of the last line**

The cursor will not go any further.

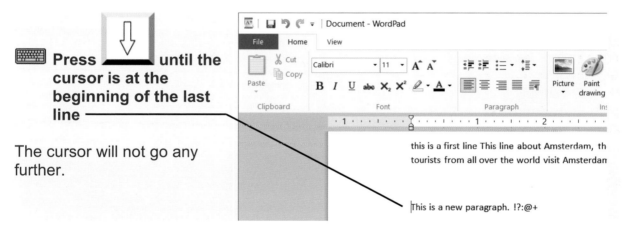

You cannot move the cursor any further than the last letter or punctuation mark:

Press ➡ **until the cursor is at the end of the last line**

Again, the cursor will not go any further.

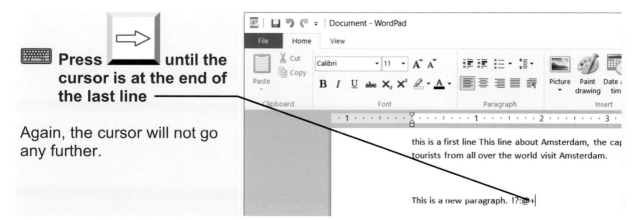

As you have seen, the cursor cannot be moved further than the beginning or the end of the text you have typed. You can, of course, type more text there.

⌨ Type a space

⌨ Type: `are special`
`characters`

The text appears at the end:

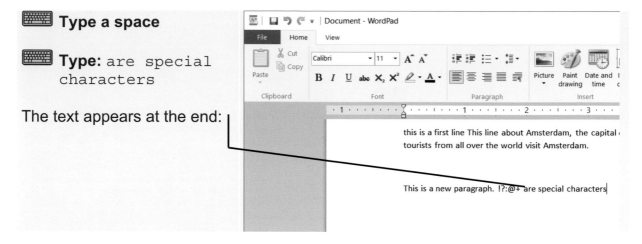

Of course, you can always add empty lines to the text. The end of the text will then be the last (empty) line:

⌨ Press Enter twice

You see empty lines appear at the bottom of the text:

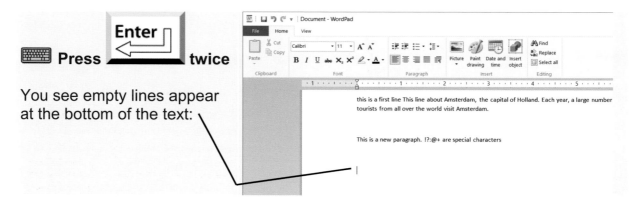

You can tell that there are blank lines there, by the blinking cursor at the very bottom.

Now you know how to move the cursor through the text. This is very handy when you want to correct errors or change the text.

3.11 Correcting More Mistakes

You can move the cursor to the spot in the text where you want to make a change. For example:

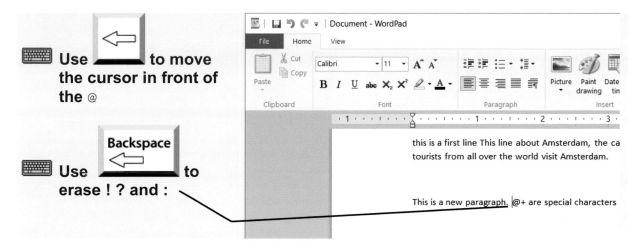

Use ⟵ to move the cursor in front of the @

Use Backspace ⟵ to erase ! ? and :

You can also change the first letter of the text into a capital:

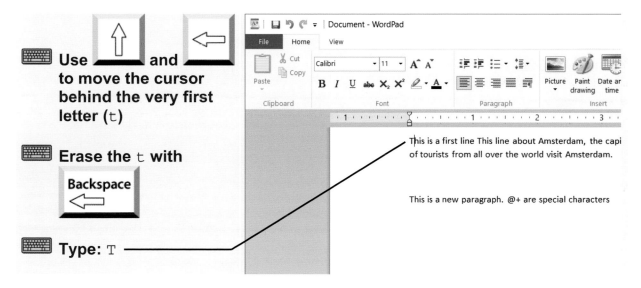

Use ⇧ and ⟵ to move the cursor behind the very first letter (t)

Erase the t with Backspace ⟵

Type: T

3.12 Removing Empty Lines

You can remove empty lines the same way. Move the cursor to an empty line and press the Backspace key:

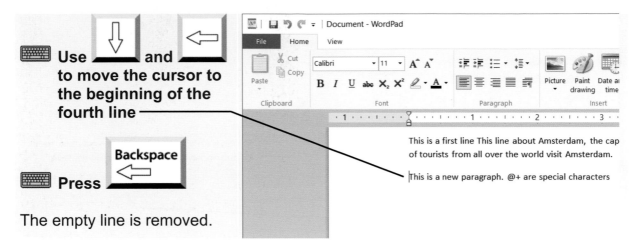

Use ⬇ **and** ⬅
to move the cursor to
the beginning of the
fourth line

Press **Backspace** ⬅

The empty line is removed.

Now you will only see the additional blank space that *WordPad* automatically inserts between two paragraphs. You cannot remove this space with the Backspace key.

3.13 Undoing

If something goes wrong while you are writing, or if you accidentally press the wrong key, nearly every *Windows* program has a command that will *undo* it. Try it:

At the top left of the window:

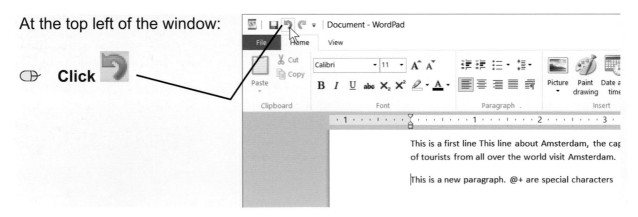

Click ↩

The line you removed in the last sections has been inserted again.

Tip
Did something go wrong?
First, always try to find out if the command can be undone:

☞ **Click**

3.14 A Larger and Different Font

A *font* is a complete set of characters of a particular size, type, and style, including numerals, symbols and the characters of the alphabet.
When you start typing in *WordPad*, the font size that is automatically used is rather small, and may be unpleasant to work with. This can easily be changed, just like almost everything else in *Windows.* You can choose a font size that is a bit bigger. Here is how you do it:

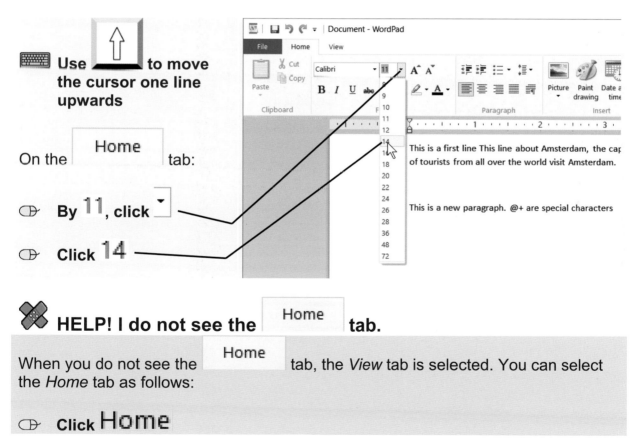

⌨ **Use** ⬆ **to move the cursor one line upwards**

On the **Home** tab:

☞ **By 11, click** ▼

☞ **Click 14**

❌ HELP! I do not see the Home tab.

When you do not see the Home tab, the *View* tab is selected. You can select the *Home* tab as follows:

☞ **Click Home**

You will not see anything happen on the window. But when you start typing, you will see that the text is somewhat larger and easier to read:

Type: This is a
larger font.

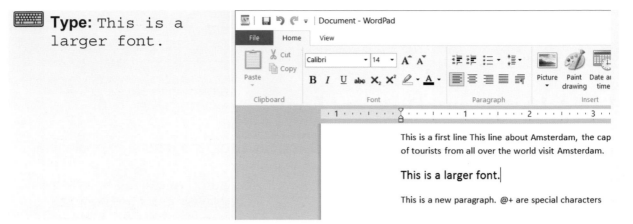

You can also change the font type:

On the [Home] tab:

☞ **By Calibri, click** ▾

☞ **Click Cambria**

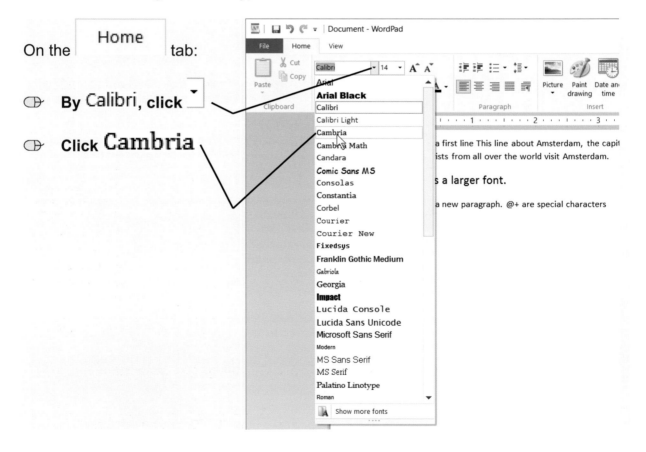

⌨ **Type a space**

⌨ **Type:** And a different font.

You will see the new font:

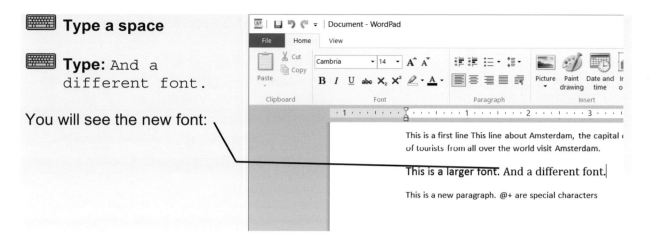

In this way, you can always use the font you like. You can also change the font afterwards. In that case, you will need to select the font first. In *Chapter 4 Word Processing* you will learn about selecting.

3.15 Opening a New Document

You have now practiced enough with the keyboard. It is time to start working with a new, blank document. This is how you do it:

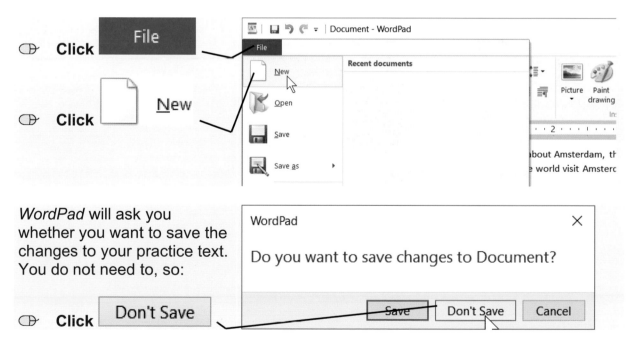

☞ **Click** File

☞ **Click** New

WordPad will ask you whether you want to save the changes to your practice text. You do not need to, so:

☞ **Click** Don't Save

Now you have a new, blank document, just like a fresh sheet of paper:

You can start typing again:

⌨ **Type a small text, for example:** This is my first document written on a computer.

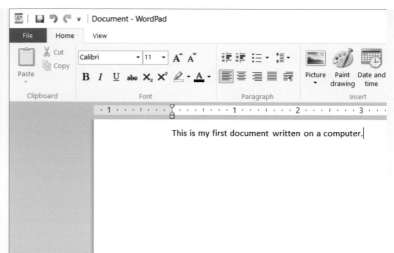

In the next section you will be saving this text.

3.16 Saving a Document

This first practice document will be stored on the computer. Storing a document (such as a letter or a report) is called *save* in *Windows*. This is how you save your document:

👆 **Click** File

A menu appears:

👆 **Click** Save

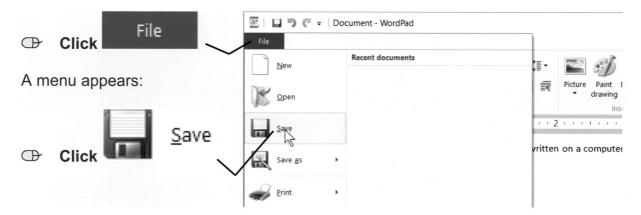

The practice document needs to have a name.

The name is entered in the box next to **File name:**:

You will change it:

⌨ **Type:** first document

☞ **Click** Save

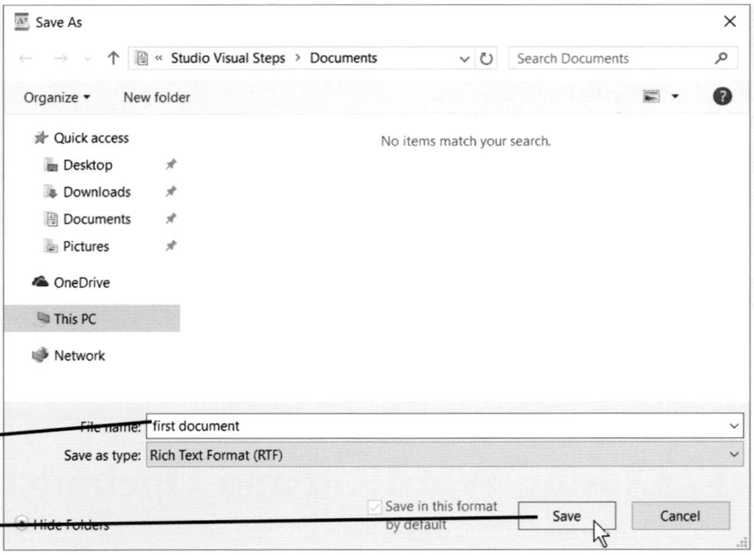

HELP! I see a small window.

In most cases you will see a large window, but in some cases you will see a small window. You enlarge the window like this so that all folders are shown as well:

☞ **Click** ▼ Browse Folders

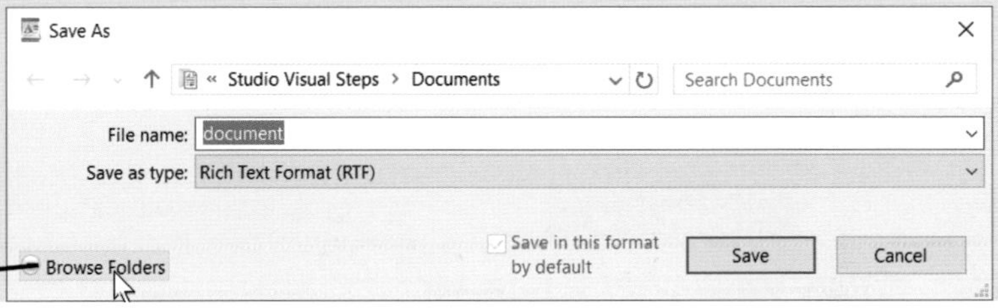

The document has been saved on your computer's hard disk. You will open this document in one of the next sections.

Now the name of your document appears at the top of the window in the title bar:

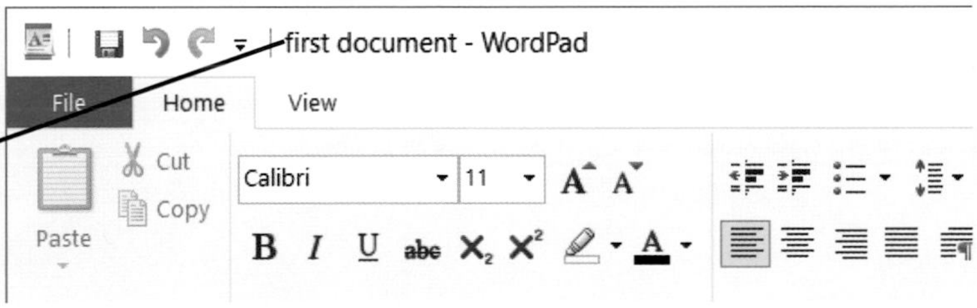

HELP! The file already exists.

Did this window appear?
If so, you (or someone else)
has already saved a text with
the name *first document*. You
can replace it with your own
document.

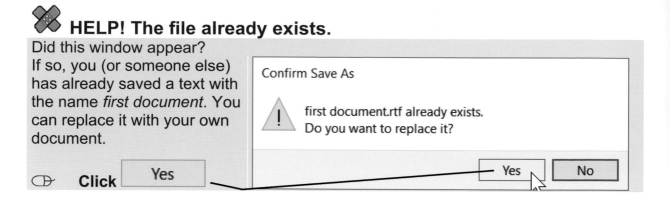

Confirm Save As

⚠ first document.rtf already exists.
Do you want to replace it?

Yes   No

👉 **Click** | Yes |

3.17 Closing WordPad and Opening it Again

Now you must close *WordPad* for the moment. This is done to show you how to
retrieve your practice document so that you can work on it another time:

At the top right of the window:

👉 **Click** ✖

WordPad is closed. Now you can open *WordPad* again:

👉 **Open *WordPad* again** 𝄞²

You see an empty window,
without your practice
document.

The name *Document* is
shown at the top:

Document is the default name for a new text. In order to get your practice document
to appear on the window, you need to open it first.

3.18 Opening an Existing Document

If you want to use a document that has been saved on the computer, you must open it first. This is how:

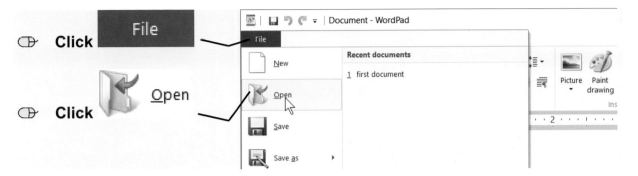

Click File

Click Open

The *Open* window appears. The name is shown in the title bar:

In the big white box in this window, you see the name of your document:

first

Click document

This icon might look different on your computer, for example like this

first document.

Click Open

You can change the way you view a document, for example in the *Open* window. You can read more about this in *Chapter 5 Files and Folders*.

Now your practice document is once again displayed on your window:

You can continue to work on it now and print it.

3.19 Printing the Document

When you write a document like a letter, most likely you will want it printed on paper.

Printing is done with a printer:

🩹 HELP! No printer?
If you do not have a printer, you can skip this section.

Before you actually print a document, it is wise to have a preview of what it will look like on paper. *WordPad* has a special command for this:

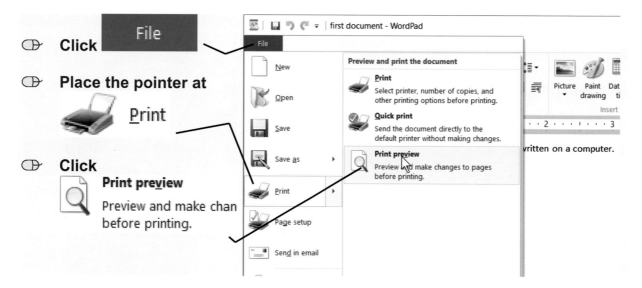

☞ **Click** File

☞ **Place the pointer at** Print

☞ **Click** Print preview

Preview and make chan before printing.

Now this window appears.
In the middle is a miniature
representation of the page as
it will be printed:

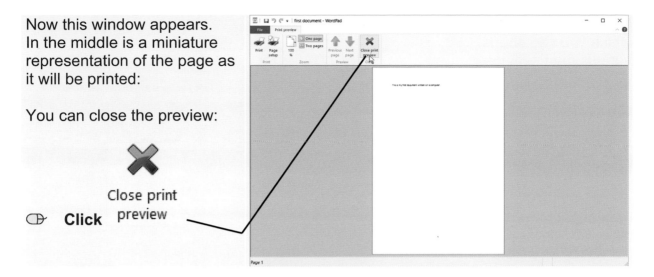

You can close the preview:

Close print
⊕ **Click** preview

For now, you can print the document the way it is. Of course, you can do a lot of
other things to make the document look more appealing, for example by typing more
text or using a different type of font. But for now, that is not necessary.

➥ Please note:

It is important to check if your printer is ready for use before you tell the computer to
print anything.

☞ **Make sure the printer is on**

☞ **Make sure there is paper in the printer**

Is everything ready? Then you can tell the computer to print the document:

⊕ **Click** File

⊕ **Place the pointer at**
Print

⊕ **Click**
Print
Select printer, number of
other printing options be

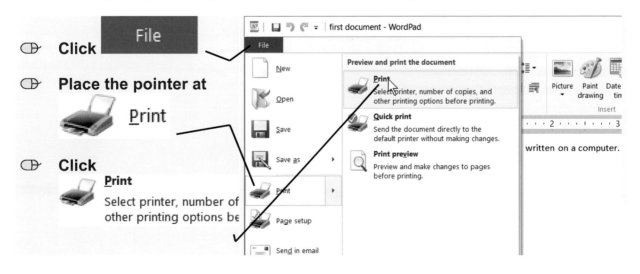

Now you see a window in which you can choose various print settings:

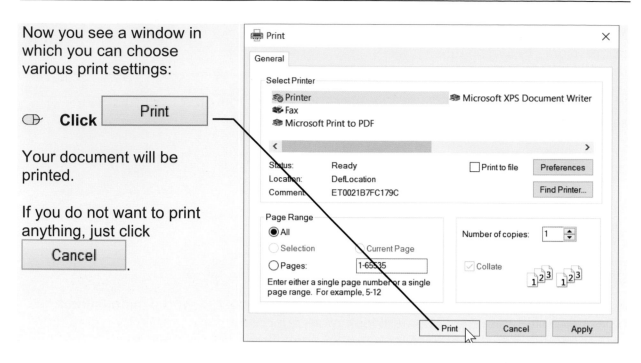

☞ **Click** Print

Your document will be printed.

If you do not want to print anything, just click Cancel.

3.20 Save Changes?

You can never accidentally lose something you have already saved. *Windows* always checks to see if something is about to be lost. You should give it a try by making a small change. If you stop the program after that, *WordPad* will warn you:

☞ **Click at the end of the sentence**

⌨ **Type a space**

⌨ **Type a new sentence, for example:** I think I did a good job!

☞ **Click** ✖

WordPad will ask you whether or not the changes should be saved:

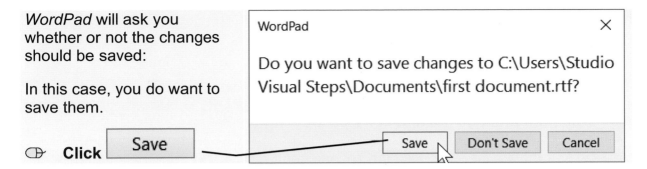

In this case, you do want to save them.

☞ **Click** Save

The changes will be saved and *WordPad* will be closed.

💡 **Tip**

Saving
To many people, this window is confusing. If you unexpectedly see this window, you apparently made at least one change. No matter how small, even if the change is simply one space, it is still a change to *WordPad*.

- If you click Save , the changes will be saved.
- If you click Don't Save , the changes will not be saved. The old text will stay saved.
- If you click Cancel , you will return to *WordPad*.

WordPad ✕

Do you want to save changes to C:\Users\Studio Visual Steps\Documents\first document.rtf?

Save Don't Save Cancel

Please note: only click Don't Save if:
- you do not want to save the text;
- the version of the text that you saved previously is better than the current version. In that case, it would be a waste to replace it.

Now you can open your practice document again to see what happens when you first save the changes yourself.

☞ **Open *WordPad* again** 𝒲²

☞ **Open the practice document** first document **again** ✇¹³

You will see the saved letter, with the second sentence. Again, make a small change to the document:

⌨ **In between 'a' and 'good', type:** pretty

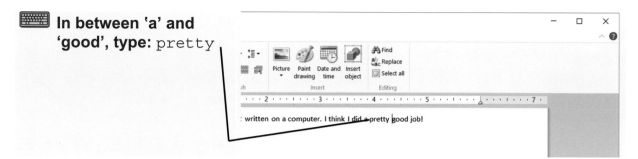

Now you can save this minor change:

☞ **Click** File

☞ **Click** Save

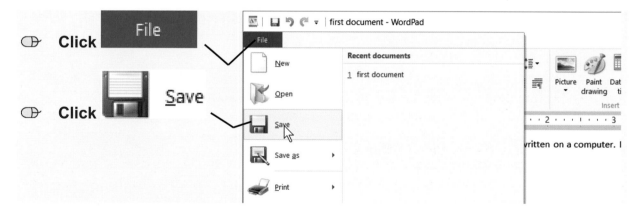

This time you were not asked to select a name. You have already given this document the name *first document* and it will be saved with that name.

☞ **Close *WordPad*** ✇⁶

Did you notice that the window asking whether to *save changes* has not appeared? That is because you saved the last changes yourself while you were working.

You have reached the end of this chapter. In the exercises on the next page, you can practice a little more.

3.21 Exercises

The following exercises will help you master what you have just learned. Have you forgotten how to do something? Use the number beside the footsteps to look it up in the appendix *How Do I Do That Again?*

Exercise 1: Typing Text

☞ Open *WordPad*. ᨒ2

☞ Type the following text:
```
Canberra is the capital of Australia. Canberra is exactly
halfway between Sydney and Melbourne, two other large
cities.
```

☞ Now insert a new, empty line. ᨒ14

☞ Type the following text:
```
Most people think that Sydney is the capital. For a long
time, people argued about whether Sydney or Melbourne
should be the capital. They finally decided to pick the
city in between the two.
```

☞ In the last sentence, erase the first **the** and type **a** in the same place. ᨒ15
```
They finally decided to pick the city in between the two.
```

☞ This is what the practice text looks like now:

Canberra is the capital of Australia. Canberra is exactly halfway between Sydney and Melbourne, two other large cities.

Most people think Sydney is the capital. For a long time, people argued about whether Sydney or Melbourne should be the capital. They finally decided to pick a city in between the two.

☞ Move the cursor to the beginning of the line. ᨒ16

☞ Move the cursor to the end of the line. ᨒ17

☞ Open a new document and do not save the changes. ᨒ18

Exercise 2: Corrections

With this exercise, you can practice correcting typing errors.

☞ Maximize the *WordPad* window. $\wp\wp^4$

☞ Type the following text including the mistakes:
Many people drink tea in the us. It is not as important
hear as in other contries where a ceremony is made of
drinkingtee, like in japan. They pay much closer attention
to the qality of the te. Other exampels of these countries
are china and Ingland.

☞ Correct the following mistakes:
Many people drink tea in the **US**. It is not as important
he**re** as in other countries where a ceremony is made of
drinking te**a**, like in **J**apan. They pay much closer
attention to the q**u**ality of the te**a**. Other examp**le**s of
these countries are **C**hina and **E**ngland.

☞ Restore the window to its previous size. $\wp\wp^7$

☞ Open a new text and do not save the changes. $\wp\wp^{18}$

Exercise 3: Saving Changes

☞ Type the following short letter:
Dear Sirs,

With this letter I want to thank you for your excellent
service.

Sincerely,

Your name

☞ Save this letter and name it *exercise*. $\wp\wp^{19}$

☞ Open a new text. $\wp\wp^{18}$

☞ Open the *exercise* letter again. $\wp\wp^{13}$

☞ Add the line printed in bold letters below:

```
Dear Sirs,
```

With this letter I want to thank you for your excellent service. **I would also like to inform you that the appliance works perfectly.**

```
Sincerely,
```

```
Your name
```

☞ Print the letter. ✂**20**

☞ Close *WordPad*, and while doing so have the changes saved. ✂**21**

3.22 Background Information

Dictionary

Cursor	Short blinking line that signals where text will appear.
Cursor keys	Move the cursor left, right, up or down through a text.
Dead key	A key that produces no output when pressed, but which modifies the output of the next key pressed.
Document	In *WordPad* a text such as a letter or a report
Empty line	Line with no text.
Font	A complete set of characters in a particular size and style, including numerals, symbols, punctuation and the characters of the alphabet.
Keyboard	The main input device used to communicate with the computer, similar to a typewriter keyboard but with extra function keys.
Open	Command to find and retrieve a document which has been saved on a hard drive, USB-stick or other memory device.
Paragraph	A paragraph is a section in a piece of writing, usually highlighting a particular point or topic. The start of a paragraph is indicated by beginning on a new line using the Enter key (or hard return) and may include indentation. The paragraph ends by using the Enter key. It consists of at least one sentence.
Print	Command to produce a copy of the document on paper with the help of a printer.
Print Preview	A feature that allows the user to view on the computer screen the document as it will appear on the printed page.
Repeat keys	Keys that keep giving characters while being pressed.
Ribbon	Toolbar seen in various programs that gives you access to a wide variety of commands for carrying out specific tasks.
Save	Command to store a file on a memory device such as a hard drive or USB stick for future use.

- Continue on the next page -

Space bar	Large key used to type spaces between words.
Undo	Command to undo the last thing you did in a program or app.
WordPad	A text editing program you can use to create and edit documents.

Source: Windows Help

Keys

In this chapter you have used the most important keys for word processing:

 Removes characters to the left of the cursor.

Shift Makes capital letters or characters on top of a key. Used in combination with another key.

Enter Makes a new line (paragraph).

 Cursor keys: move the cursor left, right, up or down through a text.

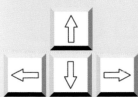

Besides, you can use the following keys to move through the text faster:

Home Moves the cursor to the beginning of a line.

End Moves the cursor to the end of a line.

File types

Your computer will save a document in a file format associated with the program in which you created the document. Each program has its own unique set of file types (or file extensions). *WordPad* in *Windows 10* can only open the following file types: .rtf, .docx, .odt, .txt.

Typing skills

It is certainly not necessary to learn to type like a professional typist in order to work with the computer. Most people have never learned to type, but learn as they go, with two or sometimes four fingers. A time comes when you can quickly find any key and then increase your typing speed.

It is striking that, despite all of the innovations of the computer era, the arrangement of the keyboard is still virtually the same as that of the typewriter.

The normal arrangement used in the United States is still QWERTY. Look at the letters at the top left of the keyboard. A long time ago, the letters were placed in this order to make sure that the typewriter keys would not get stuck even when typing very rapidly.

Apparently, people have become so familiar with this arrangement that they do not want any of it changed.

The keyboard has a separate section for typing numbers. This was designed especially for people who have to enter many numbers and amounts. This section is called the *numeric keypad*. ———

Some laptops do not have a numeric keypad.

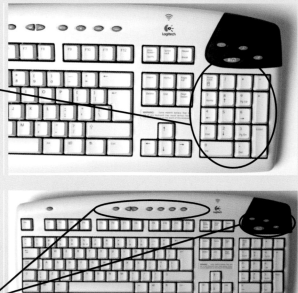

More and more keys are being added. Many of today's keyboards also have special keys used for the Internet. By pressing a single key, for example, you can collect your email. ———

Laptop keyboards may differ somewhat from regular desktop computer keyboards. Some keys, such as the Delete key, may be placed in a different spot. The descriptions in this book are based on the use of a desktop computer. If you are using a notebook, you may have to search for the key or the key combination that is described.

The proper working posture

It is important to arrange your computer properly. This not only makes it more pleasant to work with your computer, but it also minimizes the risk of various complaints. You will be surprised at the number of hours you will spend working with your PC. A proper working posture is therefore essential. Attention should be paid to the following issues:

- You need a table that is sufficiently deep and has the proper height. Your wrists should lie level with the tabletop when typing and using the mouse.
- An adjustable desk chair with arm rests is ideal because you can adjust it to achieve proper support for your back and legs. If your feet do not touch the ground, put something under them to support them - a few thick books, or a small stool or foot rest, for example.
- The keyboard should be directly in front of you. The mouse should be next to the keyboard on the correct side: on the right if you are right-handed and on the left if you are left-handed.

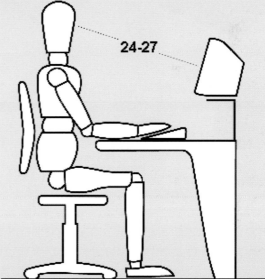

- Place the monitor straight in front of you, at about the same level as your eyes. Do not place the monitor to the left or right because this would force you to constantly strain your neck to turn your head.
- The monitor should be about one arm's length (24 to 27 inches) from your eyes.
- The monitor should not be too low or too high, forcing you to look up or down all the time. If you wear glasses or lenses that are multi-focal (with a special section for reading), having the monitor at the wrong height could force you to use the reading section instead of the 'far-off' section of the lenses. You can always raise the monitor by putting something under it (another thick book?).
- Make sure there is no direct or indirect light shining into the monitor that would make it hard to read.

Storing files on the computer

The computer has a certain amount of *working memory.* This working memory consists of chips in which the information is temporarily saved.

When you turn the computer off, however, the memory is emptied. This is why you also need to be able to save information more permanently.

That type of memory exists in various types: the computer's *hard disk* or an external hard disk, but also USB sticks (USB memory sticks), SD cards, CD-recordable/-rewritable and DVD-recordable/-rewritable and Blu-ray disks.

Hard disk   *USB stick*   *External hard disk*

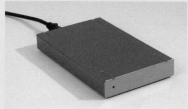

SD Card   *CD-r / CD-rw*   *DVD-r / DVD-rw*   *Blu ray disk*

The most important storage method uses the hard (disk) drive on your computer. The hard disk is a small, sealed box that has been built into your computer.

Hard disk   *Inside a computer case*   *Case (housing)*

In this box, a small disk rotates. The disk is magnetic, making it possible to save information on it.

You determine what is saved on the hard disk drive. You can save documents on it, or drawings, or computer programs. You can copy, move or delete files from the hard disk drive. You can read more about this in *Chapter 5 Files and Folders.*

Where to save?

Nowadays, every desktop computer in use contains one or more hard disk drives. In addition, many computers will have a CD drive and/or a DVD drive that can read and write (if the drive is a 'burner') CDs and/or DVDs. You can also save your work to a USB stick. USB sticks connect to the PC's USB ports.

Many modern computers have additional ports for connecting SD cards that are used in digital cameras, for example.

In the *This PC* window, you can see which items your PC contains. In this example, it contains the following items:

Hard disk:

DVD RW drive:

Removable disk:

External hard disk:

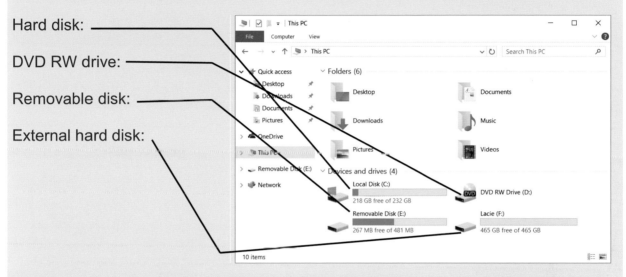

Windows gives every memory device a letter for a name.

- The hard disk drive always gets the letter C. (If there is a second hard disk, it will get the letter D.)
- The CD or DVD drive gets the next letter of the alphabet. In the example above, that's D.
- The next device gets the letter E, and so forth. In the window above, you see that the letter E has been given to a USB stick. In this example, it is a USB stick inserted into the computer. But it could also be a digital camera's memory card (SD card).

Please note: Other items or devices may be present on your computer. The letters you see on your own screen will belong to different devices.

You usually save your work on your computer's hard drive. If you want to take your work with you to another computer, or if you want to make a backup copy of a file, you can save your work onto a USB stick or a memory card. Another option for saving your work is to burn it onto a CD or DVD or save it in a location on the internet ('in the cloud').

Printers

The printer most commonly used in the home is called an *inkjet* printer.
This type of printer prints characters by spraying very small, precise amounts of ink onto the paper.

Many of these printers can also create color prints. These printers do not only have a cartridge with black ink, but also another cartridge with at least three colors. Any color imaginable can be copied by mixing the various colored inks. Each type of printer has different cartridges.

Inkjet printer

Inkjet printers can print on regular paper as well as on special types of paper, depending on the quality of print you want. You can get special photo paper to print photos, for example.

Laser printers are often used in the office sector. They are a non-impact printing device which operates in similar fashion to a photocopier, in which a laser draws the image of a page on a photosensitive drum which then attracts *toner* (an extremely fine-grained powder) on to the paper, where it is subsequently bonded by heating.

Laser printer

Laser printers are known for high quality prints, good print speed, and a low cost-per-copy. Laser printers are available in both color and monochrome varieties.

Photo printers use special photo paper to print digital photographs.

According to the manufacturers, these printers approach the professional quality of the photo printing services.

Photo printer

You can connect a printer to the computer, but there are also models that can print directly from a digital camera's memory card, through a Wi-Fi network or another network.

3.23 Tips

 Tip

Regularly save your work
If you work for a lengthy period of time, you should regularly save your work. It is also wise to save your work first before making big changes. If anything goes wrong, you will have a spare copy that has been saved. In this case, you can close the faulty document without saving it. Afterwards, you can open the previously saved document that is still in good order.

Tip

Capitals Only
The keyboard has a special key that is used to type capital letters.
This is the key that says *Caps Lock*:

Caps
Lock

This key is located on the left side of the keyboard:
It is an *on-off* key. That means: if you press it once, the capitals are on; if you press it again, you turn them off. An *indicator light* tells you whether capitals have been switched on or off.

Tip

Typing non-English letters and other special characters
When you look at your keyboard you will notice that there are no letter keys with accents or symbols such as ç, ñ, é of è. But it is actually not that hard to type these characters. You use these key combinations with the letter that needs to be accented. The + in the next examples means press the two keys at the same time.

For example:

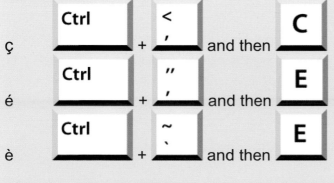

ç   Ctrl + < and then C

é   Ctrl + " and then E

è   Ctrl + ~ and then E

- Continue on the next page -

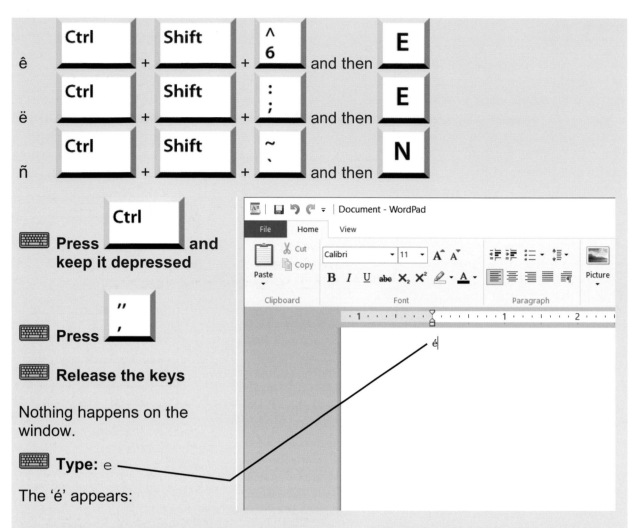

ê   **Ctrl** + **Shift** + **^ 6** and then **E**

ë   **Ctrl** + **Shift** + **: ;** and then **E**

ñ   **Ctrl** + **Shift** + **~ `** and then **N**

⌨ **Press Ctrl and keep it depressed**

⌨ **Press ″ ′**

⌨ **Release the keys**

Nothing happens on the window.

⌨ **Type:** e

The 'é' appears:

Now try to make another letter, such as the 'ñ'. It is a bit more complicated because you have to use the Shift key in order to type the '~'.

- Continue on the next page -

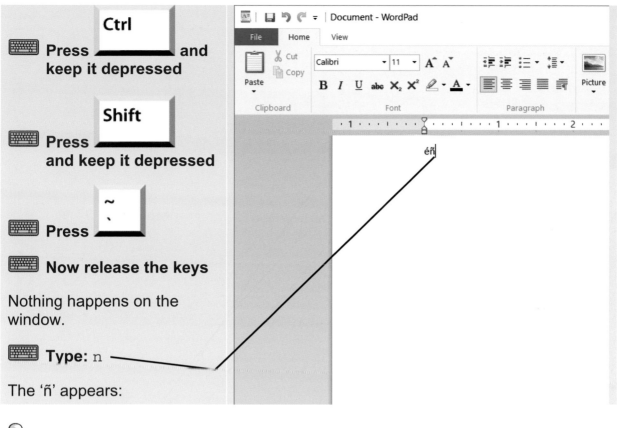

⌨ **Press** ___**Ctrl**___ **and keep it depressed**

⌨ **Press** ___**Shift**___ **and keep it depressed**

⌨ **Press** ___**~ `**___

⌨ **Now release the keys**

Nothing happens on the window.

⌨ **Type:** n

The 'ñ' appears:

💡 **Tip**

Rules for file names

What rules apply to naming a text?

File name: | Document |

A file name may not:
- be longer than 255 letters or numbers, including spaces;
- contain one of the following characters: \ / : * ? " < > . |

💡 **Tip**

Printing in black and white
If you have a printer that prints both in color and in black or white, usually it is set to print in color. If you do not want your color cartridges to empty prematurely and you are just printing text, you can choose to print in black and white. You do that like this:

👉 **Click**

Print
Select printer, number of copies, and other printing options before printing.

- Continue on the next page -

You see the *Print* window, where you can set a number of different options.
The option to print in black and white can be found in another window.

☞ **Click** Preferences

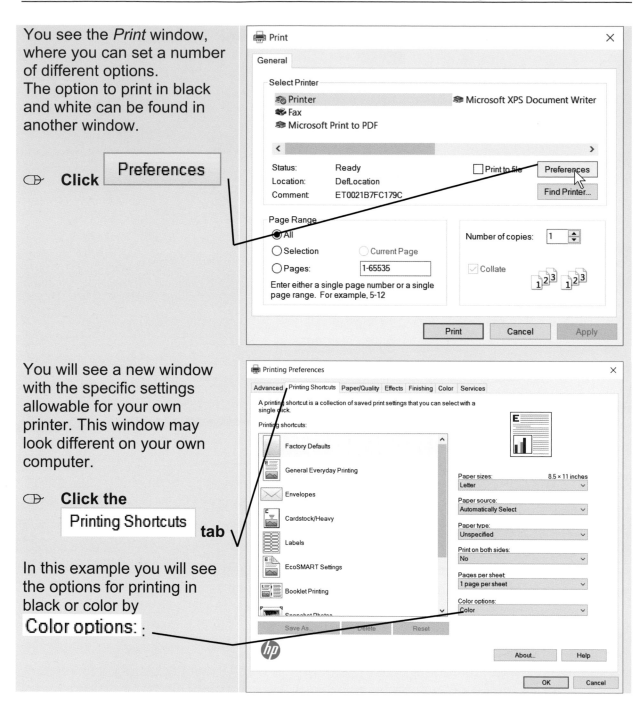

You will see a new window with the specific settings allowable for your own printer. This window may look different on your own computer.

☞ **Click the** Printing Shortcuts tab

In this example you will see the options for printing in black or color by Color options: :

☼ Tip

Quick Access Toolbar

At the top of the window, you will see various buttons. This area is called the *Quick Access Toolbar*. You can use the buttons to enter a command with a single mouse click: 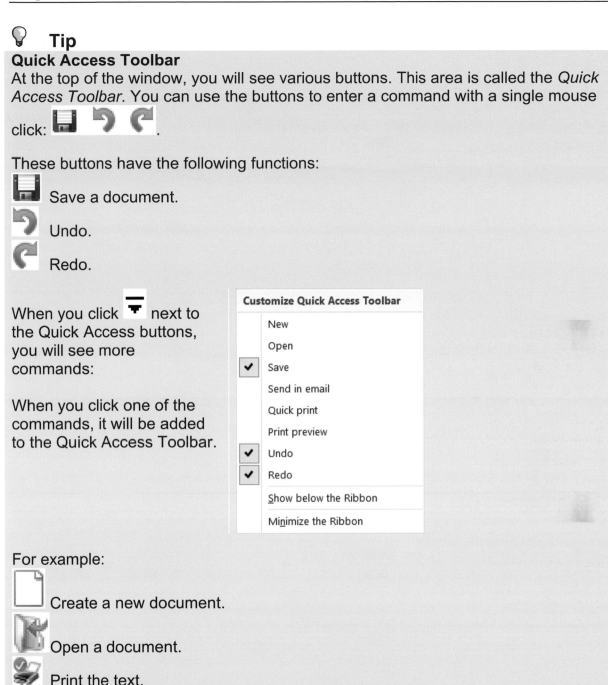 .

These buttons have the following functions:

Save a document.

Undo.

Redo.

When you click ▼ next to the Quick Access buttons, you will see more commands:

Customize Quick Access Toolbar
New
Open
✔ Save
Send in email
Quick print
Print preview
✔ Undo
✔ Redo
<u>S</u>how below the Ribbon
Mi<u>n</u>imize the Ribbon

When you click one of the commands, it will be added to the Quick Access Toolbar.

For example:

Create a new document.

Open a document.

Print the text.

See the Print Preview.

💡 Tip

Line Spacing

In *WordPad* the default line spacing is 1.15. This means there is always some space between the text lines. You can change the line space as follows:

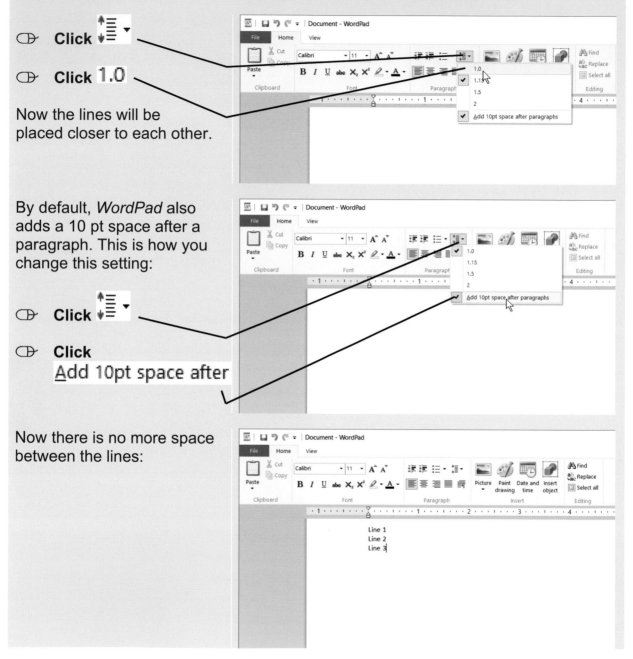

☞ **Click** ▼≣ ▼

☞ **Click 1.0**

Now the lines will be placed closer to each other.

By default, *WordPad* also adds a 10 pt space after a paragraph. This is how you change this setting:

☞ **Click** ▼≣ ▼

☞ **Click**
    Add 10pt space after

Now there is no more space between the lines:

4. Word Processing

It is very easy to modify a text using your computer. You can select a word, copy it and move it somewhere else, move sentences or paragraphs, or save the text for future use.

This chapter primarily focuses on word or text processing. You will discover how easy it is to change sentences: sometimes all you have to do is click and drag with your mouse. These actions can also be used in other apps and programs for example writing an email.

In this chapter you will learn how to:

- move the cursor with the mouse;
- select a single word or paragraph;
- delete a word;
- move a word or paragraph;
- split a paragraph and paste it back together;
- copy, cut and paste.

4.1 The Cursor and the Mouse

☞ **Open *WordPad* ⬯⬯²**

You can move the cursor with the cursor keys on the keyboard, or by using the mouse. In order to practice this, type the following words to a popular nursery rhyme.

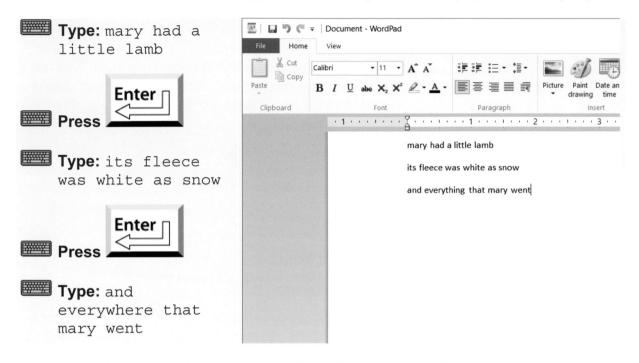

⌨ **Type:** mary had a little lamb

⌨ **Press** Enter

⌨ **Type:** its fleece was white as snow

⌨ **Press** Enter

⌨ **Type:** and everywhere that mary went

When you slide your pointer over text, the pointer changes its appearance from an

↖ (arrow) into this I. When you click the mouse somewhere in the text, the cursor will immediately move to that spot.

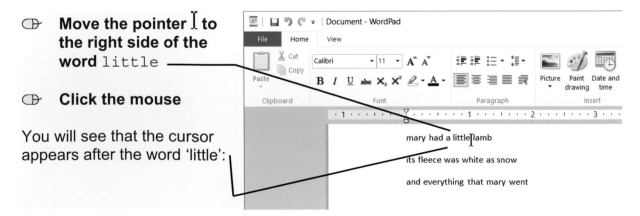

🖰 **Move the pointer I to the right side of the word** little

🖰 **Click the mouse**

You will see that the cursor appears after the word 'little':

Now you can delete the word 'little' using the Backspace key:

☞ **Delete the word**
`little` **with**

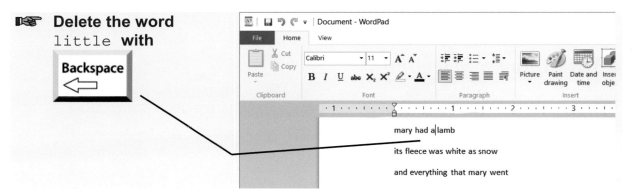

4.2 Selecting a Word

Using the Backspace key to delete a word is not very efficient. There are faster ways to delete a word or even an entire paragraph all at once.
In order to do so, you must first *select* the portion you want to delete. Selecting is done with the mouse.

🖰 **Move the pointer I to the word** `fleece`

🖰 **Double-click the mouse**

You see the word 'fleece' turn blue:

This means that the word has been *selected*.

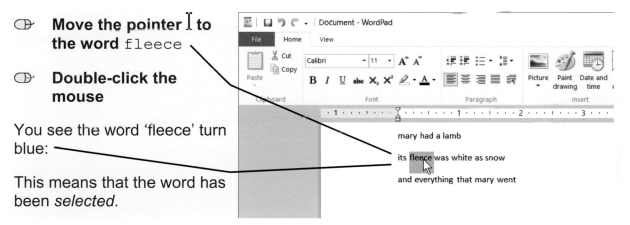

You can select a different word in the same way.

🖰 **Move the pointer I to the word** `everywhere`

🖰 **Double-click the mouse**

You see that the word 'everywhere' has now been selected:

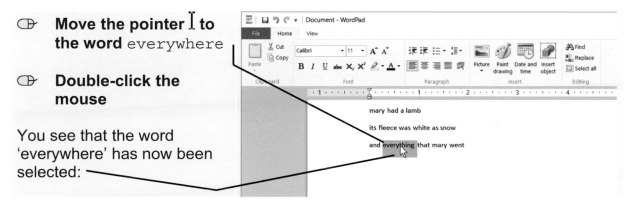

As you can see, this method allows you to select one word at a time. The word 'fleece' is no longer selected after you select 'everywhere'.

4.3 Undoing a Selection

It is very easy to undo a selection. Simply click somewhere else in the window:

☞ **Move the pointer I to an empty area in the window** ——————

☞ **Click the mouse**

You see that the word is no longer selected:

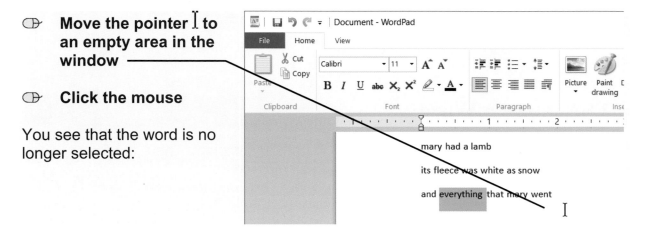

4.4 Deleting a Word

Once you have selected a word, you can do many things with it. You can delete it, for example.

Deleting is done with the Delete key:
(Sometimes it only says *Del*.)

The Delete key is located in the group of keys above the cursor keys: ——————

On a laptop computer, this key is often positioned somewhere else, for instance in the top right-hand corner.

☞ **Select the word**

white ✂22

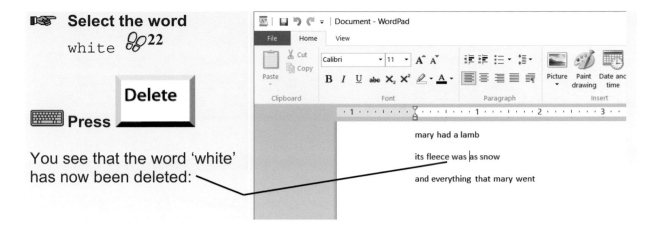

⌨ **Press** `Delete`

You see that the word 'white' has now been deleted:

4.5 Dragging a Word

You can drag a selected word to another place in the text. To practice this, first type the last line of the nursery rhyme. The words are in the right order now, but will not be after this exercise.

⌨ **Move the cursor to the end of the text**

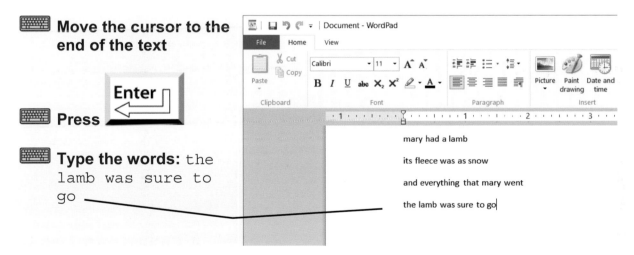

⌨ **Press** `Enter`

⌨ **Type the words:** the lamb was sure to go

Before you can drag a word, you must select it:

☞ **Select the word** the ✂22

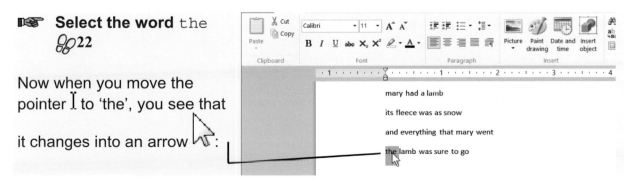

Now when you move the pointer I to 'the', you see that

it changes into an arrow ⬉ :

☞ **Press the mouse button and keep it depressed**

The pointer changes into 🖰. This indicates that the word is being dragged.

☞ **Move the pointer to the back of the word**
　　was

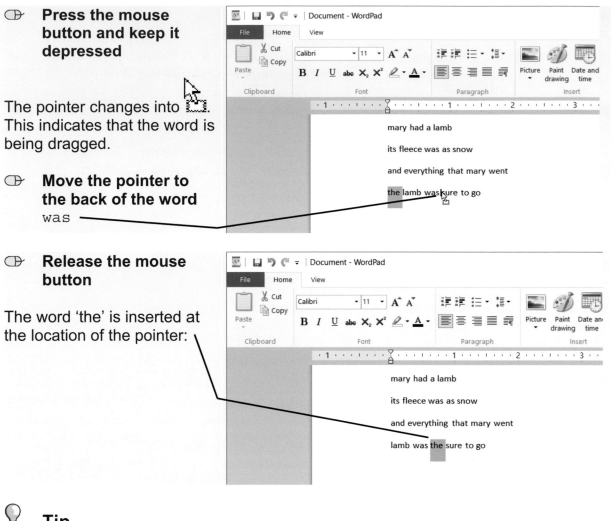

☞ **Release the mouse button**

The word 'the' is inserted at the location of the pointer:

💡 **Tip**

Does something go wrong?
For example if you dragged the word to the wrong place, you can undo it.
In the upper-left of the window:

☞ **Click** ↶

Learning to drag words will take some time. At the end of this chapter, you will find an exercise to practice dragging. You can undo the last change:

☞ **Undo the last change** 👣²³

You need to save the text if you want to practice this:

☞ **Save the text** 👣¹⁹ **and name it** *little lamb*

4.6 Typing Over a Word

If you want to replace one word with another, it is not always necessary to delete the word first. You can simply type over a word that has been selected. Try it:

☞ **Select the word** go
☪22

⌨ **Type:** walk

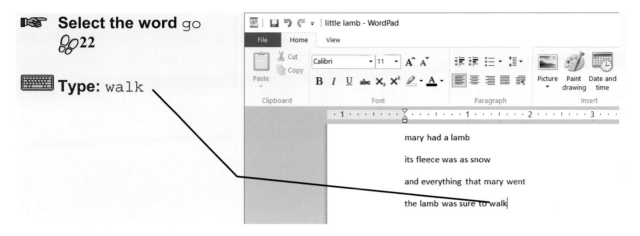

As you can see, the selected word is replaced by the new word you typed.

☞ **Open a new document, do not save the changes** ☪18

Now you have an empty window again, without text.

4.7 Selecting a Paragraph

You can also select a paragraph and delete it or drag it. You can easily practice this by placing the words of the national anthem in the right order. Type the first four lines. They have been put in the wrong order on purpose:

⌨ **Type:**
```
what so proudly we hailed
Oh, say can you see
at the twilight's last gleaming
by the dawn's early light
```

The start of a paragraph is indicated by a new line (use the Enter key). The paragraph ends by using the Enter key. A paragraph can be a group of sentences, one sentence alone or even just one line of text. In the text above every line is a paragraph.

It is easy to select a paragraph. Double-clicking with the mouse selects a word. Triple-clicking selects the paragraph:

☞ **Move the pointer I to the second paragraph**

☞ **Click the mouse three times**

Now you see that the second paragraph has been selected:

If triple-clicking does not work the first time, just try it again.

4.8 Dragging a Paragraph

Dragging a paragraph is done the same way as dragging a word. You can point to the selected paragraph and drag it to the place where it should be:

☞ **Move the mouse arrow to the selected paragraph**

☞ **Press the mouse button and keep it depressed**

The pointer changes into 🔲:

☞ **Move the mouse arrow to the front of the top paragraph**

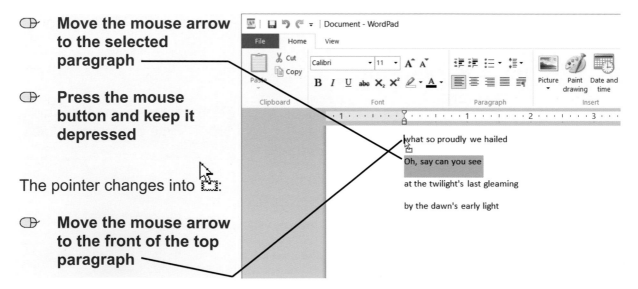

☞ **Release the mouse button**

The paragraph is entered at the top:

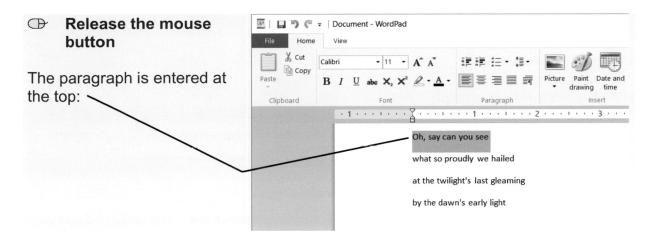

Dragging paragraphs will be easier once you give it some practice. See the relevant exercise at the end of this chapter. There you can put the entire anthem in the right order. You will be saving the text for this purpose shortly.

4.9 Splitting and Pasting Paragraphs

You have already seen that you can make empty lines (in fact empty paragraphs) by pressing the Enter key. You can also split a paragraph the same way. Sometimes this will happen accidentally when you press the Enter key. It is useful to know that you can *undo* this.

⌨ **Move the pointer to the end of the word** proudly ৪৫26

Press Enter

Now the sentence is split into two lines:

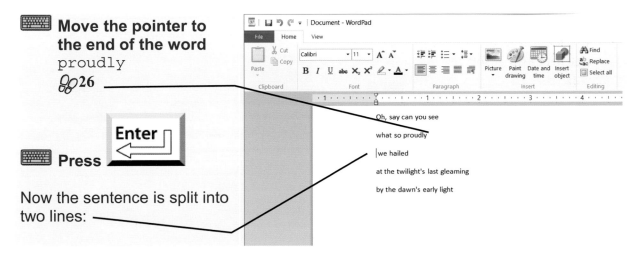

Both lines are in fact separate paragraphs. The bottom paragraph can easily be pasted back to the top paragraph using the Backspace key. In this instance, the cursor is still in the right place, at the beginning of the line.

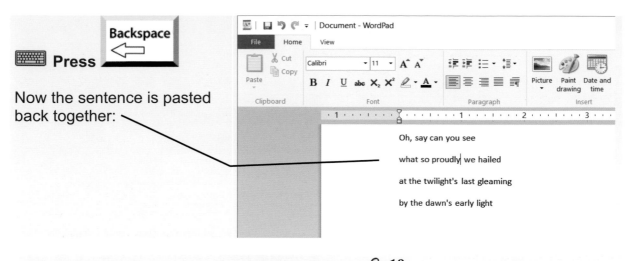

Press Backspace

Now the sentence is pasted back together:

Save this document and name it *Anthem* 𝄞19

Open a new document 𝄞18

4.10 Copying, Cutting and Pasting

Windows has three very useful commands: *copy, cut* and *paste.* Once you have copied or cut something, you can paste it somewhere else.
You can copy or cut in one program, and paste into a different program or an app. A text created in an email program can be pasted in a letter in *WordPad*, for example.

You can practice doing this in *WordPad*. Type the following three lines:

Type:
player
name
score

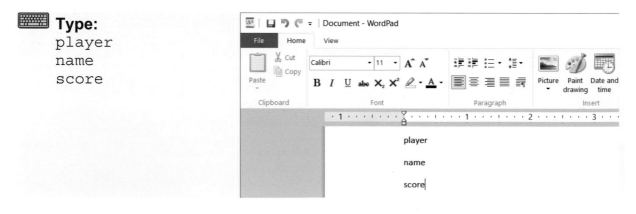

A portion of text, such as a word, is easy to copy and paste somewhere else in the text. But before you can copy something, you must select it first. Remember this rule:

Please note:
Select first ... then act.

☞ **Select the word** name
  𝒽𝒽22

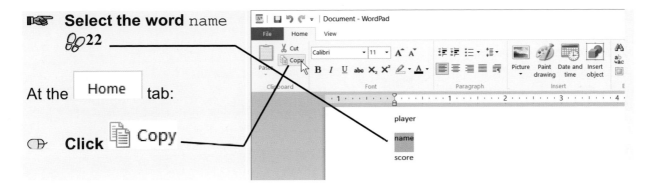

At the [Home] tab:

☞ **Click** 🗐 Copy

You cannot see anything happening, but the word 'name' has now been copied to the *Clipboard*. *Clipboard* is a temporary storage area. You can paste the word 'name' somewhere else. The cursor is used to indicate where to paste.

⌨ **Move the cursor to the end of the last line**
  𝒽𝒽26

☞ **Make an empty line at the bottom** 𝒽𝒽14

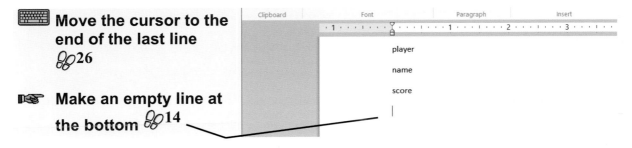

Now you can paste the word:

☞ **Click** 📋

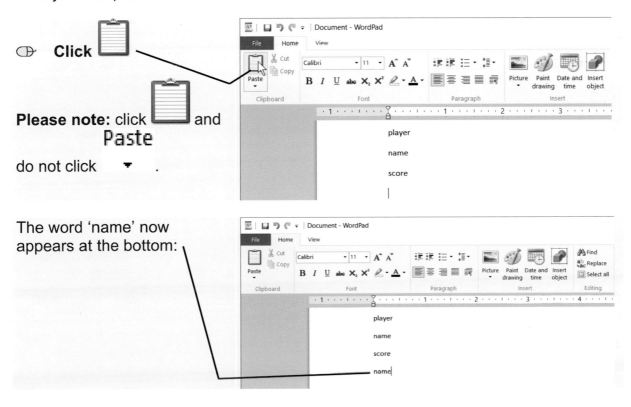

Please note: click 📋 and
  Paste
do not click ▼ .

The word 'name' now appears at the bottom:

A word that you select and copy can be pasted as many times as you want. Take a look:

☞ **Click** ⬚**again**

The word 'name' appears again:

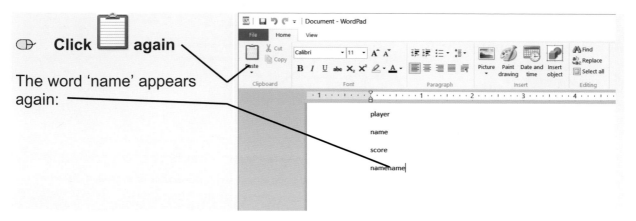

➥ **Please note:**

You can only paste the last text you copied. Each time you copy a text, any previously copied text is removed from the computer's memory.

You can also *cut* a word and paste it somewhere else. Give it a try, but remember the rule:

➥ **Please note:**
Select first … then act.

☞ **Select the word**
   player ♋**²²**

Now you can cut the word 'player':

☞ **Click ✄ Cut**

Now the word 'player' has disappeared: ────

It has now been copied to the *Clipboard*.

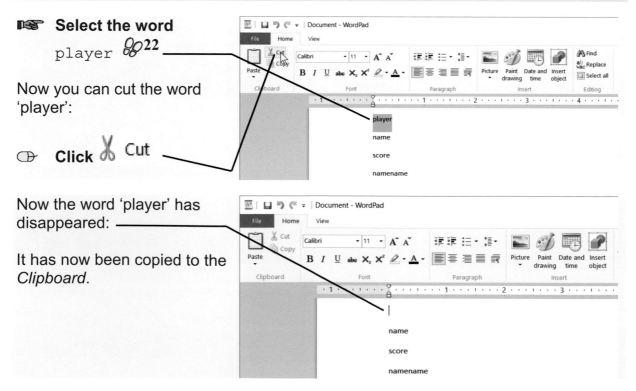

Move the cursor to the end of the last line *26*

☞ **Make an empty line at the bottom** *14*

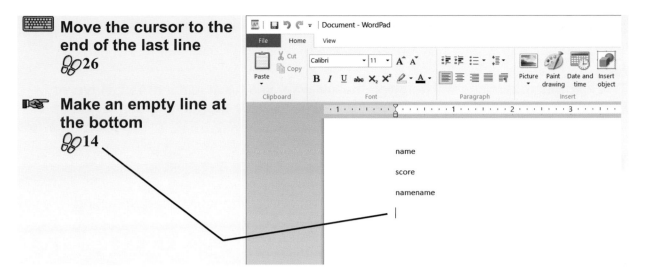

Now you can paste the word 'player'*:*

☞ **Click**

The word 'player' appears at the bottom:

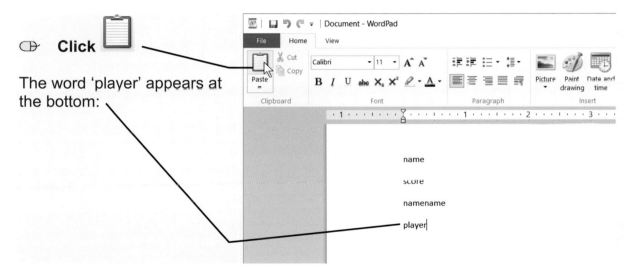

In this way you see how easily words or sentences can be moved. First select, then copy or cut, then paste your selection somewhere else.

Please note:

You can only paste the last text you copied or cut. If you copy or cut a new text, the text you copied or cut previously will be lost. You can always undo your last step, if you do not want to lose that part of the text.

☞ **Close *WordPad*, do not save the changes** *21*

With the next exercises you can practice what you have learned in this chapter.

4.11 Exercises

The following exercises will help you master what you have just learned. Have you forgotten how to do something? Use the number beside the footsteps to look it up in the appendix *How Do I Do That Again?*

Exercise 1: The Song

This exercise will help you practice deleting and dragging words and attaching portions of text to one another.

☞ Open *WordPad*. 🐾**2**

☞ Open the document with the name: 📄 little lamb . 🐾**13**

☞ Select the word 'that'. 🐾**22**

mary had a lamb

its fleece was as snow

and everything that mary went

the lamb was sure to go

☞ Delete the word 'that'. 🐾**15**

☞ Select the word 'sure'. 🐾**22**

mary had a lamb

its fleece was as snow

and everything mary went

the lamb was sure to go

☞ Drag the word 'sure' and position it behind the word 'lamb':

mary had a lamb

its fleece was as snow

and everything mary went

the lamb sure was to go

Now you can put the song on a single line:

☞ Attach the four paragraphs to make a single line. ✂[15] Add a space and a comma in the correct places.

mary had a lamb, its fleece was as snow and everything mary went, the lamb sure was to go|

☞ Save this document. ✂[24]

Note that you do not need to fill in a file name, because the file has been saved before.

Exercise 2: The National Anthem

This exercise lets you practice dragging lines of text.

☞ Open the document with the name: 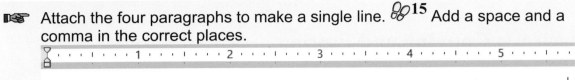 Anthem. ✂[13]

☞ Drag the paragraphs so that they are in the correct order:

Oh, say can you see

by the dawn's early light

what so proudly we hailed

at the twilight's last gleaming|

☞ Now add the following four paragraphs:
```
through the perilous fight
whose bright stars and broad stripes
were so gallantly streaming
o'er the ramparts we watched
```

☞ Now drag these paragraphs so that they are also in the correct order:

whose bright stars and broad stripes

through the perilous fight

o'er the ramparts we watched

were so gallantly streaming|

☞ Save the document. ✂[24]

☞ Open a new document. ✂ [18]

Exercise 3: Copying and Pasting

☞ Type the following three lines (paragraphs):
```
two
three
points
```

☞ Select 'points'. ✂ [22]

☞ Copy the word 'points'. ✂ [25]

☞ Move the cursor behind the word 'two' ✂ [26] and type a space.

☞ Now paste the word: 'points'. ✂ [27]

☞ Move the cursor behind the word 'three' ✂ [26] and type a space.

☞ Now paste the word 'points' here. ✂ [27]

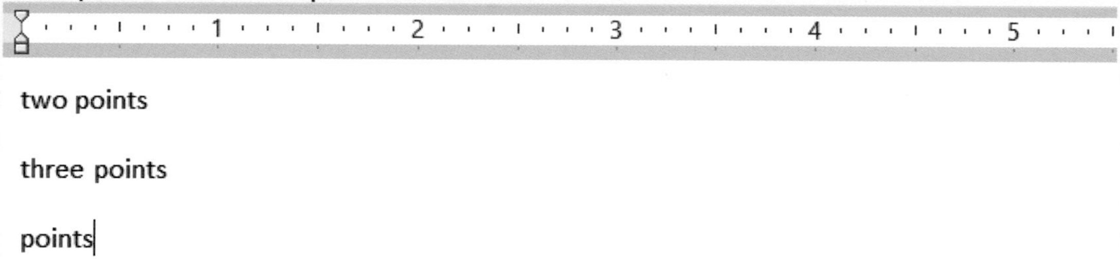

two points

three points

points|

☞ At the bottom, select the word 'points'. ✂ [22]

☞ Cut the word 'points'. ✂ [28]

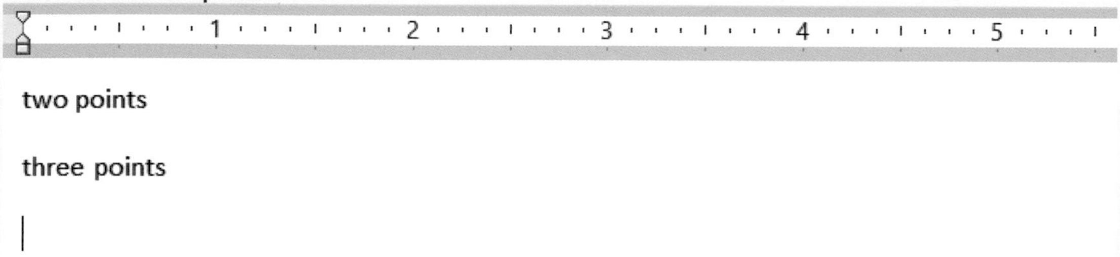

two points

three points

|

☞ Close *WordPad*, you do not need to save the document. ✂ [21]

4.12 Background Information

Dictionary

Clipboard	A temporary storage space, used by Windows. Data can be copied to the clipboard from a program or a location and subsequently pasted somewhere else. Each time you copy an item to the clipboard, the previous item will be replaced.
Copy	Command to duplicate a selected portion of a document, so that it can be inserted somewhere else.
Cut	Command to remove a selected portion of a document, so that it can be inserted somewhere else.
Delete	Action that removes a selected portion of a document.
Layout	The various elements given to a document such as font selection, font size, font color and other formatting options such as rendering text in bold, italics or with underlining
Paste	Command to insert a previously selected portion of a document which had been copied or cut.
Select	Action with the mouse that highlights a portion of a document.

Source: Windows Help

Word processing programs

Until now, you have worked with *WordPad*. It is a simple program that is more than sufficient for learning the basic principles of word processing. Its big brother is called *Microsoft Word*. This is a highly-detailed program that offers numerous functions.

You can make virtually anything you want with *Microsoft Word*: letters, minutes of meetings, folders, posters, flyers, cards, and other types of printed matter. The program has many functions for designing the layout of these items. It is very easy to make tables, for example. The program also has some extra *tools* such as an excellent spelling and grammar checker that you can turn on before you start typing. Then while you are typing, it alerts you when spelling and grammatical errors occur.

Microsoft Word is available as a separate program, but is usually sold as part of the *Microsoft Office* package. This package has a number of programs, including the popular spreadsheet *Excel* (for creating calculations) and *PowerPoint* (for creating presentations and slide shows).

4.13 Tips

💡 Tip

Selecting by dragging

You can not only select a whole word or an entire sentence, but any section of text you want:

⊕ **Move the cursor to the beginning of the section you want to select**

one two three four five

six seven eight nine

⊕ **Keep pressing the mouse button and drag the mouse to the right**

one two three four five

six seven eight nine

You will see that the letters are selected one after the other:

.

⊕ **Keep pressing the mouse button and drag the mouse downward**

one two three four five

six seven eight nine

This makes it possible to select multiple words or lines:

.

⊕ **Release the mouse button when you have selected the words or lines**

It takes some practice, but soon you will be able to select any portion of the text that you want.

💡 **Tip**

Selecting with keys

You can also select text by using the Shift key 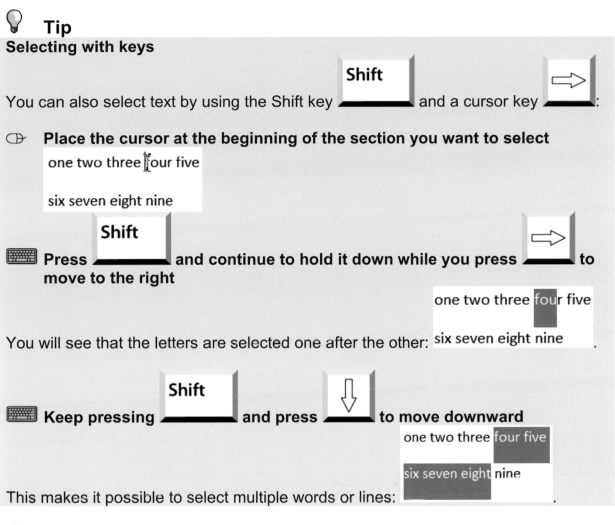 and a cursor key :

☞ **Place the cursor at the beginning of the section you want to select**

one two three |four five

six seven eight nine

⌨ **Press** Shift **and continue to hold it down while you press** ⇨ **to move to the right**

You will see that the letters are selected one after the other: one two three four five / six seven eight nine .

⌨ **Keep pressing** Shift **and press** ⇩ **to move downward**

one two three four five / six seven eight nine

This makes it possible to select multiple words or lines: .

💡 **Tip**

Selecting lines by clicking and dragging

You can also select lines or paragraphs by clicking and dragging in the margin of the text:

☞ **Place the pointer in the left margin of the document**

The pointer changes into 🔩:

☞ **Press the left mouse button and keep it depressed**

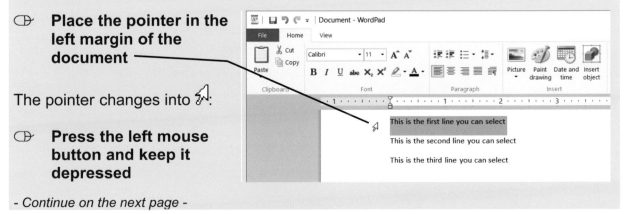

- Continue on the next page -

👈 **Drag the mouse downward**

The selected lines turn blue:

👈 **Release the mouse button**

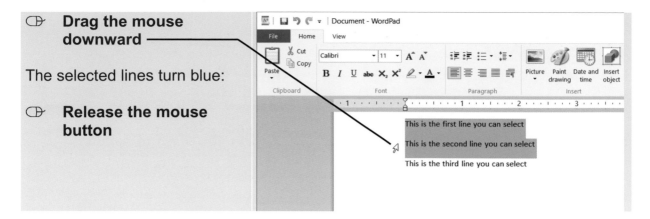

💡 Tip

Rendering text bold or in italics, underline or strike through

You can format words, lines, paragraphs, or an entire text. This is how you make a word bold:

☞ **Select a word**
    👣22

👈 **Click B**

Now the word has been made bold:

In the same way you can change a text into italics **I**, underline it **U** and strike it through **abc**.

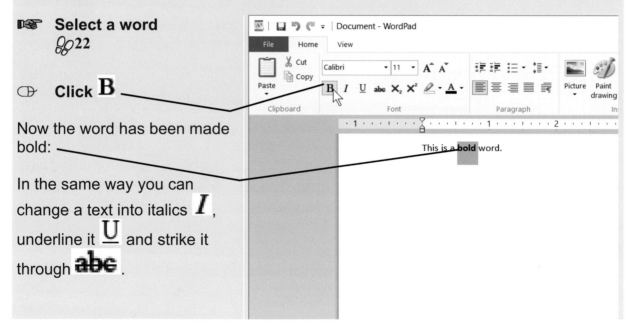

5. Files and Folders

In this chapter you will learn how to work with files and folders. A *file* is the generic name for everything saved on the computer. A file can be a program, a data file with names, text you have written, a photo or video. In fact, everything located on the hard drive of your computer is called a file.

A *folder* is little more than a container in which you store files. If you put thousands of paper files on someone's desk, it would be virtually impossible to find a particular one when you needed it. That is why people often store paper files in folders inside a filing cabinet. Arranging files into logical groups makes it easy to locate a particular file. Folders on your computer work exactly the same way.
Not only do folders hold files, but they also can hold other folders. A folder within a folder is usually called a *subfolder*. You can create any number of subfolders, and each subfolder can hold any number of files and additional subfolders.

When it comes to getting organized, you do not need to start from scratch. *Windows 10* comes with a handful of common folders that you can use as anchors to start organizing your files. Here is a list of some of the most common folders you can use to store your files and folders: *Documents, Pictures, Music, Videos* and *Downloads*.

You work with the files and folders located on your computer by using a *File Explorer* window. In this window you will be able to copy, move or delete your files and folders. Very likely at one time or another you will want to copy a text or a photo to a USB stick. You can do that in this window as well.

In this chapter you will learn how to:

- use the windows of *File Explorer*;
- add a new folder;
- move and copy a file to another folder;
- select multiple files;
- change the name of a file or folder;
- delete files;
- empty the *Recycle Bin*;
- copy a file to a USB stick.

5.1 Opening Your Personal Folder

Your *Personal folder* (also called *User Profile folder*) is a folder that contains your *Documents*, *Pictures*, *Music, Videos* folders, as well as other folders. The *Personal folder* is labeled with the name you use to log on to your computer. You can access the *Personal folder* via *File Explorer*. Take a look:

On the task bar:

Click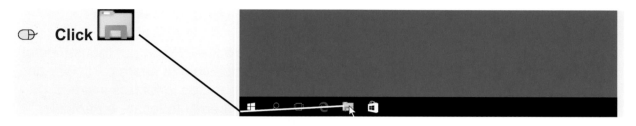

You can now see that the *File Explorer* window shows the most important folders on the computer. You will be working with your *Personal* folder:

By ⭐ **, click** ❯

Point to your profile name

In this example, it is 'Studio Visual Steps'.

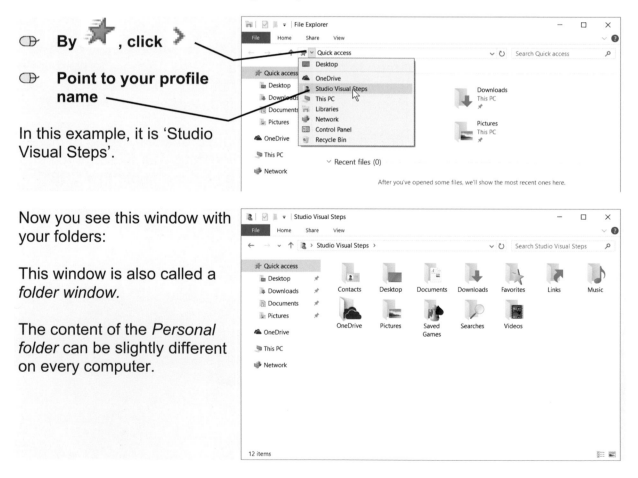

Now you see this window with your folders:

This window is also called a *folder window*.

The content of the *Personal folder* can be slightly different on every computer.

5.2 The Ribbon

Just as in *WordPad*, you will be working in a window with the ribbon. The ribbon is displayed at the top of the window. You can think of the ribbon as a very extensive taskbar containing all of the operations and commands you need to manage your files and folders. You cannot see all of these options at once. The ribbon is organized into tabs. By clicking a given tab, the tab will expand downward and all of the tab's commands will become visible.

The window consists of a number of tabs:

Take a look at one of these tabs:

☞ **Click the** Home **tab**

The corresponding groups and their commands are displayed:

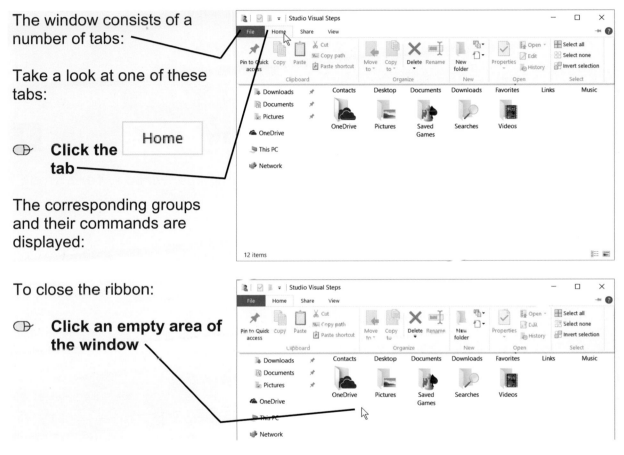

To close the ribbon:

☞ **Click an empty area of the window**

The ribbon will disappear. It is also possible to show the ribbon permanently:

☞ **Click** ⌄

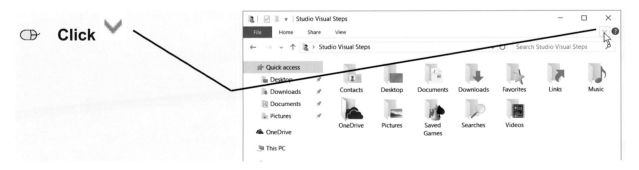

In this book the *File Explorer* window will look like this with the ribbon fully visible:

If you don't want the ribbon to be visible, you can hide it by

clicking :

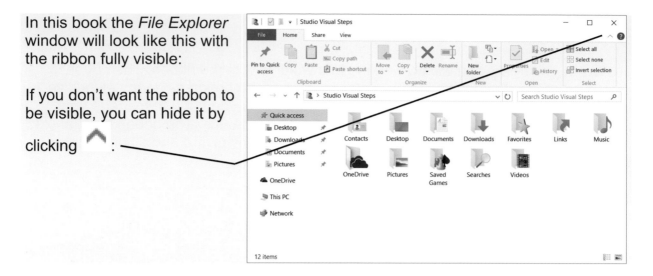

5.3 Changing the Display of the Window

There are several ways to view your folders in the *File Explorer* window. Take a look at the display settings of your window:

☞ **Click the** View **tab**

☞ **Place the pointer on**
   List

Immediately you will see an example of this display:

☞ **Click** List

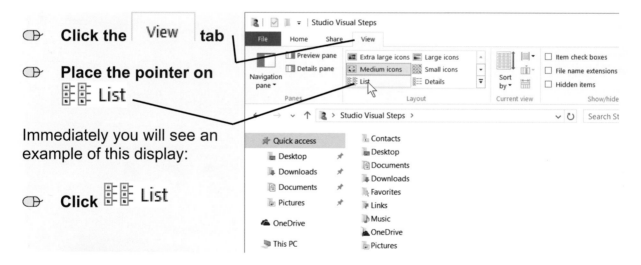

The display for this window is set to List. A blue frame appears round the option
List. This means that this option is active.

Now change the display back to medium icons:

$\oplus$ **Click**
      ⊞⊞ **Medium icons**

You will see the medium icons view again:

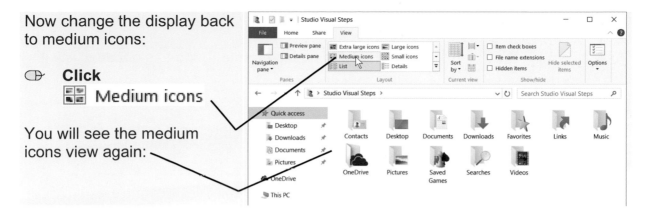

There are more options you can use to change the display of the folder. With ▯▯ **Preview pane** and ▯▤ **Details pane** you can add a preview pane or details pane to the window. Take a look at what happens when you add the details pane:

$\oplus$ **Click**
      ▯▤ **Details pane**

The details pane will appear at the right-hand side of the window. A blue frame appears round the option ▯▤ **Details pane**. This means that this option is active.

The details pane is added:

When you select a file, you can see information about it in the details pane:

Now you are going to hide the details pane:

$\oplus$ **Click** ▯▤ **Details pane**

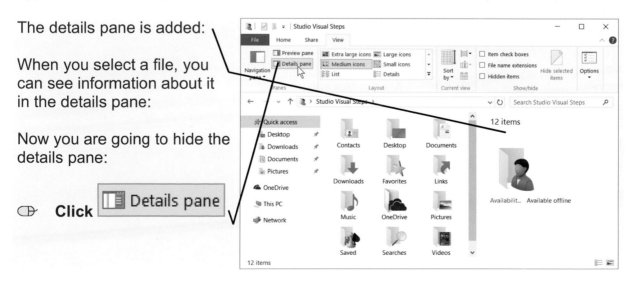

➥ Please note:

Don't click ⬚⊟ Details pane when there's no blue frame round this option. Click it only when you see a blue frame ⬚⊟ Details pane .

The *File Explorer* window on your computer should look the same as the window below:

You are going to open a folder. This is how you do it:

☞ **Double-click**

Documents

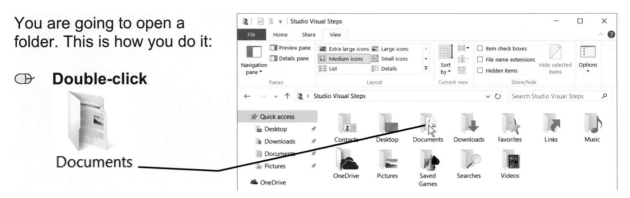

5.4 Understanding the Different Parts of the File Explorer Window

In addition to showing the contents of the folder, a *File Explorer* window has specific areas that are designed to help you navigate to the files and folders on your computer and work with them more easily. Take a look now:

The navigation pane shows some of the folders on your computer:

Notice how the address bar 📄 > Studio Visual Steps > Documents identifies the folder you are currently using:

The files in this folder are shown as icons in the file list:

By using the navigation pane on the left side, you can quickly navigate to any folder on your computer. When you click an item or folder in the navigation pane, you will see the contents of that item or folder you clicked displayed in the file list, the main portion of the window.

In the previous section, you changed the display of your *Personal folder*. Now you have opened the *Documents* folder and you see that the contents are displayed differently. In *File Explorer,* you can change the view of how the files look in any window. For example if you set the view to medium icons, your files will become more easily recognizable:

Click

Medium icons

The display of the window will be changed:

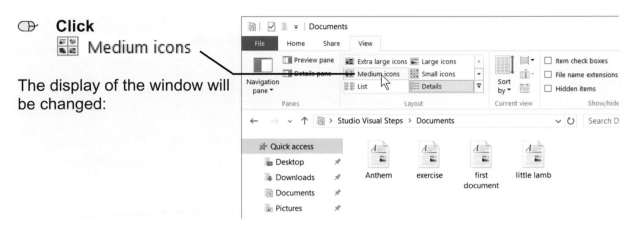

5.5 The Documents Folder

Windows has a special folder where you can save all of your text documents. This folder is called *Documents*. You have already saved some of your work in the *Documents* folder in the previous chapters.

The address bar shows which folder is currently opened

▸ Studio Visual Steps ▸ Documenten :

On your computer you will see another name for *Studio Visual Steps*.

You see the content of the *Documents* folder:

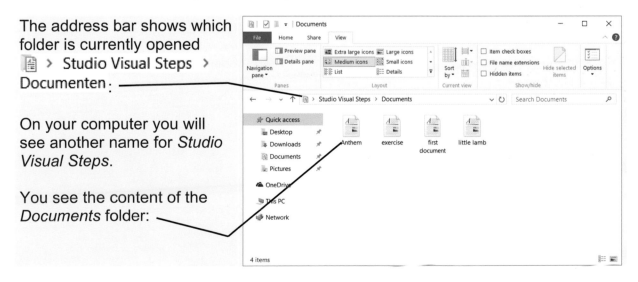

You will see at least four documents in the *Documents* folder. These are the practice text you have created and saved in the previous chapters.

Look closely at these files:

Each file is represented by an icon:

 Anthem   exercise   first document   little lamb

5.6 Creating a New Folder

A folder is a container that helps you organize your files. Every file on your computer is stored in a folder, and folders can also hold other folders. Folders located inside other folders are often called *subfolders*.

You can add new folders yourself. This can be handy, for example, to keep your letters separate from all your other documents. In following exercise, you will create a new folder inside the *Documents* folder.

☞ Click **Home** tab

☞ Click **New folder**

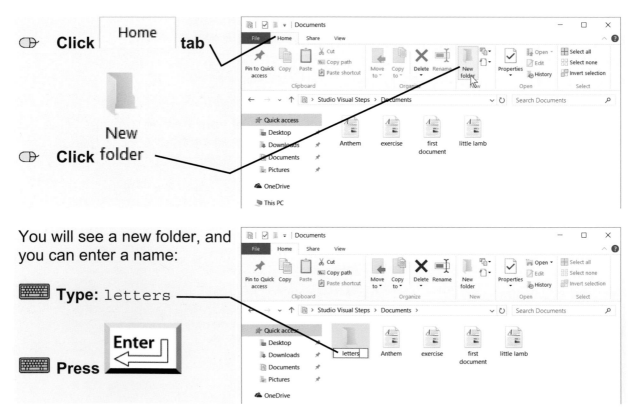

You will see a new folder, and you can enter a name:

⌨ **Type:** letters

⌨ **Press** Enter

Now you have created a new subfolder *letters* inside the *Documents* folder:

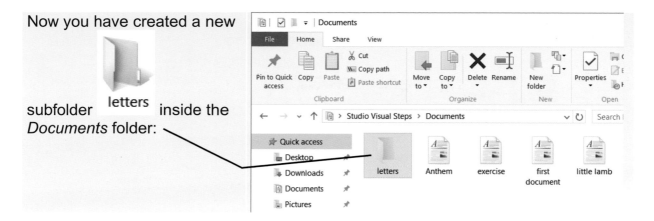

You can use this *letters* folder to save a letter that you have written in *WordPad*, for example. To do so, you can minimize the *Documents* window and then start the *WordPad* program.

☞ **Minimize the *Documents* window** 🐾³

5.7 Saving to a Folder

As an exercise, you will first write a letter in *WordPad* and then you will save it in the

subfolder you just made, **letters** .

☞ **Open *WordPad*** 🐾²

Add some 'content' to your letter, type the following short sentence:

⌨ **Type:**
Letter to be saved

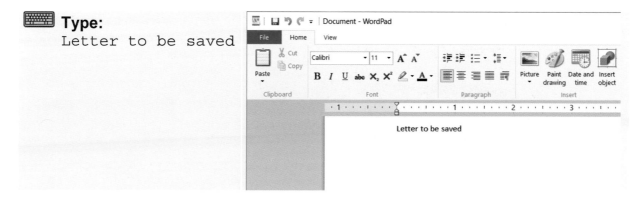

⊕ **Click** **File**

⊕ **Click** 💾 **Save**

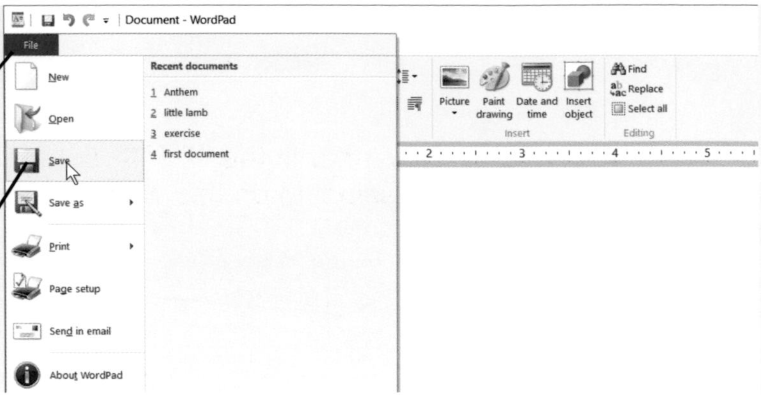

You will now see the *Save As* window:

In the address bar you see
📄 « Studio Visual Steps ›
› Documents:

This means that the
Documents folder is the
active folder.

As you can see, all the files in
the *Documents* folder are
also displayed in this window:

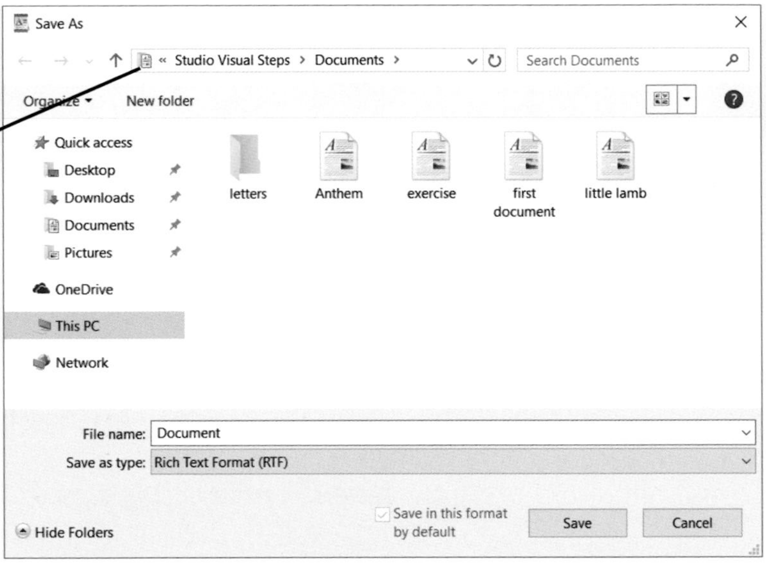

HELP! My Save As window is different.
Do you see a window without the navigation pane and file list?

⊕ **Click**
    🔽 **Browse Folders**

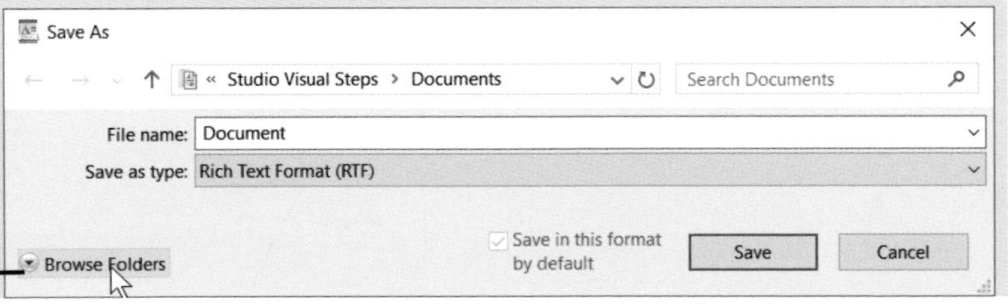

You want to save your new letter in the letters subfolder. First, you will need to open the *letters* subfolder. It is easiest to do this when the *Documents* window is already opened:

Double-click letters

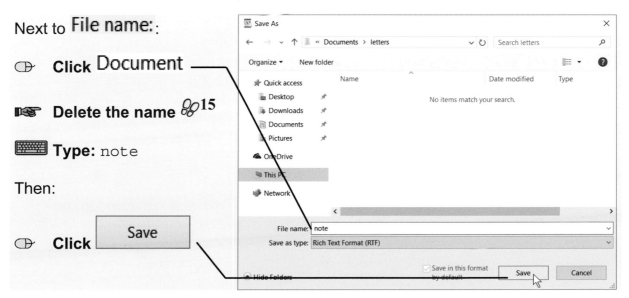

Now the *letters* folder will be opened. Notice that the folder name *letters* now appears in the address bar to the right of *Documents.* The file list is currently empty.
In the lower part of the window, a file name is already shown: Document. That is the default name the program always shows. This is how you change the name:

Next to File name::

Click Document

Delete the name ✂15

⌨ **Type:** note

Then:

Click Save

The *note* file has been saved to the *letter* folder.

☞ **Close the *WordPad* 🐾⁶**

Now you can reopen the *Documents* window, to verify that your file has been saved to the *letters* subfolder.

☞ **Open the *Documents* window with the button on the taskbar 🐾³⁰**

⊕ **Double-click** letters

In the address bar you can see that the *letters* folder has been opened: ————

In the file list you now see the *WordPad* file you have saved

note :————

To go back to the *Documents* folder:

⊕ **Click** ⬅————

➦ **Please note:**

Do the icons on your computer look larger or smaller? Then you can change the folder view. You can read how to do this in *section 5.3 Changing the Display of the Window.*

5.8 Copying Files

You can also copy files. For example, you can make a second copy of a letter that you want to change slightly. To practice, you can copy your practice text.

Now you see the files in the *Documents* folder:

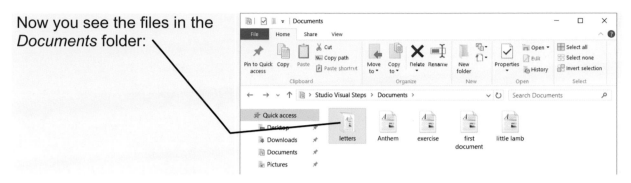

You can now copy one of the practice texts, but remember the rule: select first, then act.

➥ Please note:
Select first ... then act.

Selecting a file is easy: simply click its icon or name.

☞ **Click** **Anthem**

The file turns light blue to indicate that it has been selected.

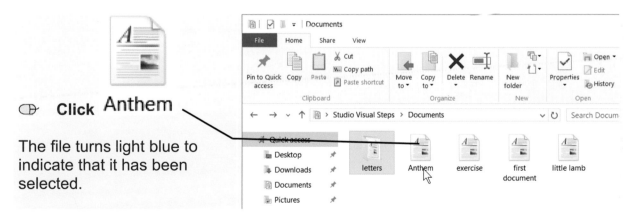

✚ HELP! There is a blue box around the name.

Do you see a light blue box around the name? Has the pointer changed into I? For example: [Anthem]

☞ **Click somewhere else in the window**
☞ **Try again**

HELP! I see another window.

Do you unexpectedly see the window for *WordPad* or *Microsoft Word*? If so, you have double-clicked the file name, and opened the program. To close the program:

☞ **Click** ✕

☞ **Try again**

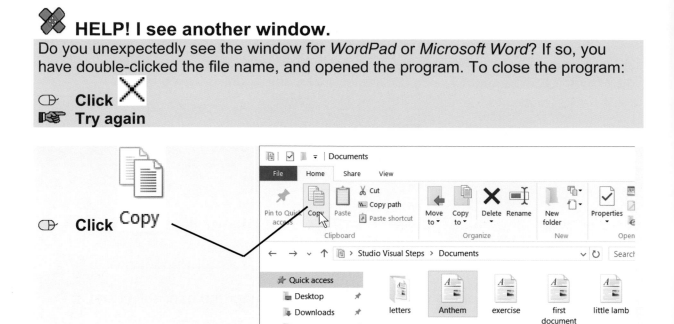

☞ **Click** Copy

Windows now knows you want to copy the file. The next step is pasting the copied file into the *letters* folder:

To open the *letters* folder:

☞ **Double-click** letters

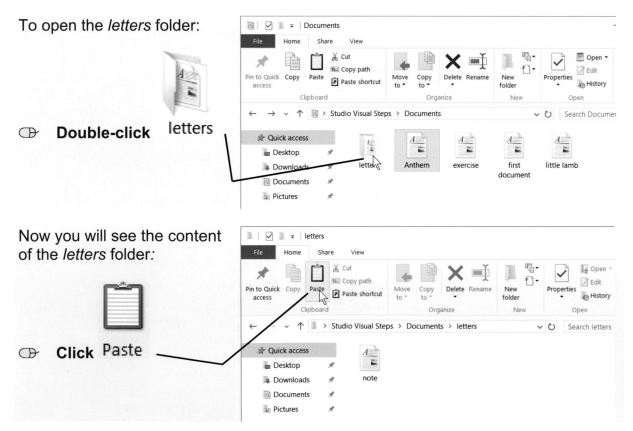

Now you will see the content of the *letters* folder:

☞ **Click** Paste

The Anthem file has been pasted:

There are more ways to copy a file. For example, you can use the right mouse button. Try that now:

☞ **Right-click** Anthem

A menu appears:

☞ **Click Copy**

☞ **Right-click a blank area of the window**

A menu appears:

☞ **Click Paste**

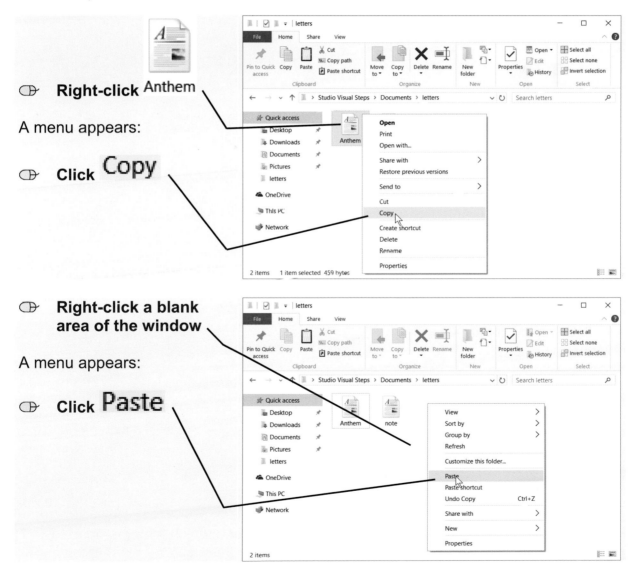

Now there is a copy of the file named Anthem - Copy in the same folder. Notice that the word 'Copy' has been automatically added to the name. This is because files with duplicate names are not allowed inside the same folder. Even though the content of the file is the same, the name of the file has to be different if it is located in the same folder.

You are going to open the *Documents* folder. Earlier in this chapter you learned how to go back to a previously viewed folder by using the ← button. You can also use the ↑ button to go up one level, to an item's parent folder. In this example you will be going up one level to the *Documents* folder. You can see that in the address bar

▯ > Studio Visual Steps > Documents > letters

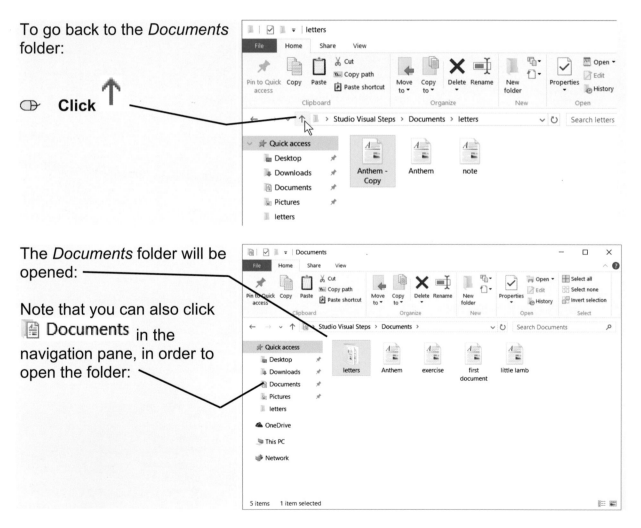

To go back to the *Documents* folder:

Click ↑

The *Documents* folder will be opened:

Note that you can also click 📄 Documents in the navigation pane, in order to open the folder:

Remember: in the address bar of the window you can see which folder is opened:

📄 > Studio Visual Steps > Documents >

5.9 Moving a File

It is also possible to use the Cut command to paste a file into another folder. This means the file will be moved from one folder to another folder. This action is very similar to copying and pasting files:

- use the ✂ Cut and Paste buttons on the ribbon;
- right-click an empty part of the window and then choose Cut and Paste.

There is also another option available on the ribbon:

☞ **Click** first document

The file is selected:

☞ **Click** Move to ▾

You might see ⬅▾.

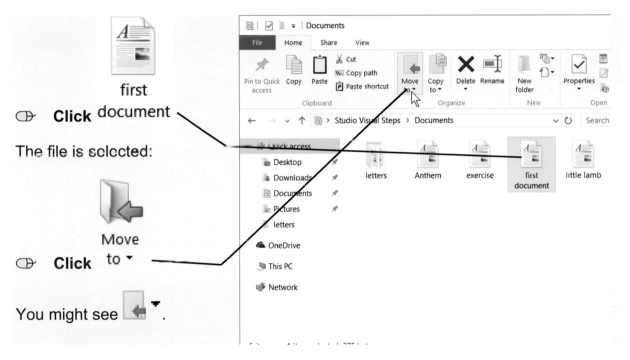

You are going to move the file into the *letters* folder:

In the menu you will see folders which you have recently opened. Including the folder *letters*:

☞ **Click** letters

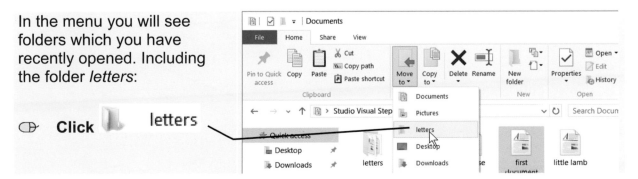

In the *Documents* folder
the *first document* file has
disappeared:

You can check if the file has
moved to the *letters* folder:

☞ **Double-click** letters

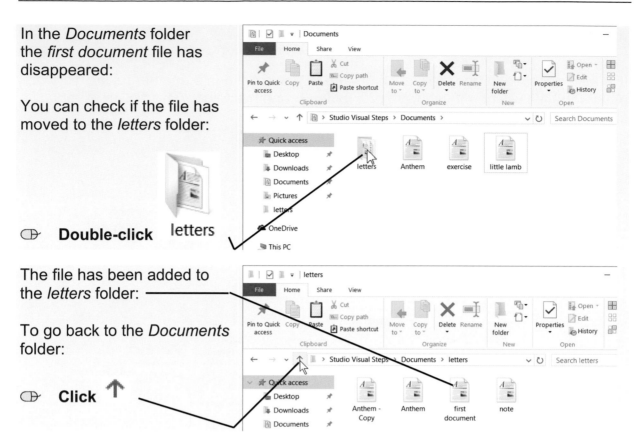

The file has been added to
the *letters* folder: ———

To go back to the *Documents*
folder:

☞ **Click** ⬆

5.10 Dragging and Dropping Files

The easiest way to move files to another folder is by *dragging and dropping*. Try it:

☞ **Point to** little lamb

☞ **Press the left mouse
button and keep it
depressed**

☞ **Drag** little lamb **to**

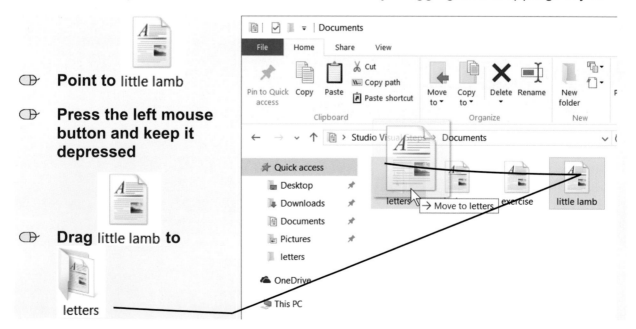

When you see this box
→ Move to letters | appear: ─────

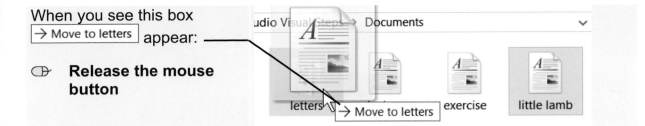

☞ **Release the mouse button**

☞ **Open the *letters* folder** ✇³¹

You will now see the *little lamb* file appear in the *letters* folder:

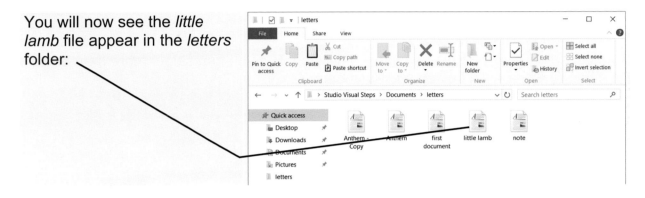

5.11 Selecting Multiple Files

You can also copy or move more than one file at a time. To do this, you must select the files first. Go ahead and try:

☞ **Click** Anthem ─────

The file is light blue, so you know it has been selected.

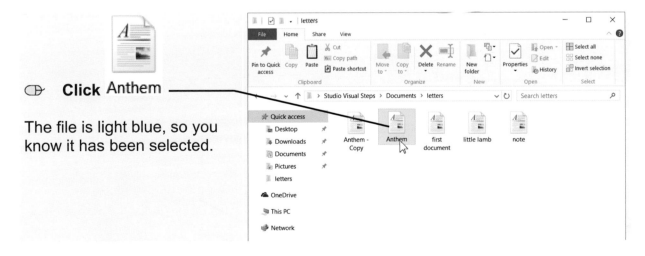

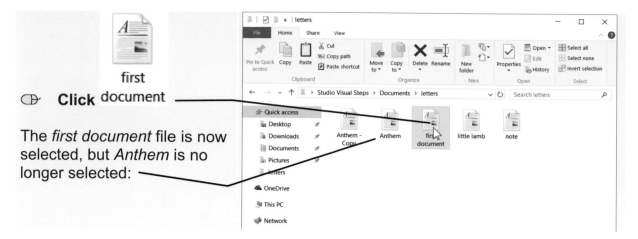

Click document

The *first document* file is now selected, but *Anthem* is no longer selected:

You can select only one file at a time by clicking. But you can select more than one file if you use a special key on your keyboard:

The *Control key*. It always shows the abbreviation 'Ctrl':

Ctrl

The Ctrl keys are located at the bottom left-hand side of the keyboard:

Use one of these keys.

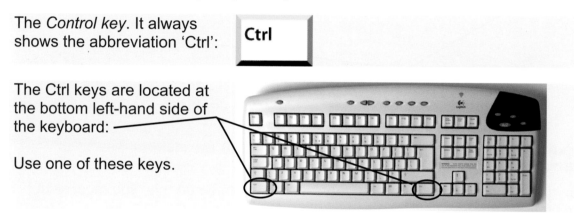

The Ctrl key is used together with the mouse. The *first document* file is still selected.

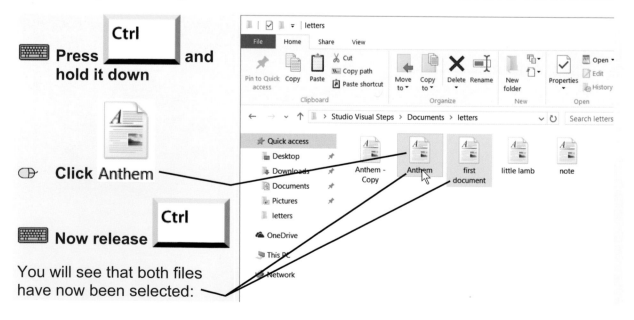

Press **Ctrl** **and hold it down**

Click Anthem

Now release **Ctrl**

You will see that both files have now been selected:

You can select even more files by using the Ctrl key. Then you can copy and paste, or cut and paste, or drag the group of selected files to their destination folder. For now, that is not necessary. This is how you clear the selection:

☞ **Click on any blank area of the window**

The selection is cleared.

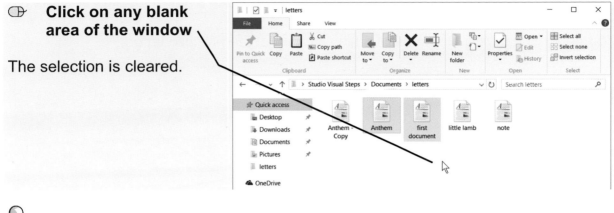

💡 **Tip**

Selecting a consecutive group of files

To select a consecutive group of files (or folders when you are working with folders):

☞ **Click the first item**

⌨ **Depress**

☞ **Then click the last item**

To select all of the files (or folders when you are working with folders):

☞ **Click** Home

☞ **Click** ⊞ Select all

5.12 Changing the File Name

Sometimes you may want to give a file a different name. Perhaps you have several documents about the same subject, for example, and you want to be able to clearly distinguish one document from another.
You can try changing the name of a file with one of the practice letters.

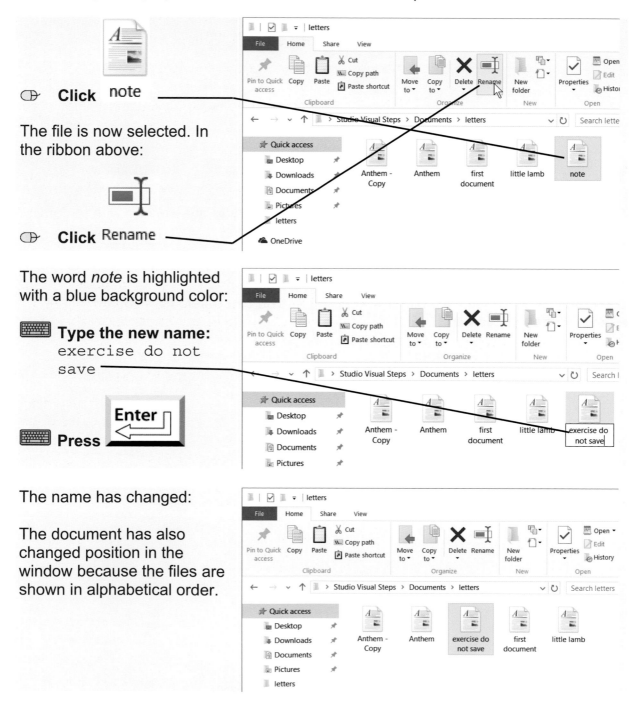

Click note

The file is now selected. In the ribbon above:

Click Rename

The word *note* is highlighted with a blue background color:

Type the new name:
exercise do not
save

Press Enter

The name has changed:

The document has also changed position in the window because the files are shown in alphabetical order.

HELP! I see another window

You cannot save more than one file with the same name to a folder.
If you try to give a file a name that already exists, you will see:

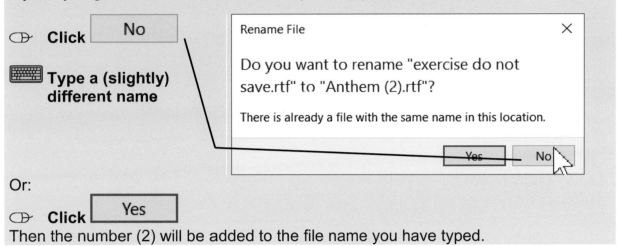

Click [No]

Type a (slightly) different name

> **Rename File**   ✕
>
> Do you want to rename "exercise do not save.rtf" to "Anthem (2).rtf"?
>
> There is already a file with the same name in this location.
>
> [Yes]   [No]

Or:

Click [Yes]

Then the number (2) will be added to the file name you have typed.

5.13 Deleting Files

It is a good idea, every now and then, to do a regular 'spring cleaning' of your computer. To keep your computer manageable, you can delete files you no longer need. To practice, you can delete the *Anthem - Copy* file in the *letters* folder, because this is a copy that you do not really need.

It is important to select the file carefully, so you will not delete the wrong files.

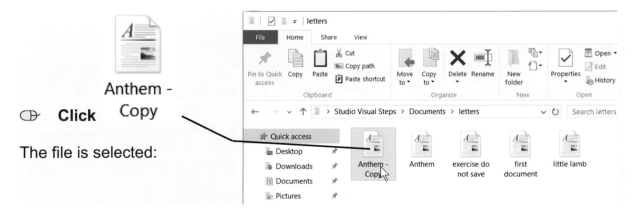

Anthem - Copy

Click

The file is selected:

Now you can delete the file. It will be 'tossed' into the *Recycle Bin*.

☞ **Click** ✖

Please note: click ✖ and
Delete

not ▾ .

Anthem -

The file **Copy** has now
disappeared from the *letters*
window:

Files that have been deleted are not gone forever. As a kind of safety measure, they
are moved to the *Recycle Bin* first. They are not really gone forever until you empty
the *Recycle Bin*. As long as a file is in the *Recycle Bin*, you can retrieve it later if you
need it.

You also have the option to remove a file directly. You do this by clicking **Delete** ▾ ,

and then ✖ | **Permanently delete** . Be careful however if you use this option,
for it means that the item is gone forever and will not be able to be recovered.

💡 **Tip**

Selecting multiple files
You can also delete multiple files at the same time. You must select them first by
clicking them while pressing the Ctrl key or the Shift key. Then you can delete them.

Tip

Selecting an entire folder

You can also select an entire folder you want to delete. You can select a folder by clicking it, then you can delete it.

Please note:

Only your files
Be careful when deleting files. Only delete files that you yourself have made.
If you did not create the file, you might not be able to delete it.
Also, you cannot delete a file (or the folder that contains it) if the file is currently opened in a program or app. Make sure that the file is not opened in any program, app, and then try to delete the file or folder again.
Never delete files or folders for programs or apps that you do not use. These files have to be deleted in a different way.

5.14 The Recycle Bin

All the files that you delete from your computer end up in the *Recycle Bin*. You can open the *Recycle Bin* to see its contents. It will contain all the files you have deleted.

You can open the *Recycle Bin* with its own icon on the desktop ![Recycle Bin]. You can also do this from within a *File Explorer* window:

☞ **Click the first** ❯ **on the left side of your name in the address bar**

☞ **Click** 🗑 **Recycle Bin**

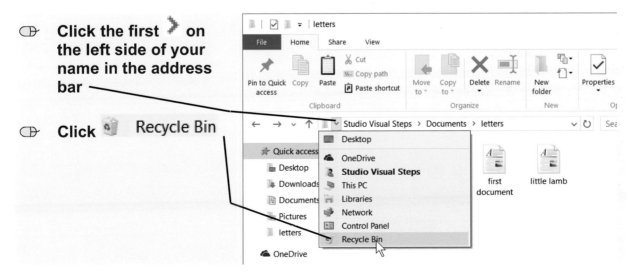

Now you will see the *Recycle Bin* window containing the *Anthem – copy* file that you have deleted:

There is also a new tab especially for files in the *Recycle Bin*. You are going to use this tab to empty the *Recycle Bin*:

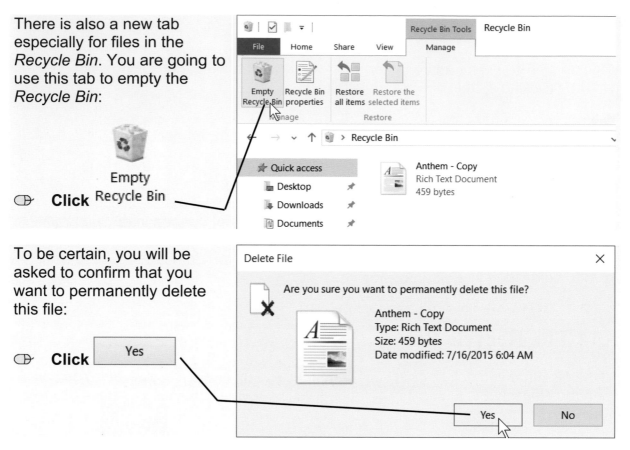

☞ **Click** Empty Recycle Bin

To be certain, you will be asked to confirm that you want to permanently delete this file:

☞ **Click** Yes

Now the file has been permanently deleted and cannot be retrieved.

💡 **Tip**

When should you empty the Recycle Bin?
You do not need to empty the *Recycle Bin* every time you delete a file. You only need to empty it when you want to permanently delete a file. It is better to collect your deleted files in the *Recycle Bin* and to wait until you do your 'spring cleaning'; then you can empty the whole bin at once.

💡 **Tip**

Is there anything in the Recycle Bin?
You can tell by the icon for the *Recycle Bin* on the desktop whether there is anything in it. The icon changes its appearance:

 not empty   empty

Tip

Restore an item from the Recycle Bin

Did you perhaps delete the wrong file, or on second thought want to restore a

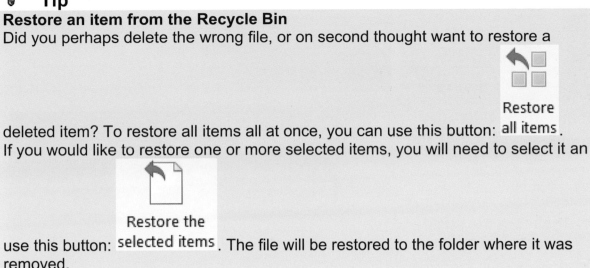

deleted item? To restore all items all at once, you can use this button: all items.
If you would like to restore one or more selected items, you will need to select it an

use this button: selected items. The file will be restored to the folder where it was removed.

5.15 Copying to a USB Stick

You may sometimes need to copy something to a USB stick. For example, you might want to transfer a file to another PC or store a backup copy of the file away from the computer. Try this now by copying the *Anthem* file to a USB memory stick.

Please note:

In order to work through this section, you will need a
USB stick. A USB stick is a small, portable device that plugs
into a computer's USB port. Just like your computer's hard
drive, a USB stick stores information. A USB stick makes it
very easy to transfer information from one computer to
another.

If you do not have a USB stick, you can just read through
this section.

If you have an external hard disk, you can execute the operations with this disk as well. An external hard disk is actually a big brother of the USB stick. You can store many times more information on such a disk.

First you have to insert the USB stick into the computer.

☞ **Locate the USB port on your computer**

A USB port can be situated on the front or the back of the computer, or both. On a laptop, a USB port could also be located on one of its sides.

☞ **Insert the USB stick into the USB port and gently push it in**

Having trouble?

☞ **Then turn the stick over and try again**

When you insert a USB stick into the computer, you will probably see a message appear on the right-side of your screen: ——— You can ignore it. It will disappear on its own.

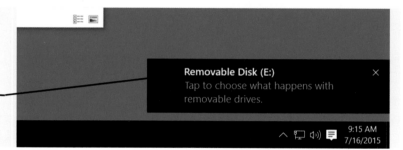

Removable Disk (E:)   ✕
Tap to choose what happens with removable drives.

∧ 🖵 ◁)) 🗩   9:15 AM
7/16/2015

You can open the folder of the USB-stick in *File Explorer* by using the navigation pane:

☞ **Click**
  🖴 Removable Disk (E:

In this example, the USB stick is named Removable Disk. It may have a different name on your computer.

You will see the content of the USB stick. In this example, there no files yet. The stick is empty.

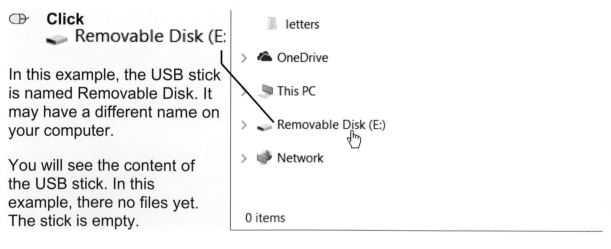

📄 letters

> ☁ OneDrive

> 💻 This PC

> 🖴 Removable Disk (E:)
        🖑

> 🖧 Network

0 items

You can copy the Anthem file from the letters folder to the USB stick.

☞ **Open the letters folder** 🦶²⁹

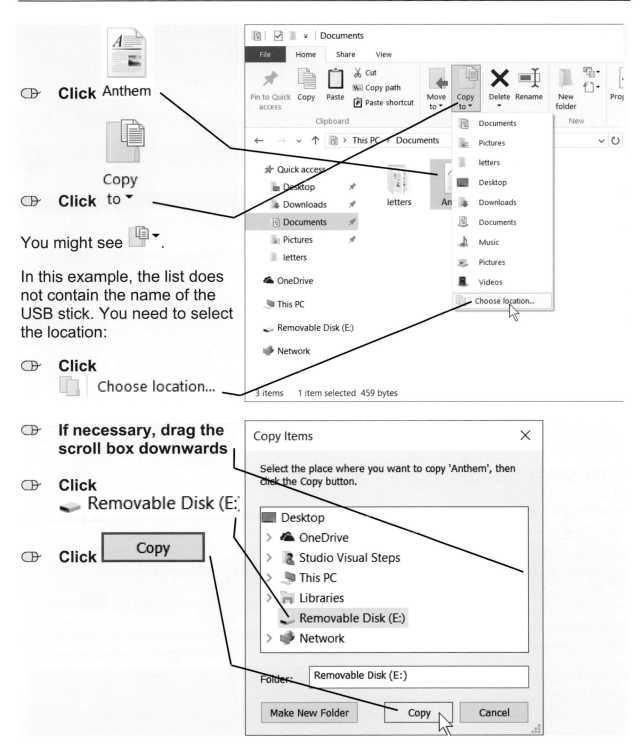

Click **Anthem**

Click **Copy to ▾**

You might see ▾.

In this example, the list does not contain the name of the USB stick. You need to select the location:

Click **Choose location...**

If necessary, drag the scroll box downwards

Click **Removable Disk (E:)**

Click **Copy**

The file will now be copied to the USB stick. You may see a message indicating this. In general, a message will appear only with larger files. The *Anthem* file is small.

➤ **Please note:**

If multiple USB sticks are inserted, you also see the names of the other USB sticks. Then choose the one at the bottom. That will be the device you connected last.

Now you can check to see if the file has been added to the USB stick. You can do this in the navigation pane on the left-side of the window.

☞ **Click**
   🖴 **REMOVABLE D (E:)**

You will see the *Anthem* file on the *Removable Disk*:

☞ **Click** ✕

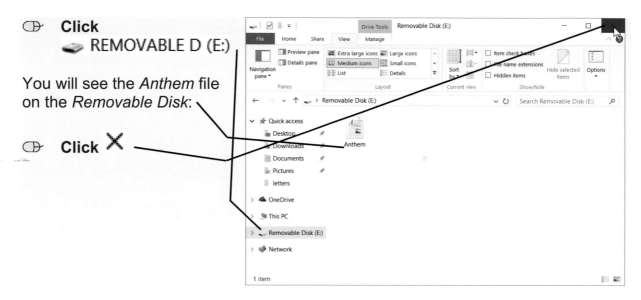

5.16 Safely Removing a USB Stick

Before removing storage devices, such as USB sticks, you need to make sure that the computer has finished saving any information to the device. If the device has an activity light flashing, wait for a few seconds until the light has finished flashing before removing it. There is also another way to ensure that the USB stick is ready to be removed. You can use the icon 🔌 that appears after you have clicked ⌃, to ensure that the USB stick will be ready to be removed. You can display the icon like this:

At the lower right-hand side of the taskbar:

☞ **Click** ⌃

☞ **Click the icon** 🔌

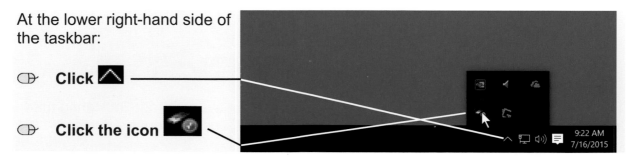

⏏ **Click the USB Stick**
🖴 Eject DISK 2.0

You may see a different name for your own USB stick. Do you see multiple devices? Then choose the one at the bottom, this is the device you have connected last.

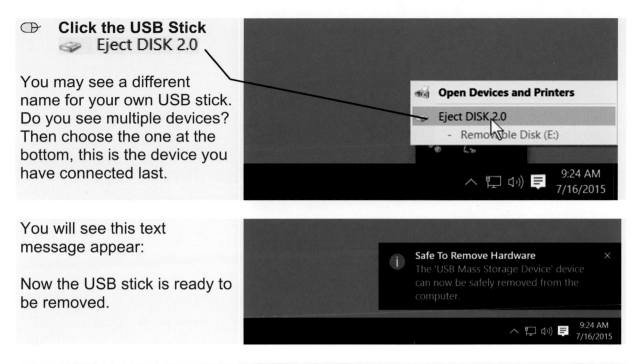

You will see this text message appear:

Now the USB stick is ready to be removed.

☞ **Remove the USB stick from the computer**

In this chapter you have learned how to move, delete and copy files working with the *File Explorer* windows. You have practiced many of these actions using your own *Personal folder.*

You can practice all of these actions a little more by doing the following exercises.

5.17 Exercises

The following exercises will help you master what you have just learned. Have you forgotten how to do something? Use the number beside the footsteps to look it up in the appendix *How Do I Do That Again?*

Exercise 1: Opening Windows in File Explorer

☞ Open your *Personal folder.* $\mathscr{W}^{32}$

☞ Open the *Documents* folder. $\mathscr{W}^{31}$

☞ Open the *letters* folder. $\mathscr{W}^{31}$

☞ Go back to the *Documents* folder using the Back button. $\mathscr{W}^{33}$

☞ Go to the *letters* folder using the Forward button. $\mathscr{W}^{33}$

Exercise 2: Creating a New Folder

☞ Open your *Personal folder.* $\mathscr{W}^{32}$

☞ Open the *Documents* folder. $\mathscr{W}^{29}$

☞ Create a new folder with the name *practice.* $\mathscr{W}^{34}$

☞ Open the new *practice* folder. $\mathscr{W}^{31}$

Exercise 3: Copying Files

Please note: in order to do this exercise, you need to do the exercise above first.

☞ Go back to the *Documents* folder. $\mathscr{W}^{33}$

☞ Copy the *Anthem* file to the *practice* folder. $\mathscr{W}^{35}$

Exercise 4: Renaming a File

Please note: in order to do this exercise, you need to do the exercises above first.

☞ Go back to the *Documents* folder. 👣^{33}

☞ Open the *practice* folder. 👣^{31}

☞ Change the name of the *Anthem* file to *song*. 👣^{36}

Exercise 5: Deleting Files

Please note: in order to do this exercise, you need to do the exercises above first.

☞ Go back to the *Documents* folder. 👣^{33}

☞ Open the new *practice* folder. 👣^{31}

☞ Delete the *song* file in this folder. 👣^{37}

Exercise 6: Renaming and Deleting a Folder

To rename and delete folders you do the same thing as you do with files. Give it a try:

☞ Go back to the *Documents* folder. 👣^{33}

☞ Rename the *practice* folder and call it *my letters*. 👣^{36}

☞ Delete the *my letters* folder. 👣^{37}

☞ Close the window. 👣^{6}

5.18 Background Information

Dictionary

Address bar	The address bar appears at the top of every window or *File Explorer* and displays your current location as a series of links separated by arrows. By using the address bar, you can see which folder is opened.
File	The generic name for everything saved on the computer. A file can be a program, a data file with names, text you have written, a photo, a video or a piece of music. Actually, everything located on the hard drive of your computer is called a *file*.
File Explorer	The program that allows you to access, save and manage your files and folders.
File list	This is where the contents of the current folder are displayed.
Folder	A folder is a container that helps you organize your files. Every file on your computer is stored in a folder, and folders can also hold other folders (subfolders).
Folder list	List of folders in the navigation pane. By using the folder list in the navigation pane, you can navigate directly to the folder you are interested in by clicking on this folder.
Folder window	The window of *File Explorer*.
Frequent folders	Through Quick access at the left-hand side of the *File Explorer* window you can directly access frequent folders. This provides quick access to the folders you frequently use.
Hard drive	The primary storage device located inside a computer. Also called a hard disk or hard disk drive, it is the place where your files and programs are typically stored.
Library	A library looks like a folder, but the difference is that in a folder, the files are actually stored in the folder only. There are no files stored in a library, but only the links to various folders. A library displays files that are actually stored in several different folders, distributed all over the computer.

- Continue on the next page -

Navigation pane	Shows a list of folders that can be opened in the *File Explorer* window.
Recent files	Through Quick access at the left-hand side of the *File Explorer* window you can directly access recent files. You can use this to quickly continue working on a file you frequently use, for instance.
Recycle Bin	When you delete a file or folder, it goes to the *Recycle Bin*. You can retrieve a file from the *Recycle Bin*. But if you empty the *Recycle Bin*, all of its contents are permanently gone.
Search box	The box in the top right-hand corner of *File Explorer*. If you type a keyword in the search box, the content of the folder will be filtered, and you will only see the files that match your keyword. The search will only extend to the current folder and any subfolders, the entire computer will not be searched.
USB port	A narrow, rectangular connection point on a computer where you can connect a universal serial bus (USB) device such as a USB stick.
USB stick	A small portable device, to store files and folders. Plugs into a computer's USB port. *Windows* will show a USB stick as a removable disk.

Source: Windows Help

USB sticks, external hard drives, SD cards, CDs and DVDs
USB sticks, CDs and DVDs are storage media often used to store files outside the computer. For example, you can use them to transfer files to another computer or to save a *backup* copy. Software manufacturers often provide their products on a CD-ROM or DVD-ROM.

USB stick
A USB stick is a small storage medium with a large storage capacity. You can insert it directly into your PC's USB port. The storage capacity can vary up to 64 GB or more, with steady improvements in size and price per capacity expected. You can write files directly to a USB stick.

External hard drive
An external hard disk is also a kind of portable storage device, but with more storage capacity. Nowadays, external hard disks have a storage capacity of up to four terabytes (approximately 4000 GB).

SD card
Memory card for use in a digital camera, smartphone, tablet or eReader. The capacity varies from 4GB to 512 GB.

CD and DVD
Some software manufacturers deliver their software packages on CD or DVD. Recently however, many software manufacturers are delivering their programs through direct Internet download.
Large files, like movies can be distributed on DVD as well.

Writable CDs and DVDs
If your computer includes a CD or DVD recorder, you can copy files to a writable disc.

The parts of the Open window
This is the window that you use in *WordPad*, for example, to open a file from your computer. It looks like the *Save As* window. You used this previously in the section *3.18 Opening an Existing Document*. Windows such as these are easy to use.

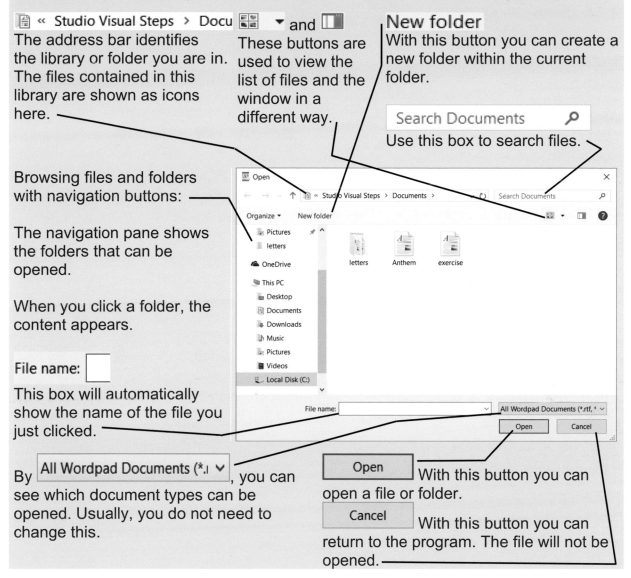

⟦ « Studio Visual Steps › Docu ⟧ ▾ and ⟦ ⟧
The address bar identifies the library or folder you are in. The files contained in this library are shown as icons here.

These buttons are used to view the list of files and the window in a different way.

New folder
With this button you can create a new folder within the current folder.

Search Documents 🔍
Use this box to search files.

Browsing files and folders with navigation buttons:

The navigation pane shows the folders that can be opened.

When you click a folder, the content appears.

File name: ⟦ ⟧
This box will automatically show the name of the file you just clicked.

By ⟦ All Wordpad Documents (*.⟧ ∨ , you can see which document types can be opened. Usually, you do not need to change this.

⟦ Open ⟧ With this button you can open a file or folder.

⟦ Cancel ⟧ With this button you can return to the program. The file will not be opened.

5.19 Tips

💡 Tip
The folder list in the navigation pane
When you use the folder list in the navigation pane, you can navigate directly to the folder that contains the folders, subfolders or files you are interested in:

All you have to do is click a folder or library name and the content will be displayed in the file list. ──

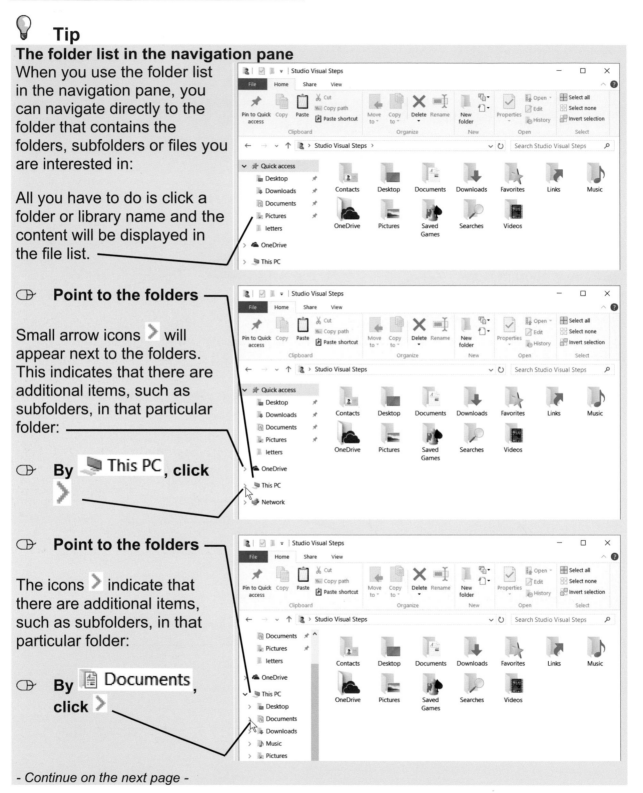

☞ **Point to the folders** ──

Small arrow icons ❯ will appear next to the folders. This indicates that there are additional items, such as subfolders, in that particular folder: ──

☞ **By** 🖥 This PC, **click** ❯

☞ **Point to the folders** ──

The icons ❯ indicate that there are additional items, such as subfolders, in that particular folder:

☞ **By** 📄 Documents, **click** ❯

- Continue on the next page -

You can see that in this example there is one subfolders stored in this folder:

Now the arrow ❯ has changed into ✔:

✔ indicates the folder is expanded to show the entire contents. Every folder with a the arrow ❯ contains one or more folders or subfolders.

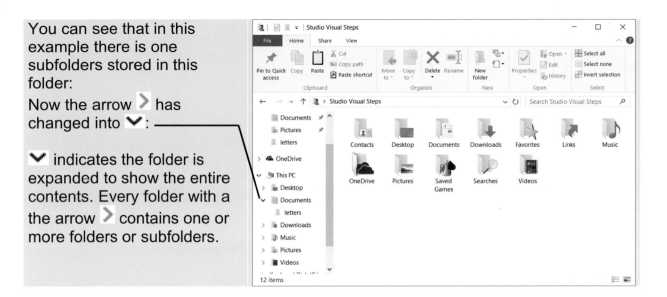

💡 Tip

Libraries

Windows 10 has already created a number of default libraries for you. A library looks like a folder, but the difference is, that the files in a folder are actually stored in that folder, whereas a library only contains links to other folders. A library displays the files that are physically distributed in folders all over the computer. For example, you can place vacation photos from the *Pictures* folder and vacation stories from the *Documents* folder in a single library. Then you will not need to navigate to different folders, in order to open and view the files concerning your vacation.

In a library you can also open files or folders, or save files. This works the same way as opening and saving files in a folder.

You can open a library as follows:

☞ **By** ⭐ **, click** ❯

☞ **Click** 🗐 **Libraries**

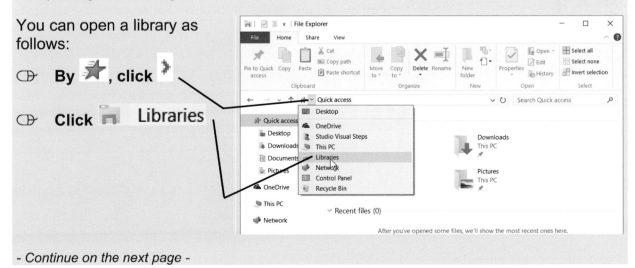

- Continue on the next page -

You see the default libraries:

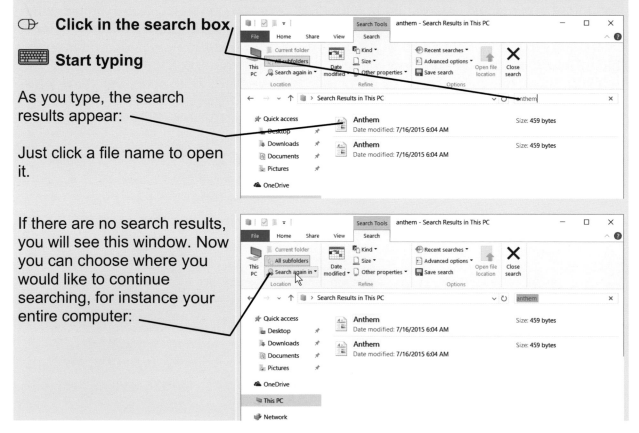

You can read more on working with libraries and creating libraries in the sequel to this *Windows 10* book. For more information on these sequel titles, visit our website at **www.visualsteps.com**

💡 Tip

Searching files in a folder

There are many ways to find your files on your computer. Most of the time, you will start by using the search box that is available within any *File Explorer* window.

👆 **Click in the search box**

⌨️ **Start typing**

As you type, the search results appear:

Just click a file name to open it.

If there are no search results, you will see this window. Now you can choose where you would like to continue searching, for instance your entire computer:

💡 Tip

Finding a file using the Search function on the taskbar
Along with the options to search for a file within a *File Explorer* window, you can also perform a search from the Search function on the taskbar:

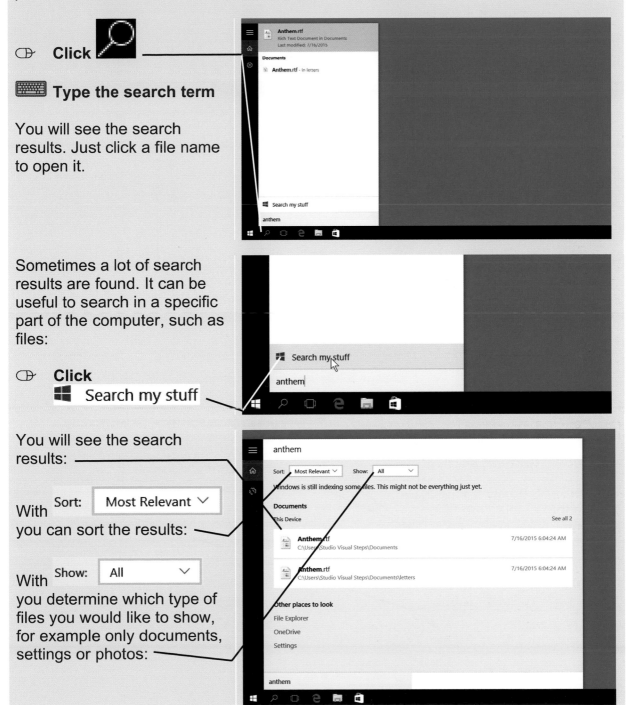

👉 **Click**

⌨ **Type the search term**

You will see the search results. Just click a file name to open it.

Sometimes a lot of search results are found. It can be useful to search in a specific part of the computer, such as files:

👉 **Click**
■■ Search my stuff

You will see the search results:

With Sort: Most Relevant ⌄ you can sort the results:

With Show: All ⌄ you determine which type of files you would like to show, for example only documents, settings or photos:

💡 Tip

Recent files and frequent folders

One of the new functions in *File Explorer* is the display of recent files and frequently used folders. You can use this function to quickly resume working on frequently used files:

If you want to view the frequently used folders and recent files, you click ⭐ Quick access:

Frequent folders:

Probably you will see more or different folders.

The recently opened files:

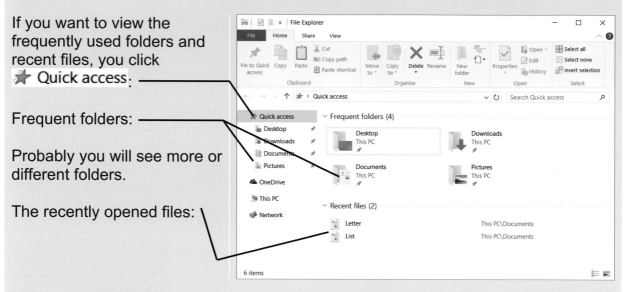

You can also disable the view of recent files and frequent folders. This is how you do it:

👉 **Click** [File], ☑️ Change folder and search options

At the bottom of the *General* tab you will find these options:

Uncheck the boxes if you do not want to display the files or folders anymore:

Only clear the current recent files and frequent folders and do not display them:

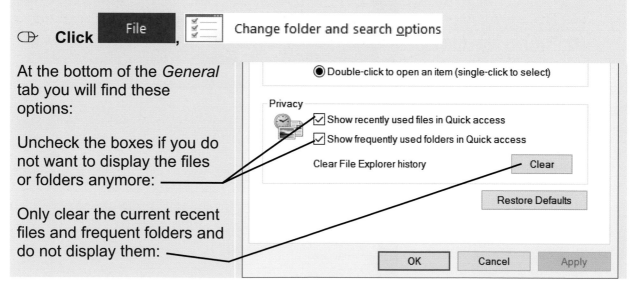

6. Surfing the Internet

The Internet is made up of thousands of computers that are all connected to one another. It is also known as the *World Wide Web* or *'the Web'*. World Wide Web indicates a spider's web of computers that all together form a huge network of information on a wide variety of topics. One of the best things about the Web is that you can open, view and share information residing on the Internet right from your own computer. It does not matter if the source of the information is located on the other side of the world. You can access it using the Internet.

These sources of information are available in what is called a *website* on the Internet. A *site* is a location. So, a website is a location somewhere on the Web. A website usually consists of multiple pages. You can browse from one page to another by clicking a hyperlink on the page. A hyperlink (or link) refers to another web page. In the same way, you can go from one website to another website. This behavior is called *surfing*. The program you use to surf the Internet is called a *browser* program. One of these browser programs is *Microsoft's Edge.*

In order to use the Internet, you will need to have an active Internet connection. This type of connection is supplied by an *Internet service provider* (ISP) or more simply *provider*. If you want to use an ISP's services, you will need to have a subscription. As soon as you are connected to the Internet, you will be *online* and you can start *surfing*. In this chapter you will learn how to do this.

In this chapter you will learn how to:

- open *Edge*;
- use a web address;
- browse back and forth between web pages;
- zoom in on a web page;
- search the Internet;
- save a web address;
- print a web page;
- work with cookies.

➤ Please note:

In order to work through this section you need to have an active Internet connection, and we assume your Internet connection has already been set up on your computer. If necessary, contact your Internet provider, computer supplier or an experienced computer user for further information.

6.1 Opening Edge

In *Windows 10* you can access the program that allows you to view web pages directly from the Start menu: the *Edge* program. You can also launch *Edge* by clicking the taskbar button . But for now you will learn how to open the program using the search function:

☞ **Click**

⌨ **Type:** edge

☞ **Click**

    Microsoft **Edge**
    Trusted Windows Store

The program will be opened and will automatically connect to the Internet.

Your screen will be filled with a *home page*.

This will usually be a page with news items. Apart from news, you may also see several advertisements on this page.

At the top of the window you will see one or two tabs:

If you see two tabs, close one of them:

☞ **Click** ✕

🡆 **Please note:**

The home page displayed above may look a little different from the one shown on your own computer. You may see a home page that was set up by someone else or yourself earlier on. Even if you do see the same web page, the content may differ. Many Internet pages are edited and updated on a daily basis.

✖ **HELP! I do not have a connection.**

If you have not been successful connecting to the Internet, even after several attempts, it is possible that the Internet connection to your computer has not been set up properly. Contact your Internet provider, computer supplier, or an experienced computer user and ask them to help you.

6.2 Typing a Web Address

Each website has its own unique *web address* on the Internet, for example, **www.visualsteps.com**. By means of this web address, a website can be found on the Internet.

Some websites have many branches to their website. A folder on your computer can contain one or more subfolders; a web address can also contain various sub addresses. The sub address is separated from the main address by a / (slash). Just take a look at the website accompanying this book:
www.visualsteps.com/windows10senior

At the top of the window:

☞ **Click**
    Search or enter
    web address

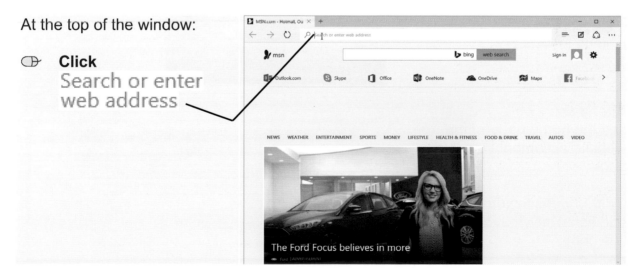

✚ HELP! I do not see Search or enter web address.

If you do not see Search or enter web address, you can click the web address that is shown, for example msn.com/en-us.

The area in which the web address is displayed is called the *address bar*. You can type the web address **www.visualsteps.com/windows10senior** in the address bar:

This is the location of the slash / character on the keyboard: ———

It can be found on the key that also has the question mark.

⌨ **Type:**
www.visualsteps.co
m/windows10senior

Enter

⌨ **Press**

You may see some suggestions while you are typing: ———

The Ford Focus believes in more

After a short while you will see the home page of the website accompanying this book:

On this website you can find additional information about this book.

6.3 The Wrong Web Address

Unfortunately it is quite easy to make a typing error when typing a long web address. The address for a website may no longer exist or perhaps it has been taken offline. These things occur more often as the number of websites on the Internet continues to grow and change every day. The addresses for private websites are also subject to constant change.

Sometimes you will see 'http://' on the left side of an address. This is additional information that tells you this is a website. In *Edge* you do not need to type 'http://'. The program understands that this is the given protocol for a website and will automatically add the correct prefix to the web address.

While typing a web address, you need to pay attention to these things:

- Check if any dots (.), slashes (/), hyphens (-) or underscores (_) are typed in the right spot. Otherwise you will get an error message.
- Never type a blank space in a web address.

Even omitting just a single dot in the web address can mean that the website or webpage will not be found. Just look what happens if you try to find the Visual Steps website while using an incorrect web address:

☞ **Click the address bar**

⌨ **Type:**
www.visualstepscom

⌨ **Press** **Enter**

You will see this web page:

This is not the web page you were looking for.

You may see a different web page on your own screen. This will not affect the following steps you need to take.

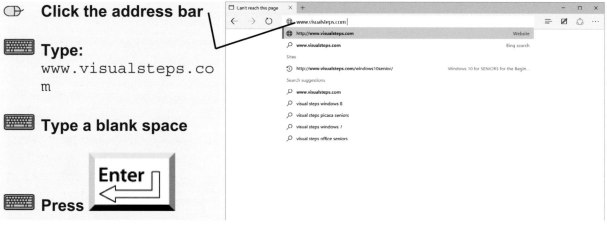

In the web address you just typed, the dot before *com* was missing. The correct address for the Visual Steps website is:

www.visualsteps.com

Now try this again, with the correct address:

☞ **Click the address bar**

⌨ **Type:**
www.visualsteps.co
m

⌨ **Type a blank space**

⌨ **Press** Enter

You will see the opening page of the Visual Steps site:

This is also called the *homepage*.

Here you can find information about the computer books from Visual Steps. Feel free to visit the website, from time to time, to explore news and information about upcoming books and more.

You have seen that even if you forget just a single dot, it can make a difference when you try to find a website.

➥ Please note:

The website above may look different on your own screen. The Internet is constantly changing.

6.4 Refreshing a Web Page

Sometimes a web page is not correctly displayed on the window. You can try to let *Edge* reload the page again. This means the web page will be refreshed. Just take a look at what happens:

In the upper left corner of the window:

☞ **Click** ↻

You will see that the window is refreshed. This can happen very fast sometimes; you may not actually see any change, but the web page is retrieved for a second time. All the items in the window will be resent to your computer. If your Internet connection is slow, this may take a while. It may sometimes seem like nothing is happening.

💡 Tip

The latest news

When you are viewing a news page, or a page with sports results, you can use the

↻

button to refresh the page and retrieve the most recent information.

6.5 Back and Forth

If you want to go back to a website you previously visited, you do not need to enter the web address again. *Edge* has two buttons with which you can navigate the Internet:

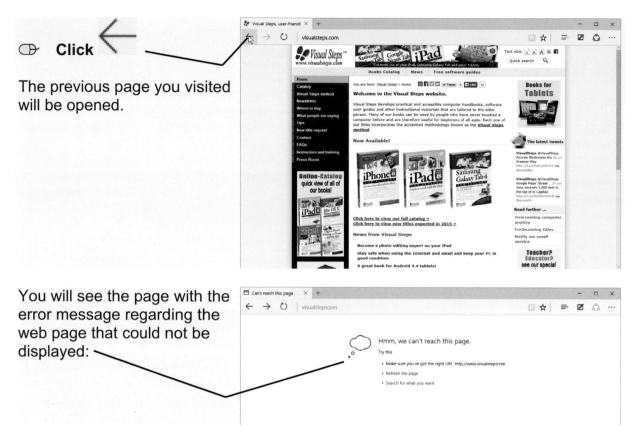

☞ **Click** ⇐

The previous page you visited will be opened.

You will see the page with the error message regarding the web page that could not be displayed:

You may have noticed how quick this happens. This is because *Edge* stores recently viewed web pages in the computer's memory. This means you can view these pages much sooner a second time, since a lot of the information does not need to be retrieved again.

☞ **Click** ⇐ **twice**

Now you see the website you have viewed first:

This was the home page:

You will not be able to go back any further from here, since this was the first website you opened.

The Back button is no longer active, the button is light grey instead of dark grey:

You can also browse 'the other way'. For this you use the button:

☞ **Click**

Now you see the website for this book again:

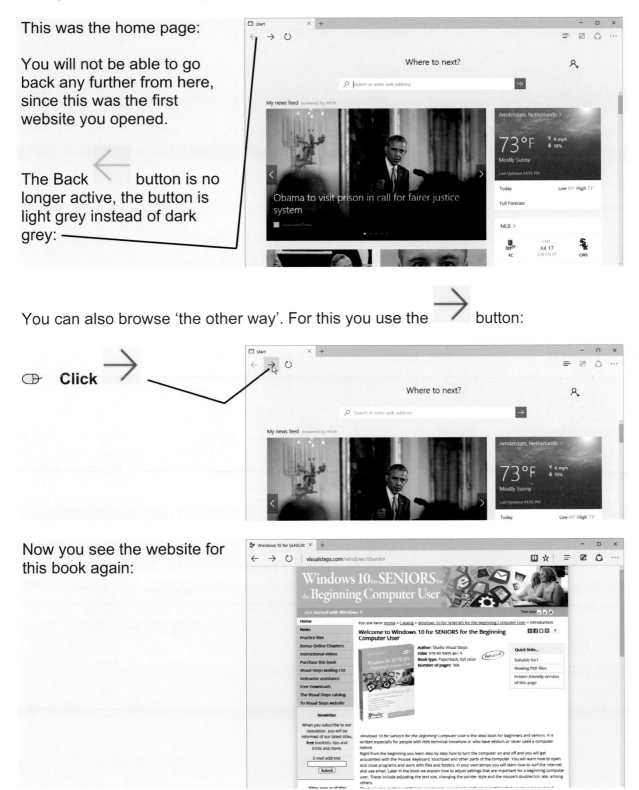

The ⬅ and ➡ buttons allow you to jump easily from one previously visited website to another. This is called 'surfing' the Internet.

6.6 Click to Leaf

Most websites have been designed in such a way that you can easily navigate through the site. You will usually find some sort of menu or list of topics in which the various pages can be found. On the left-hand site of this website you will see such a list of topics in the form of rectangular 'buttons'. By clicking such one of these buttons you can go to another page.

On the left-hand side of the window:

☞ **Place the pointer on**
   Bonus Online Chapters

You will see that the pointer ↖ turns into a hand 👆:

The color and text of the button have changed as well.

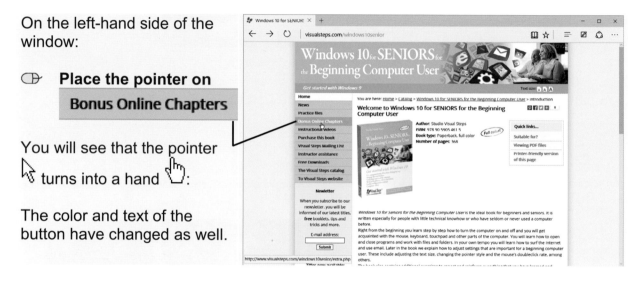

If the pointer turns into a hand, you can click. The clickable item can be a button, a piece of text or an image.

☞ **Click**
   Bonus Online Chapters

A word, button, or image that you can click is called a *hyperlink*.

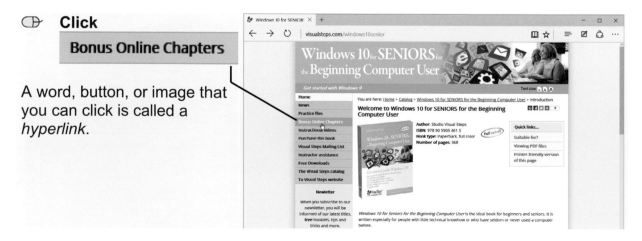

You will see a page with an overview of the bonus chapters that go with this book.

The white color of the

Bonus Online Chapters

button indicates that you are currently viewing the web page with the bonus chapters:

On this page you find hyperlinks containing the words _Start downloading »»_. These are links to the bonus chapters that go with this book.

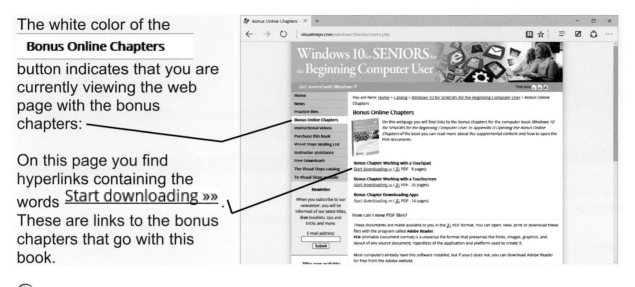

💡 **Tip**

Open the bonus chapters

You can read how to download and open the bonus chapters in *Appendix D Opening the Bonus Online Chapters* at the end of this book.

6.7 Scrolling with the Scroll Box and Mouse

You will frequently need to use the scroll box on the Internet. Your screen is often too small to display all the information on a web page. That is why you need to use the vertical scroll box to view the rest of the page:

⬲ **Drag the scroll box downwards**

Now you can read the bottom part of the text:

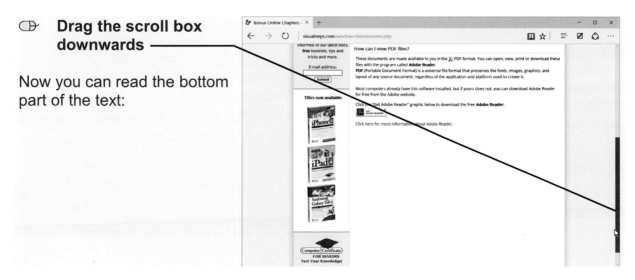

This action is called *scrolling* in computer terms.

If you have a mouse with a scroll wheel, you can easily scroll through the content of a web page.

In order to view the top of the web page again:

☞ **Place the pointer on the web page**

☞ **Roll the mouse wheel away from you with your index finger**

☞ **Stop rolling when the scroll box has arrived at the top**

You will see the top of the web page.

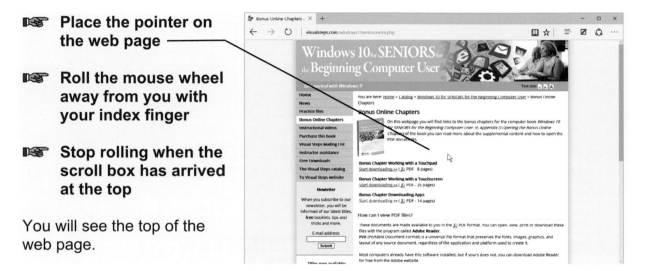

In order to go downwards again:

☞ **Place the pointer on the web page**

☞ **Roll the mouse wheel towards you with your index finger**

☞ **Stop rolling when the scroll box has arrived at the bottom**

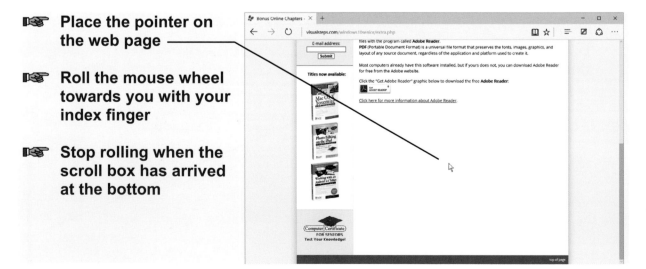

☞ **Go to the top of the web page again** 🐾**38**

A good website has been designed in such a way that you can jump from one page to another without losing your way. Usually, there is a 'Home' or 'Start' button that lets you return to the home page of the website.

On the left-hand side of the web page:

⊂⊃ **Click** | **Home** |

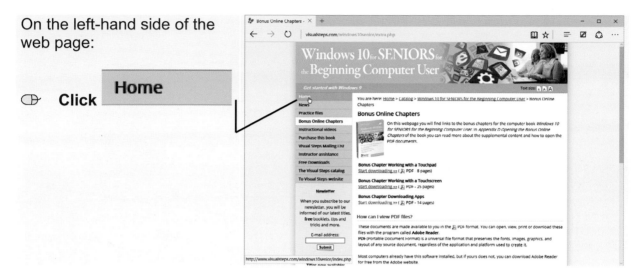

You will see the home page of this website again.

6.8 Zoom on a Web Page

Sometimes the content of a web page is difficult to read. In that case, you try zoom in on a web page. Zooming enlarges or decreases everything on a page, including the text and the images:

In the upper right corner of the window:

⊂⊃ **Click** ▪ ▪ ▪

⊂⊃ **By** Zoom, **click** + **twice**

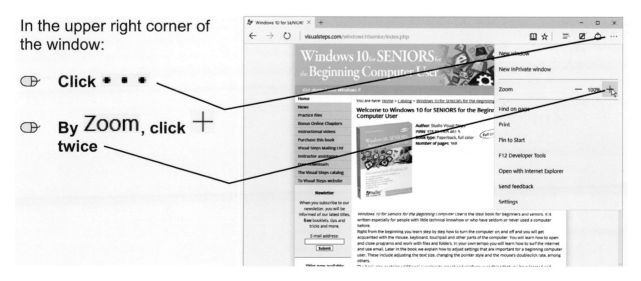

The entire page has been enlarged, including the images and buttons:

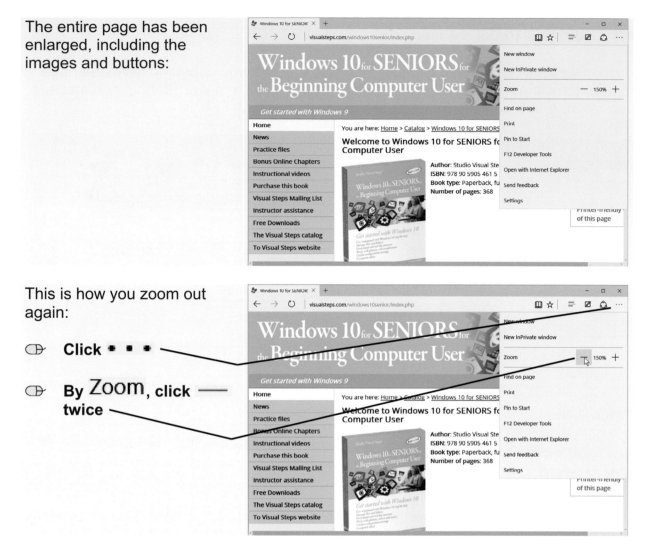

This is how you zoom out again:

☞ **Click** ▪ ▪ ▪

☞ **By Zoom, click** ——— **twice**

The page has become smaller again.

💡 **Tip**

Zooming with the mouse or keyboard
If you have a mouse with a scroll wheel, you can zoom in and out by pressing the

Ctrl

Ctrl key ▭ and rolling the scroll wheel.
You can also use the keyboard to zoom. You do this by depressing the Ctrl key

Ctrl

▭ and then pressing ▭ or ▭ .

6.9 Searching the Internet

If you want to find information on the Internet, you can use a so-called search engine. A search engine is a program that has searched through the content of millions of web pages on the Internet.

You can allow a search engine to look for a specific keyword, or a combination of keywords. The engine will go to work and present you with the web addresses of the web pages that contain that keyword.
If you are looking for a specific subject, you can enter the words directly in the *Edge* address bar:

☞ **Click the address bar**

⌨ **Type a keyword, for example:** weather in canada

As soon as you start typing, you will see suggestions for the keywords:

You can click a suggestion, or press the Enter key:

⌨ **Press**

You will see the search results:

In this example we have searched in *Bing*, the search engine powered by *Microsoft*, but it may also be another search engine, such as *Google*.

In order to open the matching web page, you click the search result:

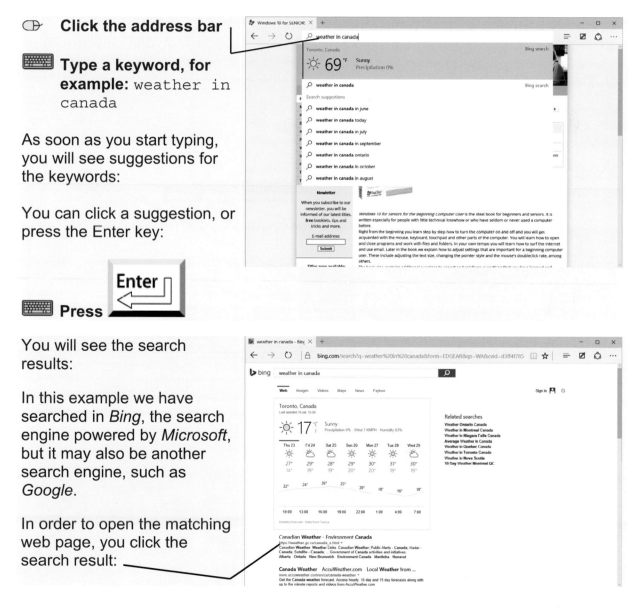

Tip

Different search engines

If you wish, you can also search for something by opening the search engine page first. For example, www.bing.com or www.google.com.
You will notice that the search engines do not always come up with identical search results. That is why it makes sense to use different search engines for a search.

6.10 Saving a Web Address

If you have found an interesting website, you can save its web address. Then you can quickly open the website without having to retype the web address again. Websites that are saved this way are called *favorites* in *Edge*. You can only save a web address as a favorite if the corresponding website is opened. You can try this with the Visual Steps website:

☞ **Open the www.visualsteps.com web page** ⚇³⁹

In the upper right corner of the window:

☞ **Click** ☆

☞ **If necessary, click**

☆
Favorites

You will see a small window. The name of the website has already been filled in:

☞ **Click** Add

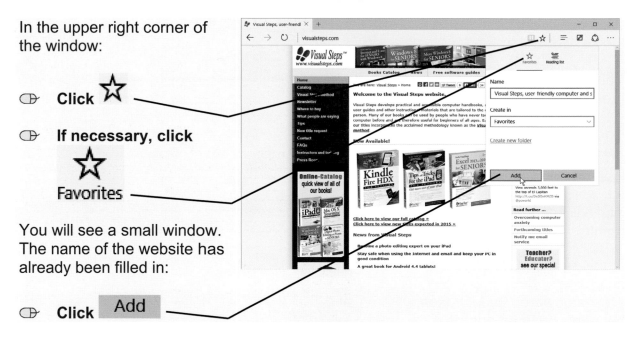

The website has been added to your favorites.

6.11 Opening a Favorite

Now you can check and see how a favorite works. First, you need to open another website:

☞ **Open the web page www.cnn.com** 👣³⁹

You will see the news website cnn.com. Now you quickly open one of your favorite websites:

In the upper right corner of the window:

⊕ **Click** ☰

⊕ **Click** ☆

⊕ **Click**
    👣 Visual Steps, user-friendly c
    http://www.visualsteps.com

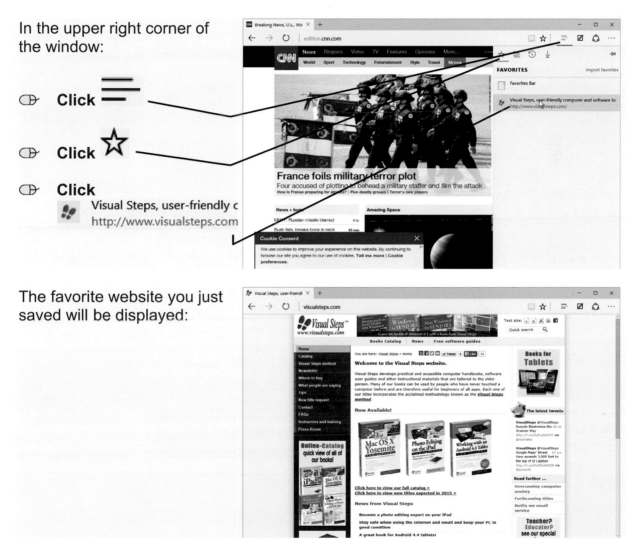

The favorite website you just saved will be displayed:

Edge remembers all your favorites, even after you have closed the program. You can collect a lot of your favorite websites in the same manner, and access them quickly at any given time.

6.12 Arranging Your Favorites

You can assemble all your favorite websites in a single long list. But this is not very practical if you have a lot of favorites. It is better to arrange your favorites in separate folders. You can save the favorites ordered by subject, for example.
You can also use these folders to separate your own favorites from those of the other users on your computer.

To practice a little, you can create a folder for the website that accompanies this book.

☞ **Open the web page www.visualsteps.com/windows10senior** 🦶**39**

You will save this web page and create the folder all at once.

In the upper right corner of the window:

🖱 **Click** ☆

🖱 **Click**
  Create new folder

Add a name for the folder:

🖱 **Click the box by**
  Folder name

⌨ **Type:** Computer books

🖱 **Click** **Add**

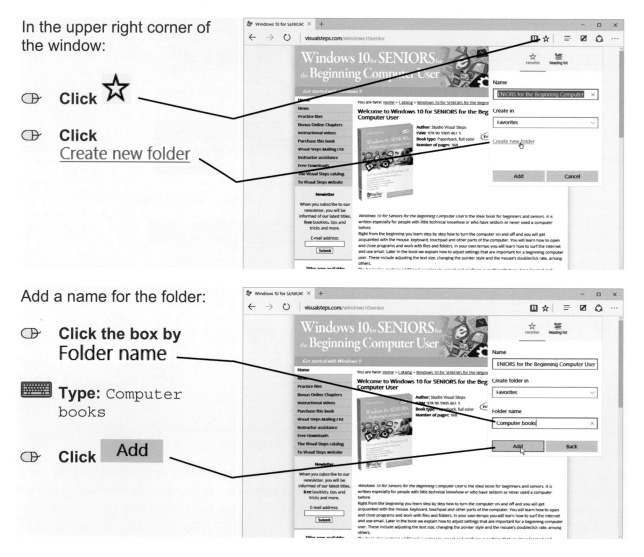

The folder has been created, and the web page has been added to the folder. You can check this right away:

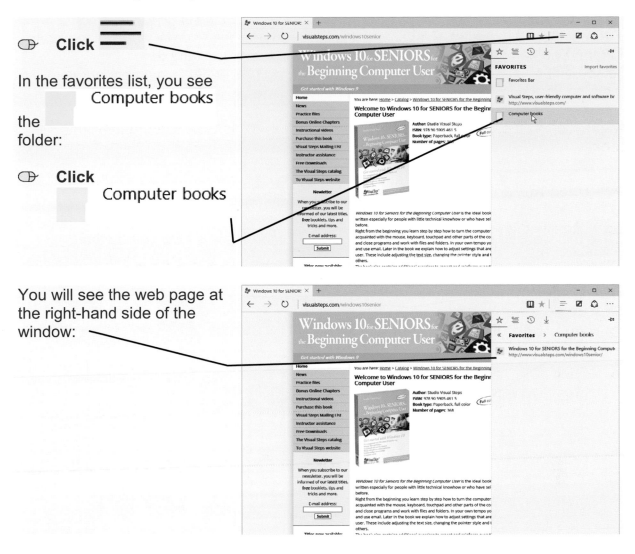

👉 **Click** ▬

In the favorites list, you see the Computer books the folder:

👉 **Click** Computer books

You will see the web page at the right-hand side of the window:

In the next section you will learn how to save web pages in a previously created folder.

6.13 Saving a Favorite in a Folder

It is very easy to save a web address in the new folder.

➥ Please note:

You can only save a web address as a favorite, if the website in question is displayed in the *Edge* window.

⊕ **Click**

The Visual Steps catalog

You will see an overview if the books published by Visual Steps:

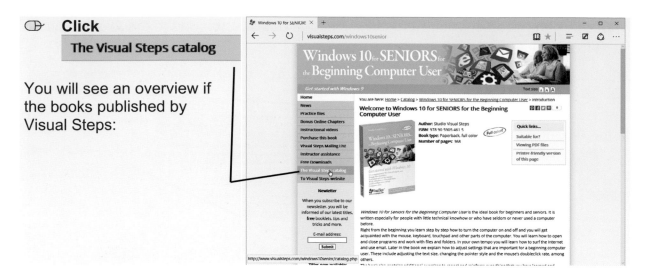

Save this website in the new *Computer books* folder. Here is how you do that:

⊕ **Click** ☆

⊕ **By** Create in, **click**

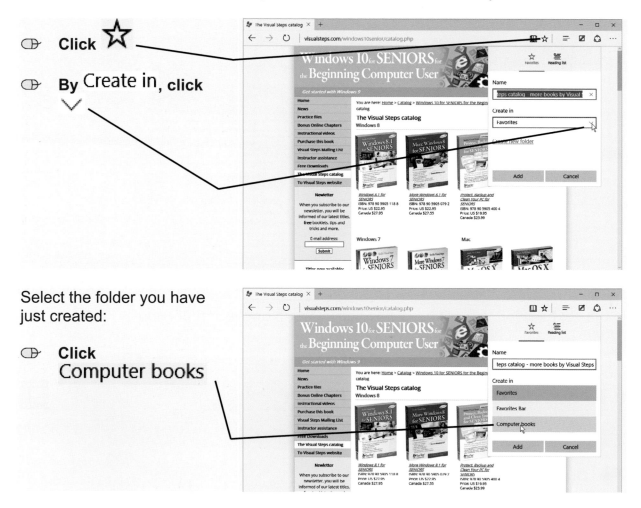

Select the folder you have just created:

⊕ **Click**
Computer books

The right folder has been selected:

👉 **Click** Add

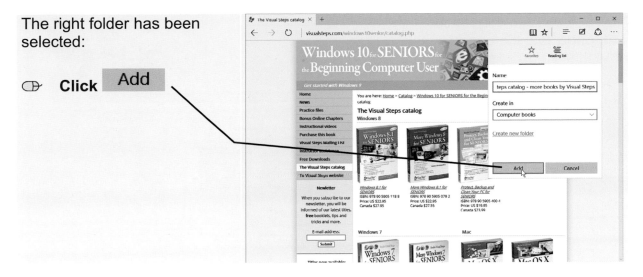

Now you can check to see if the favorite has been saved in the right folder. First you open another website, for example, the Wikipedia website:

☞ **Open the web page www.wikipedia.org** 🐾**39**

You will see the Wikipedia home page:

Wikipedia is an encyclopedia on the Internet.

👉 **Click** ☰

The *Computer books* folder is still open, and the favorite has been added:

👉 **Click** 👣 The Visual Steps catalog - moi http://www.visualsteps.com/w

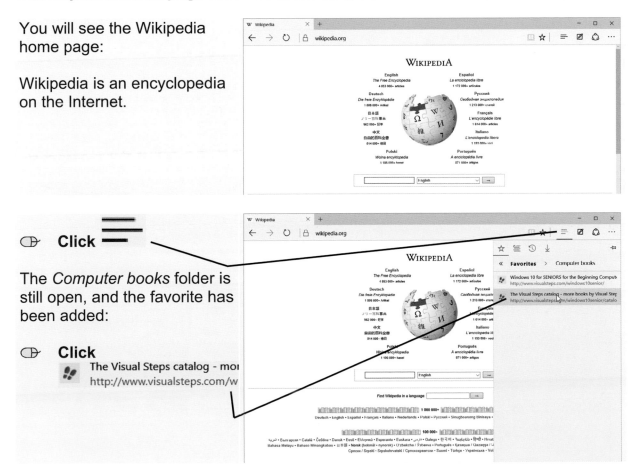

Now you will see the catalog web page with the overview of Visual Steps books again:

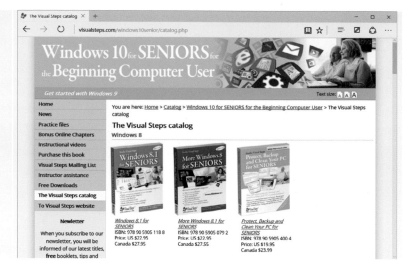

6.14 Printing a Web Page

It is not always easy to read a web page on a screen, especially if the page contains a lot of text. You may want to print the web page first, and read it later.

You do not have a printer?
If you do not have a printer, you can skip this section.

☞ **Check if the printer is turned on**

This is how you print a web page:

In the upper right corner of the window:

☞ **Click ▪ ▪ ▪**

☞ **Click Print**

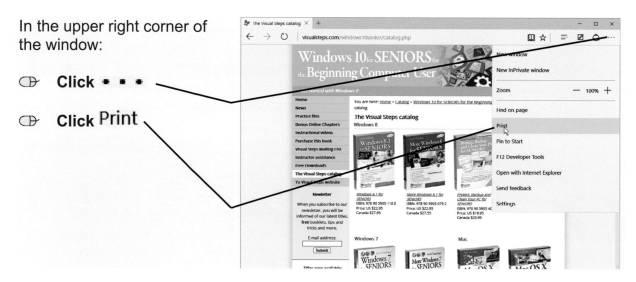

A window will be opened. On the right-hand side of the window you will see a print preview of the web page:

You can also change the print settings, if you wish.

If you want to print the page:

☞ **Click**

| Print |

If you do not want to print the page, click

| Cancel |

The page will be printed.

6.15 Cookies

When you visit a website, cookies will be stored on your computer. The main object of a cookie is to distinguish between different users.

Cookies do not pose a threat to the operation of your computer. They do not damage files or programs. Nor can they access your files. In fact, they are just simple text files and not programs. The main function of cookies is to distinguish between users.

Since May 2012, the so-called Cookie Law has come into action in the EU countries. This law requires websites to inform its visitors about the kinds of cookies that are in use on their websites, and for what purpose. The websites need to obtain informed consent of each visitor, before being allowed to place the cookies. The law does not apply to companies that operate exclusively within the US, but if they target European users they will have to comply too. There has been a lot of discussion and complaints about this law from the local business community.

You will usually not need the cookies in order to make proper use of the website, so you could decide to ignore the message and just view the web page. If the message annoys you, or if you are forced to click it in order to be able to view the website properly, you can click the message. Although you should always check whether the source of the website is trustworthy. If this is the case, it is usually safe to accept the cookies.

Asking for the visitor's permission is done in various ways. For example, a bar may be displayed above or below the window, as is seen in this example from the CNN website.

An example of a message
you can choose to ignore.
The rest of the page is visible:

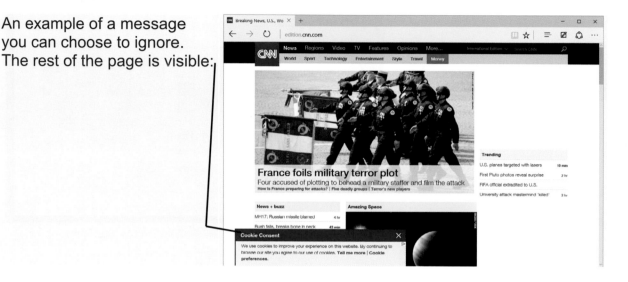

There are also messages that requires you to accept the information in the window, in order to make use of the website.

You can delete the cookies from the computer by deleting the browser history. On page 230 you will find a *Tip* on this subject.

In this chapter you have learned how to surf the Internet, add websites to your favorites, zoom in on a web page, and find information on the Internet. In the next few exercises you can repeat these actions.

6.16 Exercises

The following exercises will help you master what you have just learned. Have you forgotten how to do something? Use the number beside the footsteps to look it up in the appendix *How Do I Do That Again?* at the end of this book.

Exercise 1: The Visual Steps Favorite

In this exercise, you will open the SeniorNet website and add it to your favorites.

☞ Open *Edge*. $\wp^2$

☞ Type the web address: www.seniornet.org. $\wp^{39}$

☞ Browse through a few pages of the SeniorNet website. Click some of the hyperlinks on the pages for practice.

☞ Go back to the homepage of SeniorNet. $\wp^{40}$

☞ Make the address for Seniornet a favorite. $\wp^{41}$

☞ Close *Edge*. $\wp^6$

Exercise 2: Surfing

Going from one website to another is called surfing. In this exercise, you will surf to websites you previously visited.

☞ Open *Edge*. $\wp^2$

☞ Open the favorite www.visualsteps.com. $\wp^{42}$

☞ Open the favorite www.seniornet.org. $\wp^{42}$

☞ Open the web page www.cnn.com. $\wp^{39}$

☞ Go back to www.seniornet.org. $\wp^{40}$

☞ Go back to www.visualsteps.com. $\mathscr{QD}^{40}$

☞ Go back to www.seniornet.org. $\mathscr{QD}^{43}$

☞ Close *Edge*. $\mathscr{QD}^{6}$

Exercise 3: Zooming In and Out

In this exercise you will practice zooming in and out on a web page.

☞ Open *Edge*. $\mathscr{QD}^{2}$

☞ Open the stored favorite website www.visualsteps.com. $\mathscr{QD}^{42}$

☞ Zoom in on the page. $\mathscr{QD}^{44}$

☞ Zoom out on the page. $\mathscr{QD}^{44}$

☞ Close *Edge*. $\mathscr{QD}^{6}$

Exercise 4: Searching

You can find lots of information on the Internet by entering keywords.

☞ Open *Edge*. $\mathscr{QD}^{2}$

☞ Search with these keywords: `weather in France`. $\mathscr{QD}^{45}$

☞ Open a search result. $\mathscr{QD}^{46}$

☞ Close *Edge*. $\mathscr{QD}^{6}$

6.17 Background Information

Dictionary

ADSL	Asynchronous Digital Subscriber Line. A fast Internet connection that uses the telephone network. This type of connection is also called a broadband connection.
Browser, Web browser	A program used to display web pages and to navigate the Internet. *Edge* is an example of a web browser.
Cookie	A small text file that is stored on your computer by a website, in order to save certain information.
Download	Retrieving a file from the Internet and storing it on your computer. This could be a computer program, an app, a music or photo file or other items.
Edge	A type of browser program with which you can view web pages on the Internet.
Home page	The web page that is displayed each time you open *Edge*.
Hyperlink, Link	A hyperlink or link is a navigational element in a web page that automatically displays the referred information when the user clicks the hyperlink. A hyperlink can be text or an image such as a button, icon, photo or other illustration. You can recognize a hyperlink when the pointer turns into a hand 👆.
Internet	A network of computer networks which operates worldwide, using a common set of communications protocols. The part of the Internet that most people are familiar with is the World Wide Web (WWW). Also called simply the web.
Internet Explorer	A type of browser program with which you can view web pages on the Internet. Works in a way similar to *Edge*.
Internet provider	An Internet provider is a company that provides access to the Internet, usually at a fee. The most common way of connecting to an Internet provider is by using a phone line or a broadband connection (cable, ADSL, or optic fiber). Many Internet providers offer additional services, such as email accounts, spam filters, and space for a website.

- Continue on the next page -

Malware	A computer program intended to damage your computer. Viruses, worms, and Trojan horses are a few examples of these harmful programs.
Password	A string of characters that a user must enter to gain access to a resource that is password protected. Passwords help ensure that unauthorized users do not access your Internet connection or your computer.
Scroll	Sliding the content of a web page up and down by using the mouse's scroll wheel.
Spyware	A computer program that can display commercials and ads (such as pop-up ads). Spyware will often collect information about your surfing behavior so that it can be passed along to the spyware manufacturer or other third parties.
Virus	A virus is a program that replicates itself and tries to spread from one computer to another. It can cause damage (by deleting or damaging data) or annoy the user (by displaying messages or altering the information in the window).
Web address	The web address of a website identifies a unique location on the Internet. A web address is also called a URL (Uniform Resource Locator). An example of a web address is: **http://www.visualsteps.com**.
Web page	A web page is a resource of information that is suitable for the World Wide Web and can be accessed through a browser.
Website	A website is a collection of interconnected web pages, typically common to a particular domain name on the World Wide Web on the Internet.
WWW	World Wide Web - web of computers, connected to each other - containing an infinite amount of web pages.

Source: Windows Help

Types of Internet connections
In order to gain access to the Internet you need to have a subscription with an Internet provider. Internet providers include telephone networks (ADSL) or cable television networks that also provide Internet access. Both these types of networks are available in many countries, although in some regions, there are fewer Internet access providers than in others.
The most recent type of connection is the glass fiber or fiber-optic connection. This type of connection is becoming more common but may not be available in your area.

- Continue on the next page -

When you connect to the Internet, you need to use a special device called a *modem*. A modem enables your computer to connect to the Internet provider's computer(s). It is usually included in your Internet subscription.

A modem can be connected to a router, in order to provide a wireless Internet connection, also called a Wi-Fi connection. With Wi-Fi you can use your laptop or tablet in any room of your house and or outside in the garden. Many modems already have a built-in router, so you will not need to use two separate devices.

Notifications bar

Sometimes, you may see a notifications bar while you are surfing the Internet. Here you see an example of such a bar that appears after you have pressed a button for downloading something, that is to say, copy an item to your pc:

These notifications may display options for downloads, warn you that pop-up windows have been blocked (pop-ups often contain advertisements), and notify you about other activities.
You may see a notifications bar in the following situations, for example:

- a website tries to download a file to your computer, for example, a program.
- a website tries to open a pop-up window.
- when your security settings are lower than recommended.

Sometimes you can choose on the notifications bar in *Edge* what to do with these

messages, for example, Run . If necessary, ask an experienced computer user to help you, in case you do not know what to do. Click *Cancel* if a notification suddenly appears and especially in the case when you are asked to download something. Be cautious about downloading anything from an unfamiliar website.

Viruses, spyware, and malware

If you use the Internet regularly for surfing websites or using email, your PC is at risk of being infected with viruses, spyware, or malware. *Windows 10* provides various security measures to prevent this, but you also need to be on the alert yourself when using the Internet. There are other books that discuss this subject at length. You can find more information about these books at **www.visualsteps.com**

6.18 Tips

Tip

Browsing with tabs

You can open a web page in a new tab, and then switch between various pages by clicking the tabs. This is how you open a new tab in *Edge*:

☞ **Open the web page www.visualsteps.com** ᠔᠗**39**

In the upper left corner of the window:

◯ᗑ **Click** ╋

Because this is a new, empty tab, you do not see an address bar yet. But you do see a search box in which you can type a search term of web address.

Type a search term in the search box:

⌨ **Type:** www.cnn.com

⌨ **Press** **Enter**

The website appears in this tab:

The address bar appears again:

If desired, you can open even more tabs. If you want to go to a website shown in a different tab, just click that tab.

To close a tab:

◯ᗑ **By** Breaking News, U.S.,

   click ✕

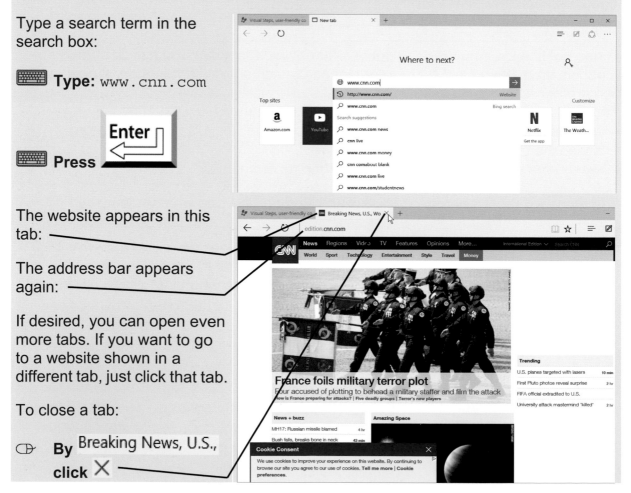

Tip

Set a home page
You can set a different home page, if you want. This can be a web page you often visit. In this example we have set the Visual Steps website as the home page:

In the upper right corner of the window:

☞ Click • • •

☞ Click Settings

☞ Click the radio button
⊙ by
A specific page or pages

In the box below:

☞ By MSN, click ✕

☞ Click Custom

⌨ Type:
www.visualsteps.com

Enter

⌨ Press

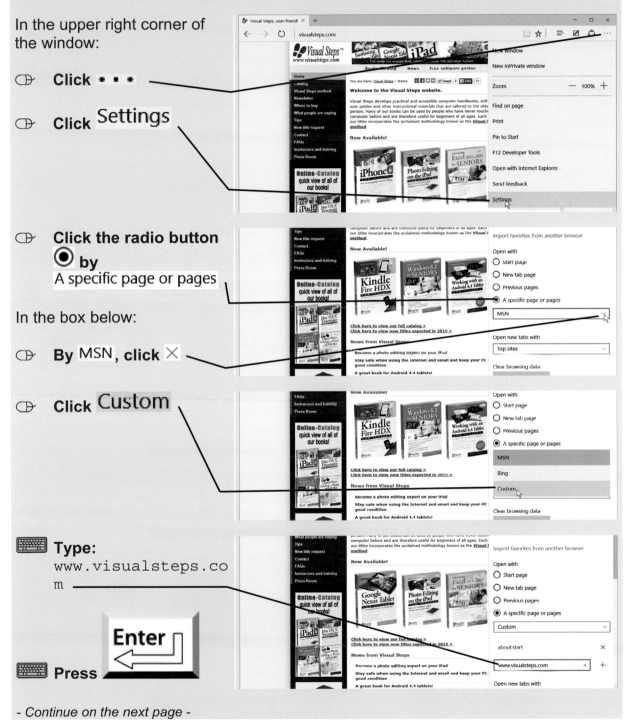

- Continue on the next page -

Now, two home pages are set: ——————————

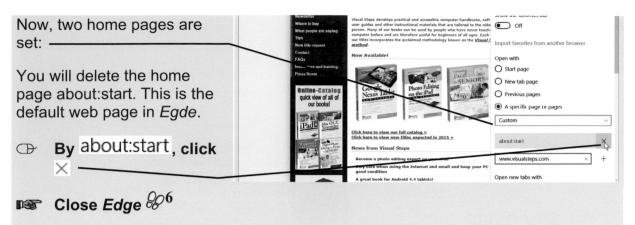

You will delete the home page about:start. This is the default web page in *Egde*.

☞ **By** about:start **, click** ✕

☞ **Close** *Edge* 🐾⁶

If you restart *Edge* right now, you will see the new home page.

💡 **Tip**

Reading list
You can also create a reading list in *Edge*. This list will contain links to the web pages you want to read later on. You do not need an Internet connection for that.

☞ **Click** ☆

☞ **Click** Reading list

You can type another name for this item, if you wish:

☞ **Click** Add

The page will be added. This is how you view the content of the reading list:

☞ **Click** ☰

☞ **Click** ☰

You will see the reading list, including the web page you just saved.
In order to open a web page from the reading list:

☞ **Click the desired web page** ——————————

💡 Tip

Add notes and markers to a web page

In *Edge* you can jot down notes, draw something, and add markers to a web page. This is how you mark something, for example, to highlight and save an important sentence:

In the upper right corner of the window:

☞ **Click**

A toolbar appears at the top of the window:

☞ **Click**

☞ **Press the left mouse button, hold it down and drag the pointer across the desired text**

The text will be highlighted:

☞ **Release the mouse button**

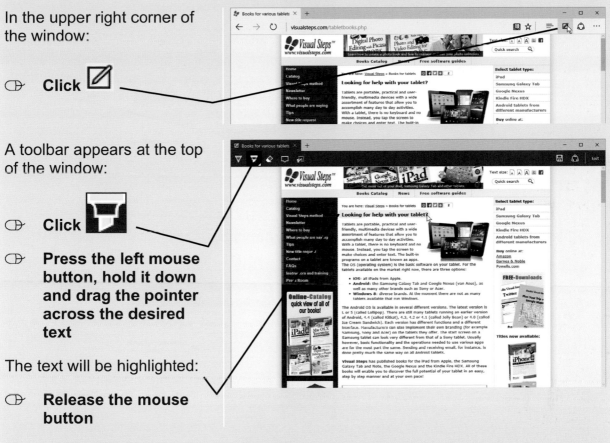

This is how you add a note to a web page:

☞ **Click**

☞ **Click the web page**

A window appears:

⌨ **Type the desired text**

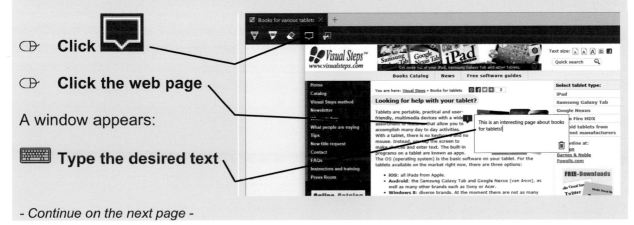

- Continue on the next page -

Save the web page with the
highlighted text and the note:

⟳   Click 🖫

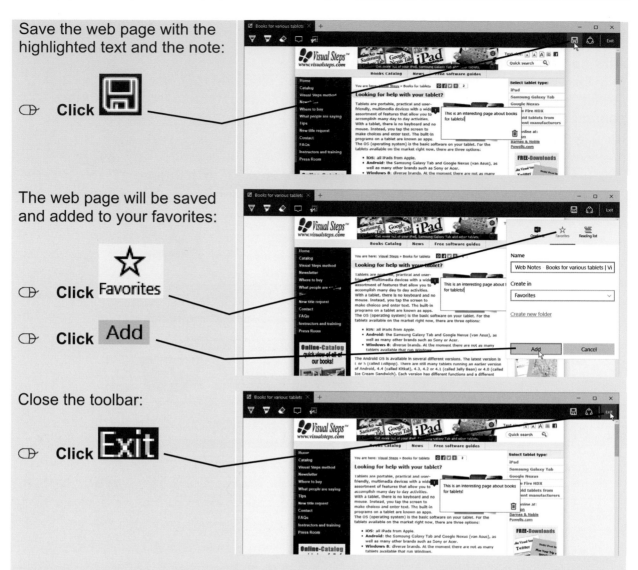

The web page will be saved
and added to your favorites:

⟳   Click ☆ Favorites

⟳   Click **Add**

Close the toolbar:

⟳   Click **Exit**

The web page has been saved as a favorite. If you have forgotten how to open a
favorite, you can go back to *section 6.11 Opening a Favorite* and read how to do so.

💡 **Tip**

Speech recognition with Cortana
Microsoft has a speech recognition assistant called *Cortana*. *Cortana* plays an
important role in *Windows 10*. It is so important, that *Cortana* is also located on the
taskbar, as part of the search box. By means of a microphone, you can pose
questions to this assistant on a variety of topics. The answers are found by utilizing
the *Bing* search engine, among others. *Cortana* can also help you find and open
files, programs and apps on the computer.

- Continue on the next page -

You need to take into account that voice recognition software, such as *Cortana*, is still undergoing development; this means some commands or questions might be misunderstood.

Cortana also stores a lot of information regarding your actions on your computer and saves it online in the cloud (a storage location on the Internet). This is intended to help you, but it also brings up privacy issues.

We will not discuss *Cortana* in this book any further, since your desktop computer may not have a microphone installed, and you would need to buy a separate microphone in order to use this function. But a tablet or a smartphone with *Windows 10* does have a built-in microphone, so you can use *Cortana* better on such a device.

If desired you can switch on and set up *Cortana* via the settings:

☞ **Click**

☞ **Click** ⚙

💡 **Tip**

Your history

Edge remembers the websites you have visited with its *History* function. This is how you open the list of recently visited websites:

☞ **Click** ☰

☞ **Click** 🕐

You will see the history:

If you have not saved a certain website as a favorite, you may be able to use this list to find it.

Click the hyperlink to visit the web page.

Tip
Delete browser history
While you are surfing the Internet, *Edge* will store information on the websites you visit. This is also called the *browser history*. The browser history consists of various elements. These may include temporary Internet files, browsing history, passwords and small files called cookies that are placed on your computer by various websites. A cookie will contain information about items you have viewed and information you have entered in forms on websites or in the address bar (such as your name, address and email address.

This is how you delete this data in *Edge*:

Click ≡

Click 🕘

If you want to delete the history page by page:

Click ✕

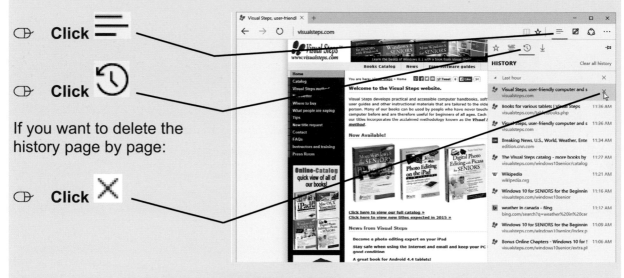

You can also delete all the history all at once:

Click
Clear all history

- Continue on the next page -

☞ **Click a checkmark ☑**
by the desired data

☞ **Click**

Clear

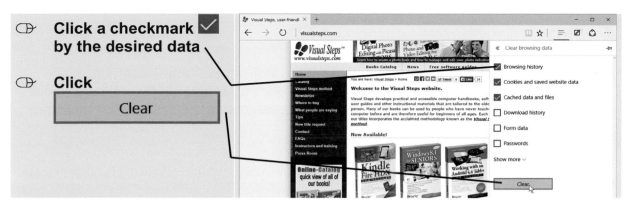

💡 **Tip**

Reading view

Lots of web pages not only contain text, but also all sorts of additional features, such as adverts and animated images. This can be very distracting if you just want to read the text. Some web pages allow you to use the *reading view* to display only text and relevant images.

An article that can be viewed in the reader view, displays

the 📖 icon in the top right-hand corner of the window:

☞ **Click** 📖

You will see the article in the reader view:

To go back to the regular view:

☞ **Click** 📖

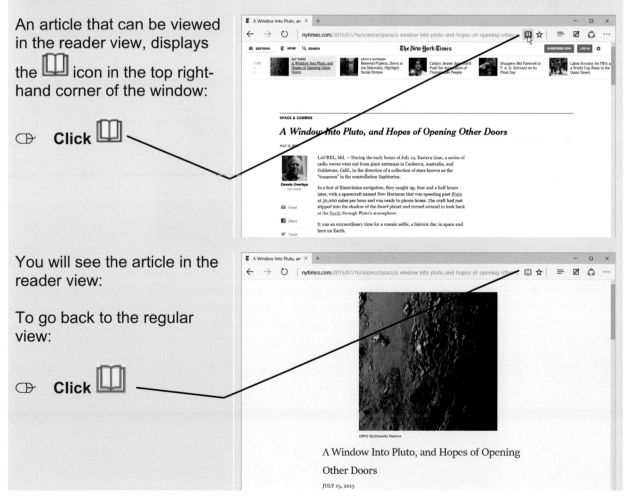

💡 Tip

Internet Explorer

You can use a different browser to surf the Internet, for example, *Internet Explorer*. This program can be found in *Windows 10* as well. You may already be acquainted with this program or have heard of it before. It works almost the same way as *Edge*.

You open *Internet Explorer* like this:

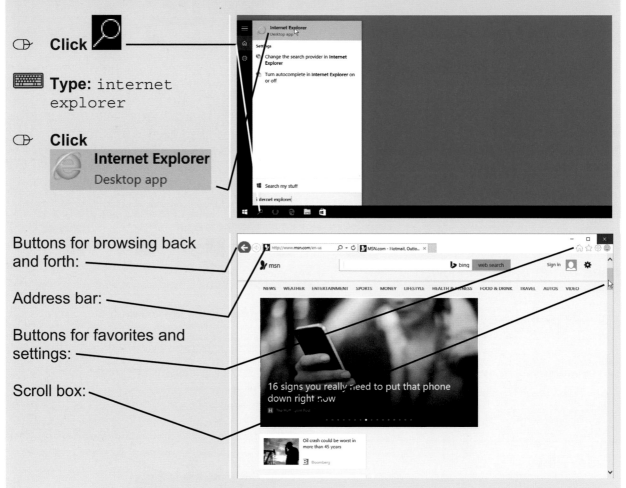

☞ **Click** 🔍

⌨ **Type:** internet explorer

☞ **Click**
Internet Explorer
Desktop app

Buttons for browsing back and forth:

Address bar:

Buttons for favorites and settings:

Scroll box:

There are a number of other browsers as well such as *Google Chrome, Apple's Safari* and *Mozilla Firefox*. If you find that a website is not correctly displayed in a specific browser, we recommend you try one of the other browsers instead.

7. Working with Mail

One of the most useful features of the Internet is the electronic mail function: email. With email you do not need a pen, paper, an envelope or stamp. You simply type your email message on the computer and send it using the Internet.

If you want to send someone an email message, they must to have an email address. It does not matter where the person lives. Sending an email to France will be just as quick as sending an email to someone in your neighborhood. Email does not cost you anything either, except for the regular fee you pay to your Internet service provider.

Mail is a simple app that lets you send and receive electronic mail, quickly and easily. In this chapter you will learn how to use this app. You will discover how easy it is to use email.

In this chapter you will learn how to:

- open *Mail*;
- set up an account;
- compose an email message;
- send, receive, and open email messages;
- reply to an email;
- send, receive and save an attachment;
- delete email messages.

7.1 Setting Up an Account in Mail

You can use the *Mail* app to send and receive email messages. You will need to have an email address available in order to use this app.

This is how you open *Mail*:

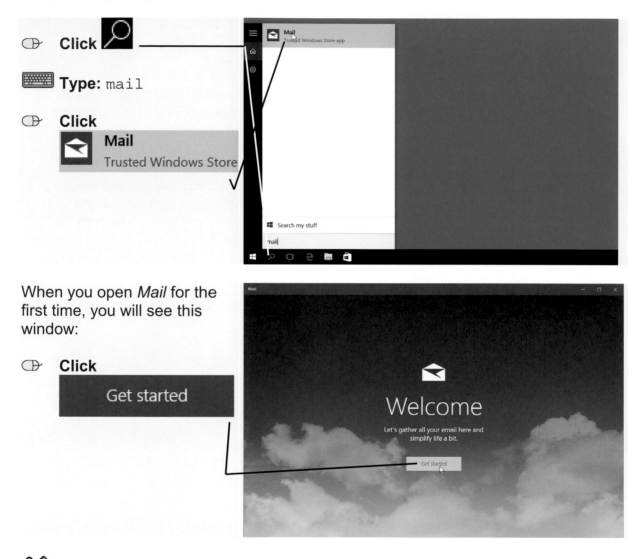

☞ **Click**

⌨ **Type:** `mail`

☞ **Click**

Mail
Trusted Windows Store

When you open *Mail* for the first time, you will see this window:

☞ **Click**

Get started

🩹 HELP! I do not see this window.

If you do not see this window, *Mail* has been previously opened. You can continue with the next step.

In order to use *Mail*, you will need to have an email account. This can be an account offered to you by your Internet provider, or you can use an account from an online email service such as *Hotmail*, *Outlook.com* and *Gmail*.

👆 **Click**

| + Add account |

🩹 HELP! I do not see this window.

If you do not see this window, an email account has already been set up. You can continue with *section 7.3 Creating an Email Message*.

You will see a window with options for various types of accounts. In this example we will set up a POP/IMAP account. This is the type of account that is offered by Internet providers, such as AOL or Verizon. If you wish, you can also select another type of account such as a *Hotmail, Outlook.com* or *Gmail* account. The email address that you will have then ends with hotmail.com, live.com, outlook.com or gmail.com. In the next section you can read more about these accounts.

When you set up the email address you have received from your Internet provider, you will need to have the email address and the corresponding password available.

This is how you set up the account:

👆 **Click**
✉ Other account
POP, IMAP

If you want to use an email account provided by *Hotmail, Outlook.com* or *Gmail*, you can read how to do so in the next section.

Choose an account

◎✓ Outlook.com
Outlook.com, Live.com, Hotmail, MSN

E⊠ Exchange
Exchange, Office 365

✉ Google

✉ Yahoo! Mail

✉ iCloud

✉ Other account
POP, IMAP

Close

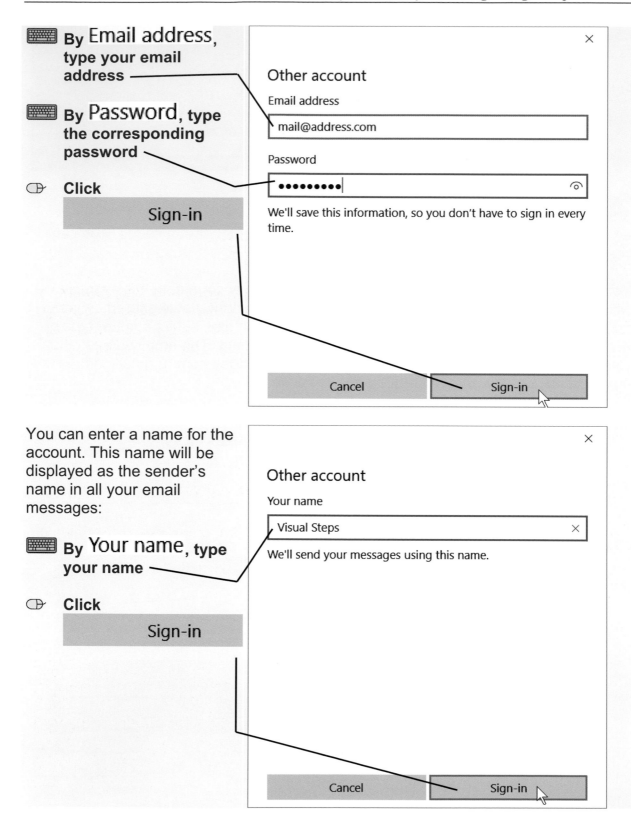

By Email address, type your email address

By Password, type the corresponding password

Click Sign-in

Other account

Email address

mail@address.com

Password

•••••••••

We'll save this information, so you don't have to sign in every time.

Cancel   Sign-in

You can enter a name for the account. This name will be displayed as the sender's name in all your email messages:

By Your name, type your name

Click Sign-in

Other account

Your name

Visual Steps

We'll send your messages using this name.

Cancel   Sign-in

Now the account has been set up:

At the bottom of the window:

Click Done

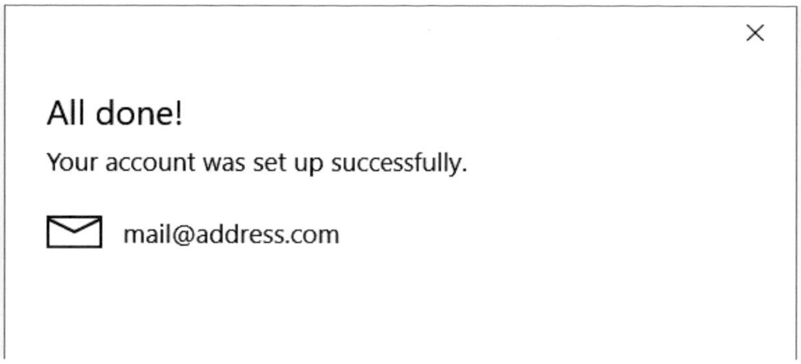
All done!
Your account was set up successfully.
mail@address.com

HELP! I see a message in the next window.

If you see a message in a window, after you have clicked Done, there may have been some problem while you were setting up your email account. At the end of this chapter you will find the *Tip Setting up a POP/IMAP account if sending and receiving mail fails*, where you can read more about the advanced settings for email accounts offered by Internet providers.

Close *Mail* 6

Continue with *section 7.3 Creating an Email Message*

7.2 Setting Up a Hotmail, Outlook.com or Gmail Account

If you are using an email address that ends in hotmail.com, outlook.com, live.com, or gmail.com, you can set up an account like this:

If necessary, open *Mail* 2

When you see the window below:

Click Add account

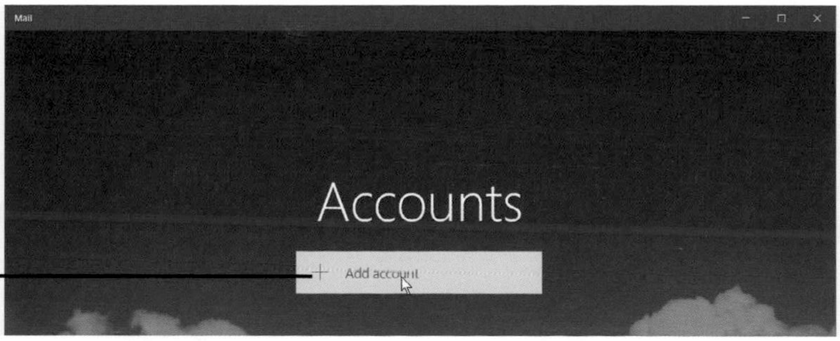
Mail
Accounts
Add account

Or if you see this window:

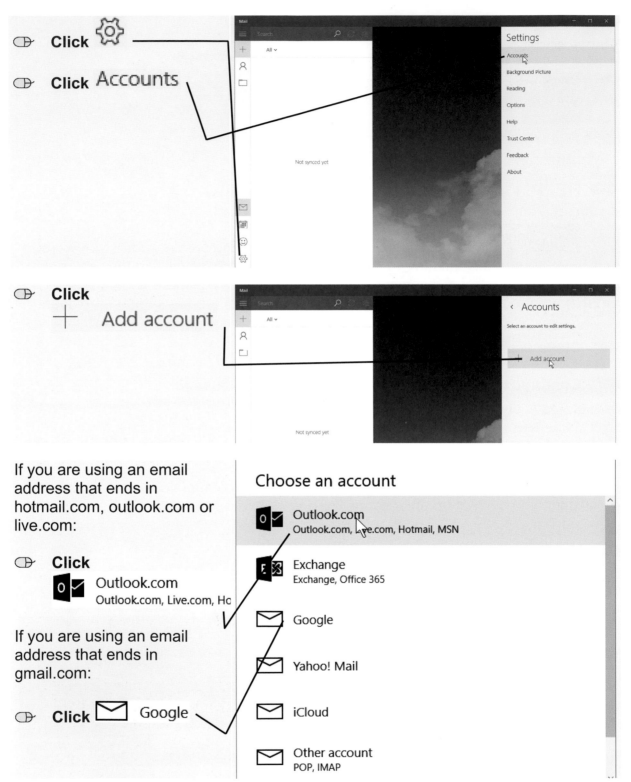

☞ **Click** ⚙

☞ **Click** Accounts

☞ **Click**

+ Add account

If you are using an email address that ends in hotmail.com, outlook.com or live.com:

☞ **Click**

O☑ Outlook.com
Outlook.com, Live.com, Ho

If you are using an email address that ends in gmail.com:

☞ **Click** ✉ Google

Choose an account

O☑ **Outlook.com**
Outlook.com, Live.com, Hotmail, MSN

E☒ **Exchange**
Exchange, Office 365

✉ **Google**

✉ **Yahoo! Mail**

✉ **iCloud**

✉ **Other account**
POP, IMAP

Log in with the account:

Use the login information for your account:

⌨ **Type your email address**

⌨ **Type the corresponding password**

🖰 **Click**

> **Sign in**

If you are using *Gmail*, click **Sign in**.

Add your Microsoft account

Sign in with your Microsoft account. You can use this account with other apps on this device. Learn more.

mail@address.com

••••••••

Forgot my password

No account? Create one!

Microsoft privacy statement

Sign in

If you have selected *Outlook.com*, you will see this window:

You can set up your account for automatic synchronization of settings and files. In this example we will skip this step:

🖰 **Click**
Sign in to just this app i

Make it yours

Sign into this device for a highly personalized experience. Cortana will assist you, you can find your device if you lose it, and your files and settings will sync automatically.

We'll need your current Windows password one last time to make sure it's really you. If you don't have a password, leave it blank.

Your Windows password

Sign in to just this app instead
Next time you sign in to Windows you'll use your Microsoft account.

🩹 HELP! What does synchronizing mean?

Synchronizing means equalizing the content. This content can be settings or files, among other things. You can synchronize data between apps, but also for your entire user account. If you have done this and are going to use another device, such as a tablet, for example, you will see the same settings and files as on your computer. Since beginning computer users will not readily use this option, we will not discuss it any further.

If you are using *Gmail*, you will need to give the *Mail* app permission:

☞ **Click** Accept

The account has been added. You will see a message in the window:

At the bottom of the window:

☞ **Click**
Done

All done!

Your account was set up successfully.

mail@address.com

Close *Mail*:

☞ **Close** *Mail* ✂⁶

7.3 Creating an Email Message

After you have set up an email account, you can send and receive mail with *Mail*:

☞ **Open** *Mail* ✂²

You may see this window:

You will see one or more email accounts you have set up:

☞ **If necessary, click the desired account**

☞ **If necessary, click**
Ready to go

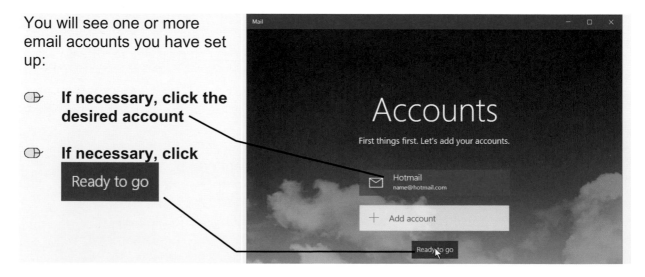

Accounts

First things first. Let's add your accounts.

Hotmail
name@hotmail.com

+ Add account

Ready to go

The *Mail* window appears:

In this example you do not see any incoming email messages. Your own window may contain a few email messages.

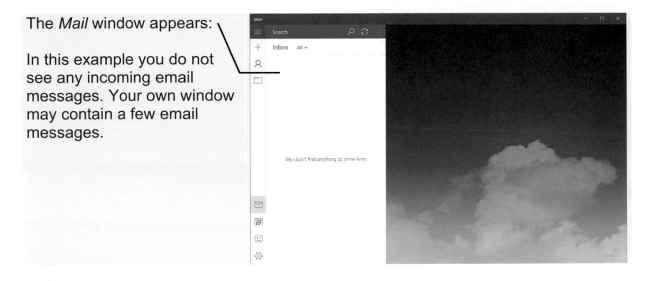

✖ HELP! My window looks different.

If your window looks different, you can widen the window by dragging the window border. Then you will probably see a window similar to the one above.

If you see different buttons in the *Mail* window, the *Mail* app on your computer may not be fully up to date. In this case, you may need to update the app first. You can read about this in *section 9.6 Updating Apps*.

You can practice sending an email by sending a message to yourself. In this way you will see how the sending and receiving part of email works. You will receive the message right away. You start by creating a new email message:

In the upper left corner of the window:

☞ **Click** +

The right-hand side of the window is the formatting area where you can create a new email message:

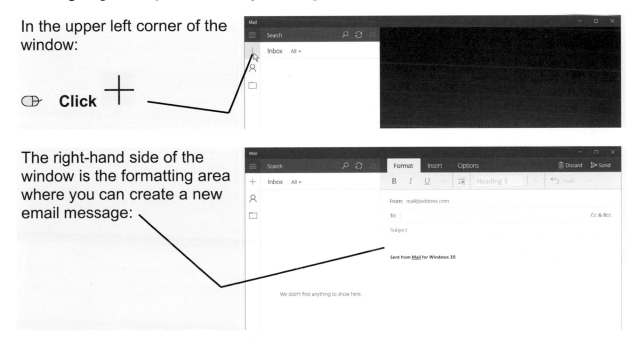

First, your message needs to have an address: the email address. Every email address consists of a number of words and the well-known 'at' sign @ somewhere in the middle.

This is what an email address looks like:

yourname@provider.com

The name of the person is on the left side of the @ symbol. On the right side of the @ symbol, is the name of the email provider that gave you the email address, for example, aol.com or verizon.com.

➥ **Please note:**

Email addresses cannot contain any blank spaces. This is why names or words are often separated by a dot (period), hyphen or underscore. It is important that you type the email address correctly. If you omit just one dot, for example, the email message will never arrive at the right address.

The best way of testing whether your email account is working, is by sending an email message to yourself:

⬭ **Click to the right of**
     To:

⌨ **Type the first letters of**
     your own email
     address

One you have typed a few letters, your own email address will appear in a small popup window:

⬭ **Click your email**
     address

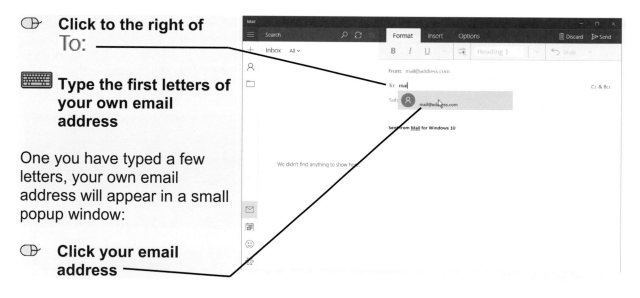

Your email address has been added:

Each email address has a subject as well:

👆 **Click** Subject

⌨ **Type:** test

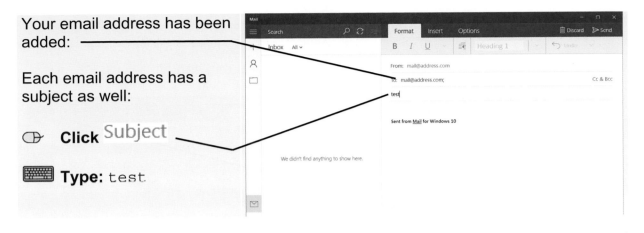

💡 Tip

Adding multiple email addresses
You can send an email to multiple addresses. If you want to send an email to more than one person, you just type the next email address after the previous one. Just make sure to type a blank space between the email addresses.

Type the message text:

👆 **Click the white area below the subject**

Here you can type the message:

⌨ **Type:** This is my first email, as a test.

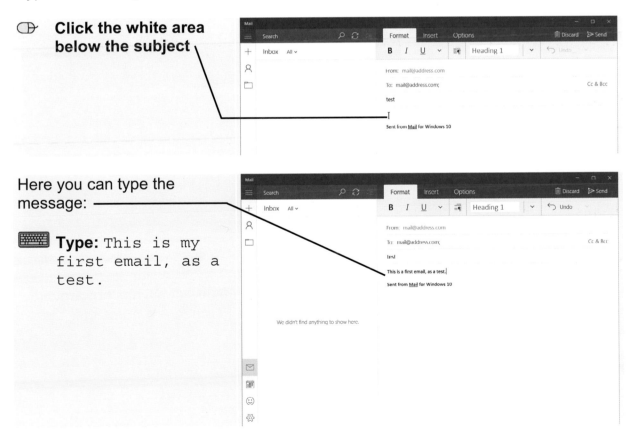

7.4 Sending and Receiving the Email

When you have finished typing the email message, you can send it:

In the upper right corner of the window:

Click ▷ Send

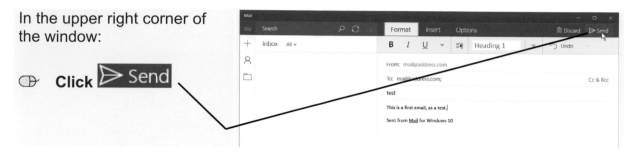

The message will be sent. The app will connect with your email provider. The app will also check to see if any new email has been received. If that is the case, *Mail* will retrieve the email message(s).

7.5 Reading an Email Message

All incoming email is saved in the folder named *Inbox*:

In the message list, you will see the email you just sent:

The sender and the subject are stated. The time of receipt is also noted.

✚ HELP! No mail.

If you do not see any messages in the *Inbox*, it may mean the email has not arrived yet. With some email providers, it can take a little while to process a message. You can also try using the refresh button:

Click

HELP! I have waited for a long time, but still no mail.

If you have waited quite a while and have not yet received anything, it may mean that your email account has not been properly set up. You may find the solution to this problem in the *Tip Setting up a POP/IMAP account if sending and receiving mail fails* at the end of this chapter.

You may see this message in a conversation. A conversation is a series of messages that belong together. You can recognize them by the arrow by the message:

☞ **By the conversation,**

    click

The conversation is opened:

now looks like this :

Here the message is the top item. You can tell, because by the other item you see

Sent :

☞ **If necessary, click the message**

You will see the email message:

Now you have created, sent, and received your first email.

7.6 Replying To an Email

If you have received an email message and you want to reply back, you do not need to retype the sender's email address. *Mail* has several options for replying to an email. You can click any of the following buttons located at the top of the window:

← Reply

An answer message is created, where the correct email address is already filled in. The original email is also included.

≪ Reply All

You can send an email to multiple persons. Use this button if you want to create a new email message that will be sent to all the recipients in the original message. The original email will also be sent along with this message.

→ Forward

The original email will be turned into a new email message that can be sent to someone else.

In most cases you will want to reply to a message. Let's give it a try:

👆 **Click** ← Reply

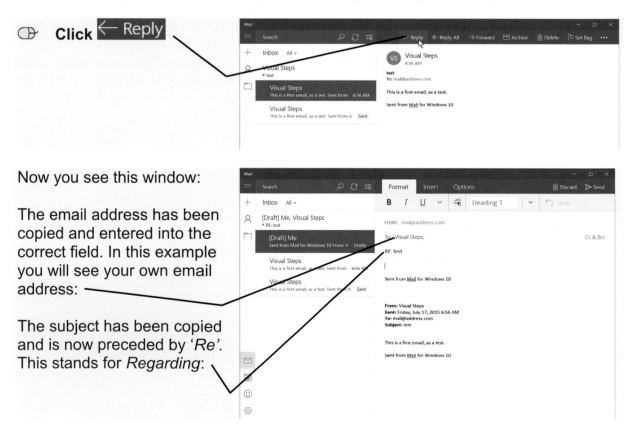

Now you see this window:

The email address has been copied and entered into the correct field. In this example you will see your own email address:

The subject has been copied and is now preceded by '*Re*'. This stands for *Regarding*:

The text of the original message is automatically inserted into the reply. In itself this can be quite useful. The person who receives your reply will immediately see what the original message was all about. The downside is that this message will become longer and longer, as the correspondence continues.

You can type your reply at the top of the message:

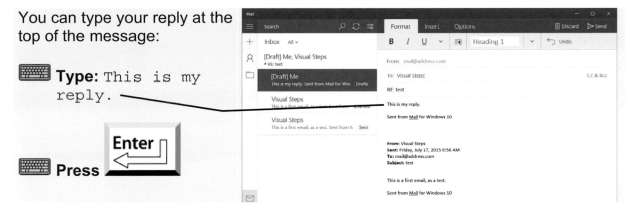

Type: This is my reply.

Press Enter

Now you can send the message, in the same manner as you learned earlier in the previous steps. You do not actually have to do that right now. You can delete the message:

☞ **Click** 🗑 Discard

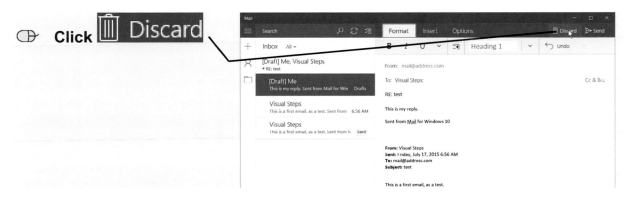

The message is deleted.

7.7 Including an Attachment

A very handy feature of an email app or program is the ability to send one or more files along with your email message. For example, you can add a photo or a document to your message. An item included with an email message is called an *attachment*.

You can practice working with attachments by sending an email to yourself.

☞ **Create a new email message** ✂️⁴⁷

⌨ **By To: , type your own email address**

🖱 **Click** Subject

⌨ **Type:** Test with attachment

🖱 **Click the white area below the subject**

⌨ **Type:** This is a beautiful photo!

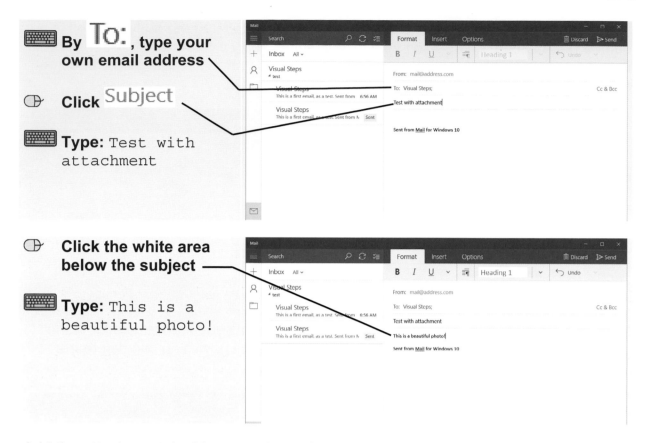

Add the attachment. In this example we have used an image. You can choose your own image:

At the top of the window:

🖱 **Click** Insert

🖱 **Click** 📎 Attach

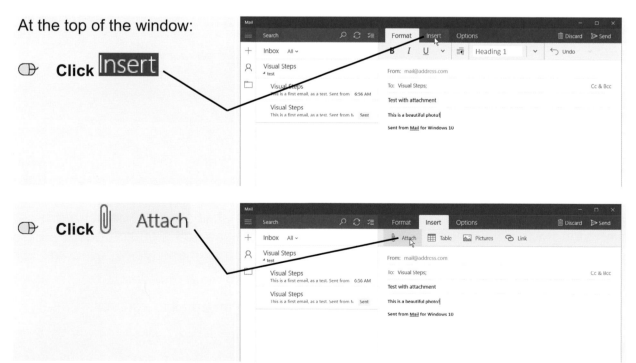

You will see the *Open* window, and now you can select the image folder:

On the left-hand side of the window:

⊕ **Click** 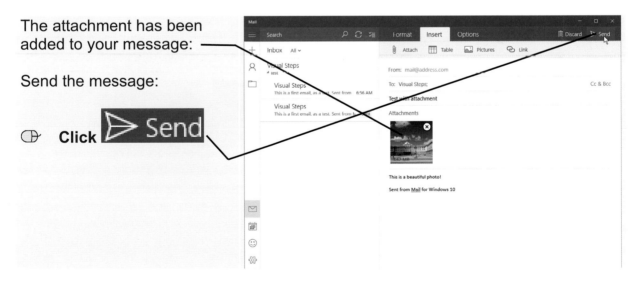 Pictures

⊕ **Click the desired photo**

⊕ **Click** Open

You will see the content of the *Pictures* folder. You may already have saved some photos in this folder. In this example, an image has already been saved in this folder. If you do not (yet) have any images on your computer, then just read *section 7.8 Opening an Attachment* and *section 7.9 Saving an Attachment*.
Or open the *Documents* folder and select a text file you have created in a previous chapter.

The attachment has been added to your message:

Send the message:

⊕ **Click** ▷ Send

The email message with the image will be sent.

7.8 Opening an Attachment

An email you send to your own address will often be received right away, in the same session. But it can take a little while, especially if the attachment is a large file. When you see the message:

☞ **Click the message**

You will see the message on the right-hand side of the window:

HELP! No mail.

If you do not see any messages in the *Inbox*, it may mean the email has not arrived yet. With some email providers, it can take a little while to process a message. You can also try using the refresh button:

☞ **Click** ⟳

In the case of a photo, you will see a thumbnail image of the photo:

The message on the left-hand side of the window includes a paperclip 📎, which means an attachment is included.

Usually you will immediately see the paperclip 📎 by the incoming email message.

In order to display the photo a bit larger:

☞ **Click the photo**

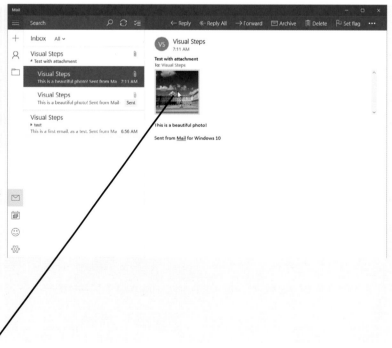

HELP! I do not see a photo.

If you see an icon instead of a photo, this is what you do:

⊕ **Click**

In this example, the photo is displayed in the *Photos* app. This is the default setting in *Windows 10*. The app is one of the many apps included in *Windows 10*. You can use the app to view, share, and print digital photos. In *Chapter 8 Introduction to Photos, Video and Music* you will learn more about this app.

After you have viewed the photo, you can close the window:

⊕ **Click** ✖

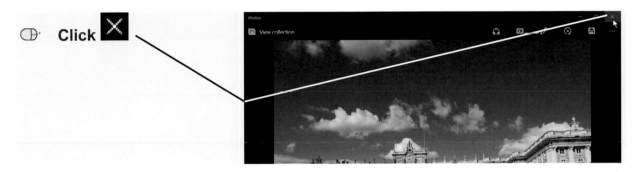

You will see the *Mail* window again.

7.9 Saving an Attachment

You can save an attachment that has been included in an email message and store it in a folder on your computer. Then you can use this attachment yourself, in a photo editing program, for example. This is what you need to do in the window of the open message:

⊕ **Right-click the photo**

⊕ **Click** Save

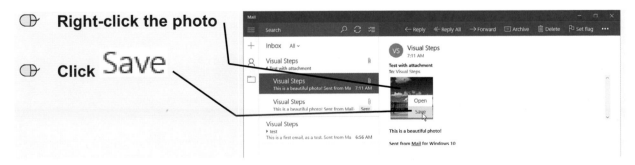

You will see the *Save As* window:

Here you see the name of the attachment:

On the left-hand side of the window you can click on the folder in which you want to save the photo:

By **File name:** you can change the name of the attachment:

If you want to save the photo, you click Save .

In this case, it is not really necessary to save the photo, since this photo is already stored on your computer.

☞ **Click** Cancel

You will see the email message again:

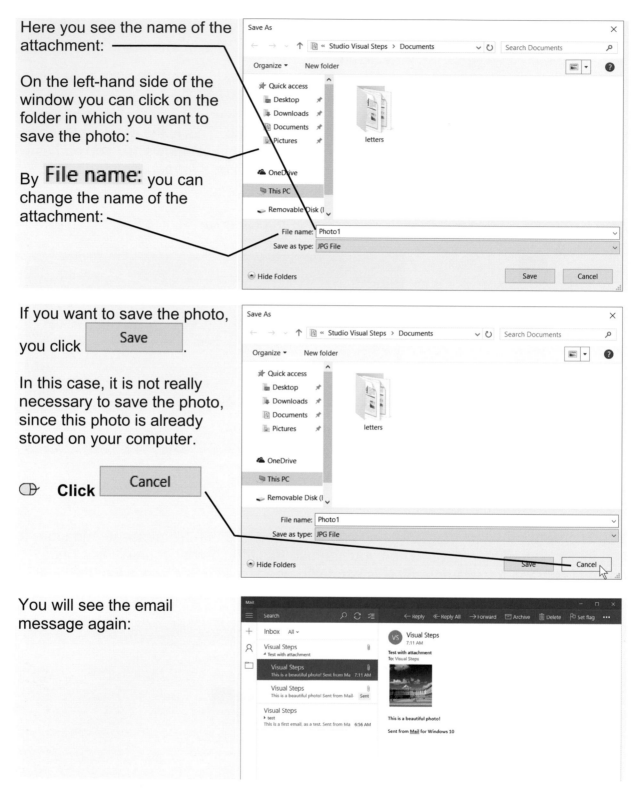

7.10 The Folders

Mail uses a system of folders for arranging your email messages: the folder list. Apart from the *Inbox*, there are some additional folders.
In the *Outbox*, the messages that still need to be sent are saved, for instance, if your Internet connection is temporarily unavailable.
Mail saves all the email messages you have sent in a separate folder, called *Sent items*.
Messages that appear to be unwanted, commercial email messages are moved to the *Junk* or *Spam* folder.
You can also delete sent and received messages from these folders. Deleted messages are saved in the *Deleted items* folder.
Finally, there is a folder for messages that have not been completed yet, these are saved in the *Drafts* folder.

➥ Please note:

Depending on your type of email account, you may see folder names that are a little bit different. You may also not be able to see some folders, such as the *Unwanted mail* or *Spam* folders.

The Sent Items folder contains copies of the emails you have sent. This folder also contains the messages you have just sent to yourself.

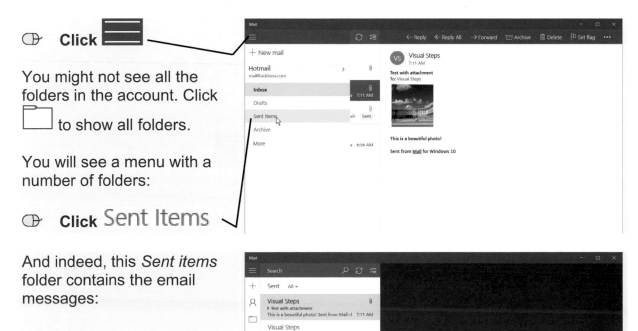

☞ **Click** ▤

You might not see all the folders in the account. Click ☐ to show all folders.

You will see a menu with a number of folders:

☞ **Click** Sent Items

And indeed, this *Sent items* folder contains the email messages:

To practice working with some of these other folders, you will be deleting an email message in the next section.

7.11 Deleting Email Messages

The *Inbox* and *Sent items* folders provide a very useful archive for lots of users. These folders contain all your email correspondence, and you can easily find email messages. You can save a large number or messages in these folders.

In practice, you will regularly delete all superfluous messages, in order to keep your folders neat and 'clean'. Before you can delete an email, you will need to select it first. In this example the sent message *Test with attachment* message will be deleted:

Click the Test with attachment message

The message is blue, which means it has been selected:

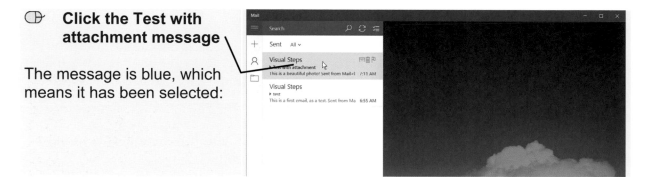

Let *Mail* delete this message:

Place the pointer on the email message

Click

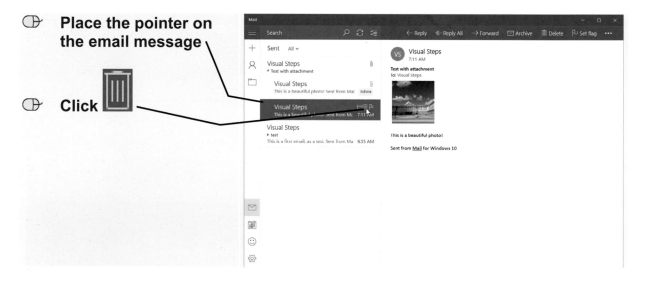

Now you just have one message left in the *Sent items* folder:

If you delete an email message in this way, it will not be permanently deleted. *Mail* saves all the deleted email messages in the *Deleted items* folder. This is an additional security measure. In case you have accidentally deleted a message, you can always retrieve it from this folder.

In next couple of steps you will learn how to permanently delete an email:

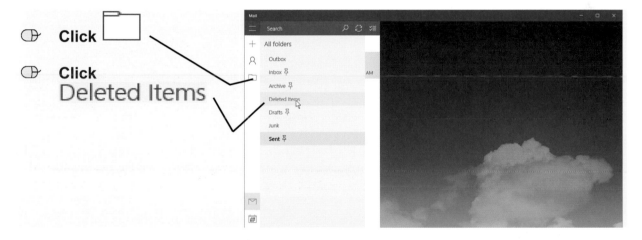

☞ **Click** 🗀

☞ **Click**
Deleted Items

You will see your email. You can delete a message in the *Deleted items* folder in the same way as you previously did:

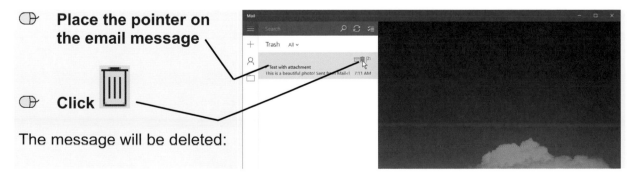

☞ **Place the pointer on the email message**

☞ **Click** 🗑

The message will be deleted:

Now the folder is empty. You can go back to the *Inbox*:

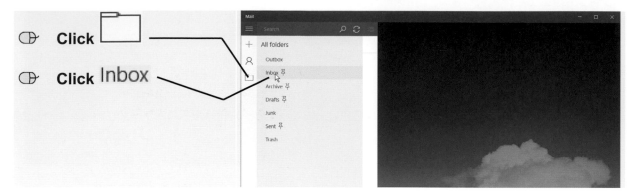

You will see the *Inbox* again. Now you can close *Mail*.

👉 **Close** *Mail* 🦶🦶⁶

In the next few exercises you will practice some more with sending and receiving email.

7.12 Exercises

✎

Have you forgotten how to do something? Use the number beside the footsteps to look it up in the appendix *How Do I Do That Again?*

Exercise 1: Creating an Email Message

In this exercise you will be creating a new email message.

☞ Open *Mail*. ✎[2]

☞ Create a new email message, address it to yourself and add the subject practice. ✎[47]

☞ Send the message. ✎[48]

☞ Check whether you have received the message in the *Inbox*. ✎[49]

☞ Read your email message. ✎[50]

Exercise 2: Sending With Attachment

In this exercise you will be creating a new email message with an attachment.

☞ Create a new email message, address it to yourself and add the subject practice with attachment. ✎[47]

☞ Add the file *Anthem* as an attachment. ✎[51]

☞ Send your message. ✎[48]

Exercise 3: Viewing the Attachment

☞ Check the *Inbox* and see if you have received the email with the attachment. ✎[49]

☞ Open the email message with the file *Anthem*. ✎[50]

☞ View the attachment. $\mathscr{O}\!\mathscr{O}$**52**

☞ Close the window containing the document. $\mathscr{O}\!\mathscr{O}$**6**

Exercise 4: Deleting an Email Message

☞ View the *Inbox*. $\mathscr{O}\!\mathscr{O}$**49**

☞ Delete the message practice with attachment. $\mathscr{O}\!\mathscr{O}$**53**

☞ Close *Mail*. $\mathscr{O}\!\mathscr{O}$**6**

7.13 Background Information

Dictionary

Attachment	A file that can be linked to an email message and sent along with it. It can be a document, picture, video or other type of file. Messages that contain attachments can be recognized by the paperclip icon in the message pane, next to the message title.
Conversation	A number of messages that belong together, such as emails with the same subject. These may be displayed together in *Mail*, in the *Inbox*.
Deleted items folder	Deleted emails are moved to the *Deleted items* folder. In order to permanently delete these items from your computer you will also need to delete the messages in this folder.
Drafts folder	Email message that are written and saved first, instead of being sent right away, are stored in the *Drafts* folder.
Email	Short for *electronic mail*. These are the messages you send and receive using and email app and the Internet.
Folder list	List of folders in *Mail*. Contains among others, the *Inbox* with received messages and *Deleted items* folder with the messages you have deleted.
Gmail	A free email service provided by *Google*.
Hotmail	A free email service provided by *Microsoft*.
IMAP	A method used by computers to send and receive email messages. This method will give you access to your email without having to download the messages to your computer.
Inbox	The *Inbox* is the folder in which all incoming email messages are stored.
Junk mail	Unwanted, commercial mail, also known as *spam*.
Junk folder	*Mail* filters all messages that resemble unwanted, commercial email, and moves them to the *Junk* folder.
Message list	A list of messages stored in the folders of *Mail*.
Outlook.com	A free email service provided by *Microsoft*.

- Continue on the next page -

Password	A string of characters with which users can sign on to an email program and gain access to their email messages.
Phishing	A trap to get computer users to disclose personal or financial information.
POP	Post Office Protocol. A standard method used by computers to send and receive email messages. POP messages are stored on an email server, until you download them to your computer. Then they are deleted from the server.
Sent items folder	In the *Sent items* folder, a copy of each sent message is stored, in case you may need it later on.
Signature	A signature can contain your name, email address, phone number and any other information that you want to include at the bottom of your email messages.
SMTP server	SMTP servers (Simple Mail Transfer Protocol) take care of sending your email messages to the Internet. The SMTP server processes outgoing email and is used alongside a POP or IMAP server for the incoming email.

Source: Windows Help

How does email work?

All email messaged are delivered to a so-called *mail server*. This is a computer owned by the email provider and specially designated for processing electronic mail.

Once you have written and sent an email message, the message will be sent on through your email provider's mail server, and through a number of intermediate stops, until it reaches the mail server of the recipient's email provider, where it will be stored.

It works both ways: your own email is stored on your email provider's mail server, until you retrieve it with *Mail*.

This means that email only arrives on the recipient's computer when this person retrieves his or her email from the email provider. Some people check their email on a daily basis, but others may check their mail only once a week. It is possible to change the settings in such a way that email is automatically retrieved. But just bear in mind that your email can be stored on the recipient's mail server for a week or so, before he or she opens their email and reads your message.

Phishing

Phishing is a method of persuading unsuspecting computer users to disclose their personal data or financial information by posing as a legitimate person or organization. In fact, phishing is a way of 'fishing' for information.

A familiar tactic in phishing is to send a fake email message that looks like a real message sent by a familiar, trusted source. This might be your bank, credit card company, a web store, or another website you have previously visited. These fake messages are sent to thousands of email addresses.

In the email, the recipients are asked to check their bank data, for instance. The message contains a hyperlink for this purpose. If the link is clicked it may lead you to a website that may look like a bank's website. There you will be asked to enter personal information, such as name and address, bank account numbers, and PIN codes, supposedly to check if everything is OK.

An example of a phishing mail:

This mail asks the clients from this bank to enter their personal information on a certain website. Criminals can then gain access to these accounts and empty them out.

If you fall for this trick and enter your data, the information will be sent immediately to the criminals who have set up this trap. Next, they may use your data to purchase items, open new credit card accounts in your name, or abuse your identity in other ways. These phishing mails and websites have a deceptively genuine look. They often use the bank's logo in the email, and the website may look like the legitimate website.

Another frequently used phishing method is to receive a phone call from someone who speaks poor English, and tells you there is a problem with your computer or bank account. You should not react to this either.

Netiquette

The word *netiquette* is a contraction of *internet* and *etiquette*. It stands for a set of rules that people are urged to follow when they use email services.

In order to communicate in an effective way, it is best to follow these rules:

• Think before you send. Writing and sending email messages is terribly easy. Make sure you have thought about what to write beforehand, and avoid writing emails while you are angry. Once you have sent the message you cannot take it back.

• Use a brief, clear description in the subject field. This will provide people who receive lots of email messages with a quick overview of the main topics, and enable them to select the most important emails first.

• Avoid using only CAPITALS. Many people think that sentences that use nothing but capital letters are 'loud', rude, and offensive.

• Be careful with sensitive and confidential information. The recipient may well share his computer with other people. In such a case, anyone will be able to forward your mails, on purpose or by accident.

Icons

Various icons are used in Mail. Below is an explanation of the meaning of these icons:

←   a message to which you have replied;

→   a message you have forwarded;

   the message contains an attachment;

   a message marked as important by the sender.

The smaller the attachment, the faster it is sent and received
This is the rule on the Internet: the smaller the message is, the faster it will be sent from A to B. The same goes for attachments. In this case 'small' refers to the file size.
This is something you or the recipients of the message need to take into account, especially if you have a slow Internet connection. Nowadays most people in North America, Europe and Australia use a fast Internet connection, but there are some countries where this kind of connection is not available.

When you send an attachment, you will always be able to see the file name and the size, in kB or MB. This is a measure, just like meters and grams, feet and gallons.

One kilobyte equals (approximately) a thousand bytes.
20 kilobytes equal 20.000 bytes. Kilobyte is abbreviated to kB.
One megabyte equals (approximately) a thousand kilobytes.
This means that a megabyte equals (approximately) one million (a thousand times a thousand) bytes. The abbreviation for megabyte is MB.

The speed with which something is sent or received depends on a number of factors, among others, the speed of your modem, the type of Internet connection, and the degree of traffic on the Internet. An email message that consists of only text, takes just a few seconds to send. A picture (unedited), taken with a modern digital photo camera (for example, 10 megapixels), is usually much larger. Sending such a photo will take up a lot more time. This can be especially hard on recipients who do not have a fast Internet connection, retrieving such a large file may cause them serious problems.

You can include many types of files with an email message, audio files and video files too. But be careful. Video files especially can be extremely large.
But if you have a fast broadband connection, such as DSL or cable, sending large files will not pose a problem.

There are other options for sharing files. You may want to create a web album or use *OneDrive* or *Dropbox*. You can add the desired files and then upload them to the Internet. You can then create a list of users that have access to your files and can download them if they want.

Please note: some Internet providers set a limit to the amount of data you can send along with an email. If the limit is exceeded, the message will not arrive. Usually you will receive a warning message when this happens.

7.14 Tips

💡 **Tip**

Setting up a POP/IMAP account if sending and receiving mail fails
If you are using an email address given to you by your Internet provider, such as
AOL or Verizon, you may not be able to receive any email right away. In this case,
you can check or change a number of settings.
You will need to have your email address, the corresponding password, the name of
your email provider's POP or IMAP server, and the name of your email provider's
SMTP server. You will often have received this information from your provider. You
can also find most of this information on the provider's website. Look for 'email
settings' on the website, for example.

If you do not succeed in changing the settings, ask an experienced computer user
for help.

This is how you change the settings:

☞ **Open** *Mail* 🦶²

⊕ **Click** ⚙, Accounts

On the right-hand side of the
window:

⊕ **Click the account**

In this example, it is an AOL
account.

- *Continue on the next page -*

You will see a window with account settings. Change the settings:

⌨ **Type your password**

Your password may already be filled in, but you still need to type it again.

☞ **Click**
Change mailbox sync set·
Options for syncing email, contac

If this option is grey on your own screen, then click

Save at the bottom, and open the window once again.

AOL account settings

✉ mail@address.com

Password

••••••••••

Account name

AOL

Change mailbox sync settings
Options for syncing email, contacts, and calendar.

Delete account
Remove this account from your device.

You will see this window. You can change the email settings:

☞ **Drag the scroll box downwards**

☞ **Click**
Advanced mailbox se·
Incoming and outgoing mai

Visual Steps

We'll send your messages using this name.

Sync options

Email

🔘 On

Advanced mailbox settings
Incoming and outgoing mail server info

| Done | Cancel |

- Continue on the next page -

Now you can choose between setting up your email account as a POP or an IMAP account:

- IMAP stands for *Internet Message Access Protocol*. This means you manage your email messages on the mail server. Messages that you have read will be saved on the mail server, until you delete them. IMAP is useful if you manage your email on multiple computers or devices. Your mailbox will look the same on all your devices.
  If you create any folders in which you arrange your email messages, these same folders will be present on every device. If you want to use IMAP, you will need to set up your email account as an IMAP account on all your devices.
- POP stands for *Post Office Protocol*. This is the traditional way of managing email. When you retrieve your messages, they will be deleted from the mail server right away. However, the default setting for POP accounts is for saving a copy on the mail server, even after the message has been retrieved. This means you can still retrieve the message on another device.

In this example we have chosen to use an IMAP account:

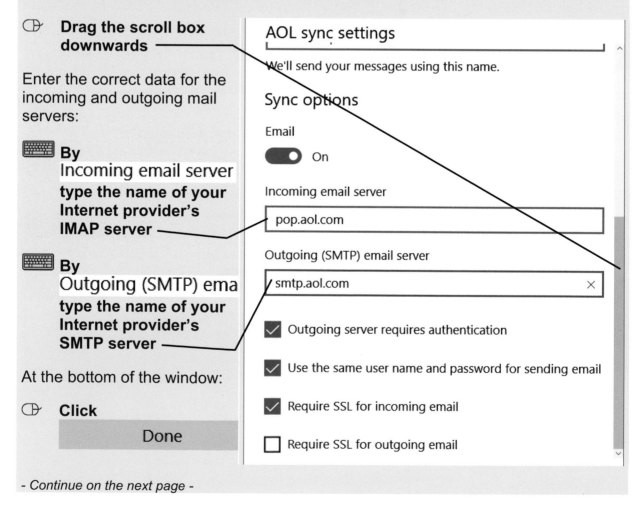

⊕ **Drag the scroll box downwards**

Enter the correct data for the incoming and outgoing mail servers:

⌨ **By** Incoming email server **type the name of your Internet provider's IMAP server**

⌨ **By** Outgoing (SMTP) ema **type the name of your Internet provider's SMTP server**

At the bottom of the window:

⊕ **Click** Done

AOL sync settings

We'll send your messages using this name.

Sync options

Email

⬤ On

Incoming email server

pop.aol.com

Outgoing (SMTP) email server

smtp.aol.com ✕

☑ Outgoing server requires authentication

☑ Use the same user name and password for sending email

☑ Require SSL for incoming email

☐ Require SSL for outgoing email

- Continue on the next page -

The settings have been changed:

⌨ **Type your password**

Maybe your password has already been filled in, but you should just retype it.

At the bottom of the window:

☞ **Click**

Save

The new settings are saved.

AOL account settings

✉ mail@address.com

Password

●●●●●●●●●

Account name

AOL

Change mailbox sync settings
Options for syncing email, contacts, and calendar.

☞ **Send an email to yourself, as explained in *section 7.3 Creating an Email Message* and *7.4 Sending and Receiving the Email***

If sending and receiving an email is still not working, contact your email provider's support desk, or ask an experienced computer user for help.

💡 **Tip**

Formatting text in an email message
This is how you can change the font, the font size, and the style of the text in an email message:

☞ **Select the desired text** 👣²²

Here you see the formatting options for rendering text bold or in italics, underlining it, or changing the text color. These options are similar to the ones you have used to edit text in *Chapter 3 Working with Text*.

To see more options:

☞ **Click** ⌄

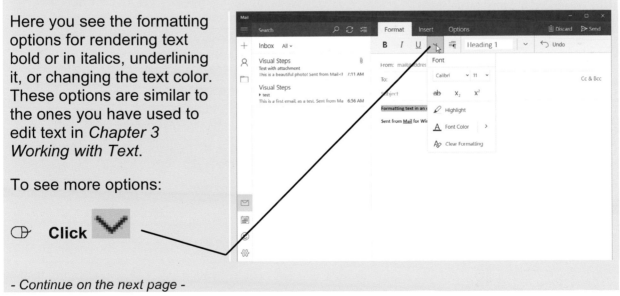

- Continue on the next page -

If you click ≡¶, you will see a window with options for lists and line spacing.

You can select a different text style with ∨ by Heading 1.

💡 Tip

CC and BCC
There are several ways of sending an email to multiple recipients:

☞ **Click** Cc & Bcc

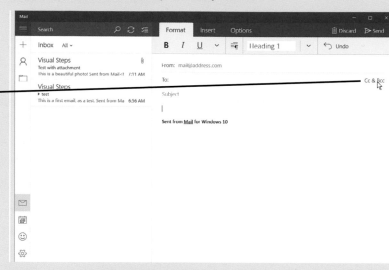

CC: (*Carbon Copy*) can be used if you want to send a copy of an email to another person or persons. In the email you can see to whom this message has been sent, and this goes for the CC's too. ―

BCC: The recipients in the BCC (*Blind Carbon Copy*) box are invisible to the other recipients of this email. ―

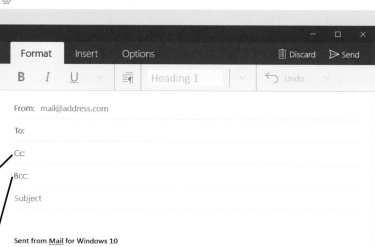

💡 Tip

Open an attachment

By double-clicking the attachment, you will automatically open a program or app with which you can view the attached file. The exact program or app to be opened depends on the settings on your computer.

If the attachment is a text document, in most cases *Microsoft Word* will be opened, or *WordPad* if *Word* is not installed on your computer.
If the attachment is a photo, the default setting in *Windows 10* is to open the *Photos* app. If you have installed a photo editing program on your computer, this default setting may have changed and the editing program will be opened instead.

If you receive an attachment that can only be opened with a program that is not installed on your computer, you will not be able to open the attachment. For some file types it is possible to download a so-called *viewer*. The viewer lets you view the file, but you cannot edit it. For example, on www.microsoft.com you can download free viewers for *PowerPoint* files (extension: PPS or PPT) and *Excel* files (XLS).

If the attachment is a computer program (for instance, an .EXE file), access to this file will usually be blocked by your antivirus program. You will see this on your screen and if you want you can unblock the files. But be cautious, especially with any files containing the extension .exe. These files could contain viruses. It is always best to download files or programs directly from the manufacturer's website or from the CD or DVD included in the program's packaging.

💡 Tip

Your signature

By default, each email you send includes the text *Sent from Mail for Windows 10*. This text is called the default signature. You can replace this text with a default signature of your own, including a salutation and your name and address. This is how you change your email signature:

👉 **Click** ⚙️, Options

By  you see that the use of a signature in enabled.

- Continue on the next page -

You can easily change this signature. In this example we have used 'Kind regards', and the name:

☞ **Delete the text in the box by**
Use an email signatur

⌨ **Type:** Kind regards, Your name

Press the Enter key to move the text to a new line, if you wish.

🖰 **Click an empty section of the window**

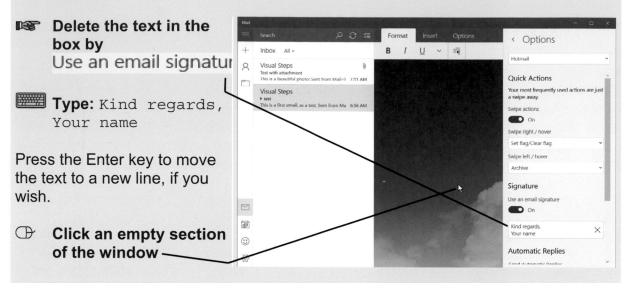

Now the signature will automatically be added to every email message you send.

💡 **Tip**
Switching between email accounts
When you have set up multiple email accounts in Mail, you can swith between them:

🖰 **Click** 👤

🖰 **Click the account**

You will see the folder of the account. If it is not the *Inbox*, you can select the *Inbox* using 📁:

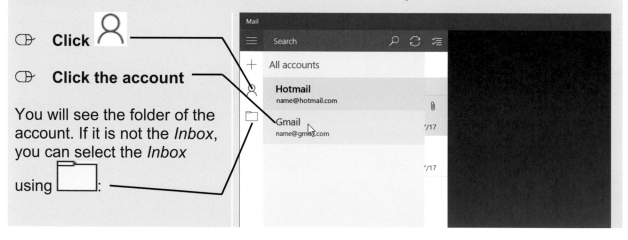

8. Introduction to Photos, Video and Music

In this chapter you will be introduced to a few of the options offered by *Windows 10* for working with photos, video, and music.

Many people have large collections of digital photos stored on their computer. You can open these photos in the *Photos* app, and view them one by one, or in a more creative way as a slideshow. If a photo is upside down, you can rotate it in *Photos*. You will also see how to crop a photo, and read about the other photo editing options available in this app.

Windows 10 also offers various options for sharing your photos with others. We will show you how to use the *Photos* app to print your photos or send them as attachments in an email.

Do you have photos stored on your digital camera? In this chapter you will learn how to transfer these photos to your computer.

You will also become acquainted with the *Movies & TV* app and *Windows Media Player*. You can play your video files with *Movies & TV* and listen to music on a CD with your computer using *Windows Media Player*.

In this chapter you will learn how to:

- view photos in *Photos*;
- rotate a photo;
- crop a photo;
- use other photo editing options;
- view a slideshow;
- print and email photos;
- connect your digital camera to the computer;
- import photos from your digital camera;
- play a video file in the *Movies & TV* app;
- play a CD in *Windows Media Player*.

➡ **Please note:**

In order to be able to follow all the examples in this chapter, you will need to copy the practice files to your computer. In *Appendix C Downloading the Practice Files* at the end of this book you can read how to do this. You also need to have a music CD available.

8.1 Opening a Photo

With the *Photos* app you can view the photos that are stored on your computer. Open *Photos*:

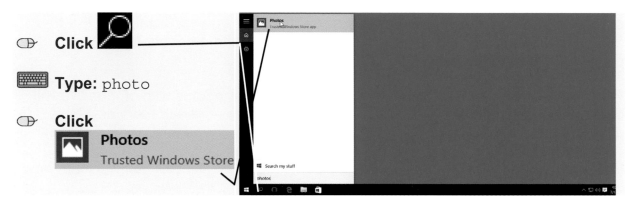

Click 🔍

⌨ **Type:** photo

Click

📷 **Photos**
Trusted Windows Store

The *Photos* app will be opened. You will see a collection of photos. In this example, you see the practice photos. If you also have photos of your own saved on your computer, you may see different pictures in this window. This will not affect the following actions you need to perform.

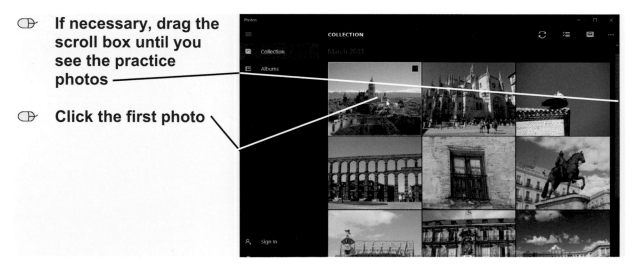

If necessary, drag the scroll box until you see the practice photos

Click the first photo

HELP! I see a window about a Microsoft account.

You may see a window about adding a *Microsoft* account. You can skip this step:

If necessary, click  Cancel

HELP! My window looks different

If your window looks different, you can widen the window by dragging the window border. Then you will probably see a window similar.

You will see a large image of the first photo in the folder:

Use the button on the right-hand side of the window to view the next photo in the folder:

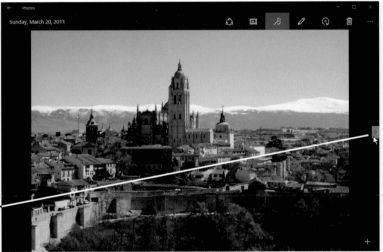

Click ❯

HELP! I do not see this button.

If the mouse has not moved for a while, the buttons will disappear. If you move the mouse a little bit, the buttons will re-appear again.

You will see the second photo:

You can view all the photos:

Click repeatedly on

❯

You will see all the practice photos. When you have reached the last photo, you will no longer see the button on the right-hand side. But you will see a button on the left-hand side 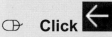. This button indicates that you can browse back to the previous photos.

Now you see this photo:

In the next section you will start working on this photo.

HELP! I do not see this photo.

If you do not see the photo above, you need to go back to the first screen of *Photos*:

☞ **Click** ←

☞ **If necessary, drag the scroll box upwards or downwards**

☞ **Click**

8.2 Rotating a Photo

Photos taken with your digital camera or photos that you have scanned may not be displayed in the correct orientation. You can easily solve this problem easily. To do this, you need to use the buttons that are displayed in the window. You can rotate the photo a quarter turn like this:

In the upper right corner of the window:

 Click

Now the photo is shown in the correct vertical orientation, also referred to as portrait mode:

☞ **Browse to the first photo** $\mathcal{QQ}$ 55

8.3 Cropping a Photo

You will often see minor blemishes on a photo, things nobody really notices. In *Photos* you can easily crop a photo and remove some of these irksome blemishes. Here is how you do that:

☞ **If necessary, click the photo**

At the top of the window:

☞ **Click**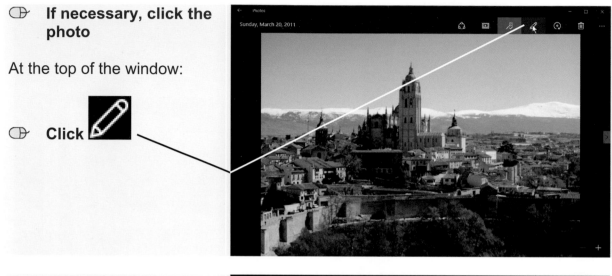

The photo will be placed in the center of the window, and to the left and right you will see photo editing buttons. You can practice working with the cropping option:

☞ **Click**

A frame appears, all around the photo. If you intend to print the cropped photo afterwards, it is a good idea to crop the photo to the correct size. To do this you need to select a fixed height-width ratio:

☞ **Click** ▪▪▪

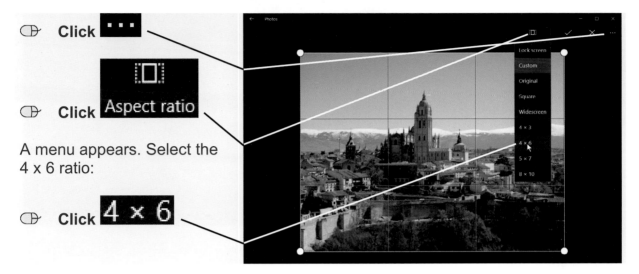

☞ **Click** Aspect ratio

A menu appears. Select the 4 x 6 ratio:

☞ **Click** 4 × 6

Now the frame will be adjusted to the 4 x 6 ratio. If you make the frame a bit smaller, the 4 x 6 ratio will remain unchanged:

☞ **Place the pointer on the corner handle in the lower right corner**

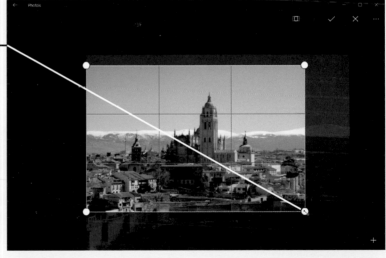

The pointer turns into ⬉:

☞ **Press the mouse button and hold it down**

☞ **Drag the handle to the left a bit**

☞ **Release the mouse button**

You can move the photo within the frame, so that you no longer see the city walls:

☞ **Place the pointer in the frame**

The pointer turns into

⊹:

☞ **Press the mouse button and hold it down**

☞ **Drag the photo to the left and downwards**

☞ **Release the mouse button**

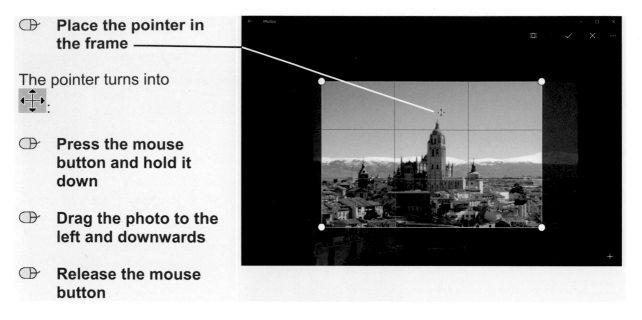

If you are satisfied with the size and position of the frame, you can crop the photo:

☞ **Click** ✓

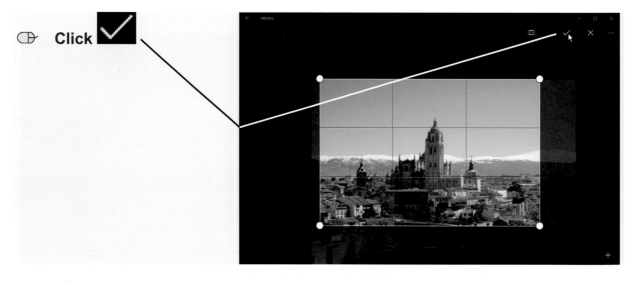

The photo will be cropped. If you are not satisfied with the cropped photo, you can restore the photo with the ↺ button. Use the 🖫 button to save the edits with the name of the original photo (the original photo will be overwritten). This means that the original photo will not be saved. This may not be what you want. Another option is to save the photo by copying it.

You can save a copy of the photo. Then the original will remain untouched:

Click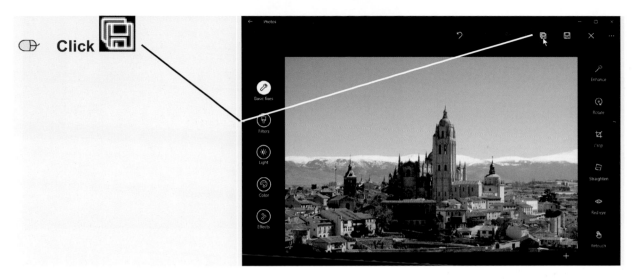

A copy of the photo has been saved in the same folder as the original photo. The file name now has the extension (2).

8.4 Photo Editing Options

Along with rotating and cropping, *Photos* has some other editing options. Take a look at these options:

If necessary, click the photo

Click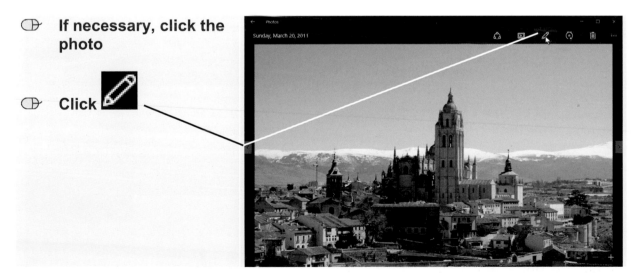

You will see the options on the left-hand side, for example, simple enhancements, filters, adjusting the exposure and colors, applying effects:

On the right-hand side you will see the functions of the selected option:

Click the desired edit. You will immediately see the effect of the edit in the window.

This is how you add a filter, for example:

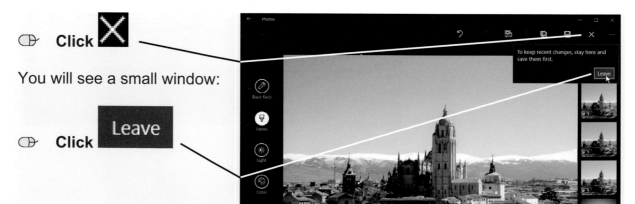

☞　**Click** Filters

On the right-hand side of the window:

☞　**Click the desired filter**

You will see the result:

You can practice using these options later on, if you wish. For now you can cancel the edit of this photo:

☞　**Click** ✕

You will see a small window:

☞　**Click** Leave

8.5 Viewing a Slideshow

A slideshow is a great way of viewing a series of consecutive photos. Your photos will be displayed on a full screen. Here is how you open a slideshow:

☞ **If necessary, click the photo**

☞ **Click**

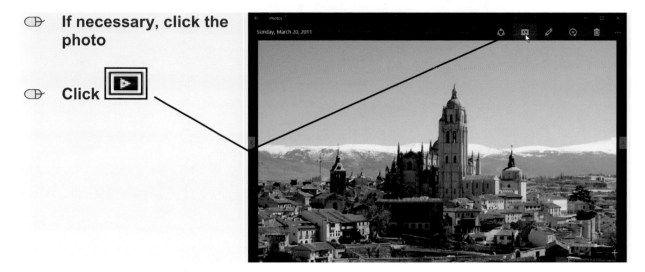

The window will turn dark for an instant, and then the slideshow will begin:

The photos will be displayed one after the other:

The series of photos will be repeated over and over again. You can stop the slideshow at any time by clicking a photo, like this:

☞ **Click the photo**

8.6 Printing Photos

In the *Photos* app you can also print a photo. You do that as follows:

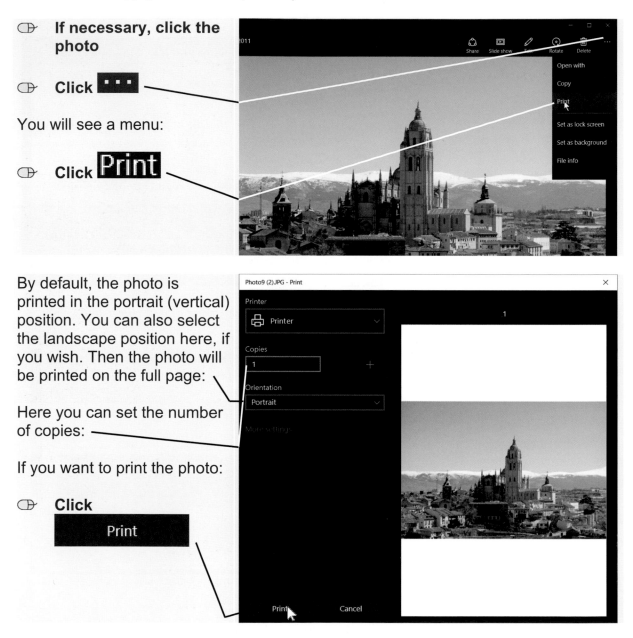

☞ **If necessary, click the photo**

☞ **Click** ▪▪▪

You will see a menu:

☞ **Click** Print

By default, the photo is printed in the portrait (vertical) position. You can also select the landscape position here, if you wish. Then the photo will be printed on the full page:

Here you can set the number of copies:

If you want to print the photo:

☞ **Click**

Print

The photo is printed.

8.7 Sending Photos by Email

You can quickly share your photos with others by sending them by email. Just try it:

⊕ **If necessary, click the photo**

⊕ **Click**

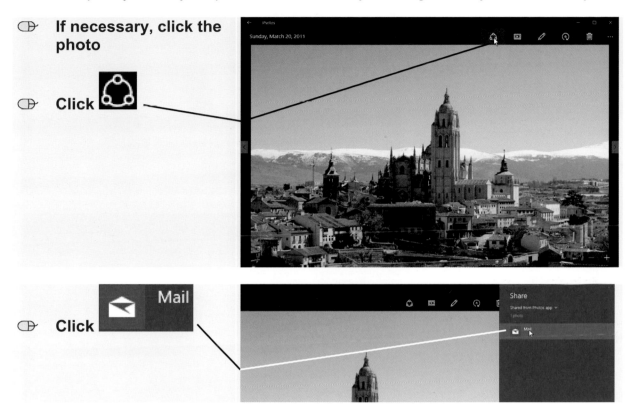

⊕ **Click**

A new email message is opened:

The photo has been added to the email as an attachment:

Now you can add a recipient, a subject, and type a message if you wish. Then you can send the email message. For now this will not be necessary.

This is how you close the window with the email message:

⊕ **Click Discard**

You can go back to the photos overview:

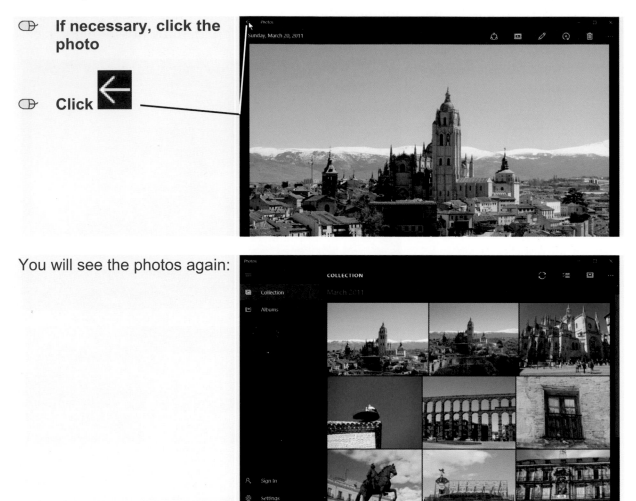

☞ **If necessary, click the photo**

☞ **Click** ⬅

You will see the photos again:

8.8 Connecting Your Digital Camera To the Computer

If you want to view the photos that are stored on your digital camera in *Windows 10*, you need to *import* these photos to your computer. Importing means that the photos are transferred from the camera to your computer. There are two ways of doing this. By connecting the camera to the computer with a cable, or by directly copying the photos from the *memory card* on which they are stored. The memory card is a small card that can be taken out of the camera.

Most digital cameras come with a USB cable that can be connected to the computer's USB port. Some digital cameras can be connected with a firewire cable, to the computer's firewire port. The other end of the cable is plugged into a slot on the camera.

➥ Please note:

In this section we will discuss importing photos from a digital photo camera. Devices such as a cell phone (smartphone), a digital video camera, or a tablet operate in a similar way. If you have stored your photos on one of these devices, you can transfer these as well. If necessary, ask an experienced computer user to help you, if you do not succeed in transferring the photos.

The most frequently used cable connection with a digital camera is the USB connection:

Firewire is the alternative connection between a digital camera and a computer. The firewire plug is smaller:

☞ **Make sure the device is turned off**

☞ **Connect the cable to the camera**

☞ **Connect the USB or firewire cable to a corresponding port on the computer**

If you have a different cable, other than a USB or firewire plug, you need to connect it to the correct port on your computer (read your camera manual).

☞ **If necessary, turn on the device**

➥ Please note:

Some cameras need to be switched to connect mode or play mode. In your camera's manual you will find the correct settings for your own camera.

Now *Windows* connects to your camera. If the camera has never been connected to the computer before, *Windows* will try to install a driver for the camera. This will happen automatically. You may see a message informing you of this procedure. The driver takes care of the correct communication between the camera, cell phone or external hard disk and the computer.

Once the device is correctly connected and has been recognized by *Windows*, you can import the photos to your computer. In the next section you can read how to do this.

HELP! My camera is not recognized.

If *Windows* cannot connect to the camera, despite having installed the driver, you can try to do the following things to solve the problem:

1. Check whether the camera's battery is fully charged.
2. Check if the camera has actually been turned on and whether the camera has some sort of special connection mode that needs to be enabled first (read the camera manual).
3. Turn off the camera and restart the computer. Turn on the camera again.
4. Make sure the latest version of the driver program for your camera has been installed. It is recommended to download the driver from the Internet. If necessary, ask an experienced computer user to help you.
5. Check if something is wrong with the cable. Try to connect the cable to a different port on the computer, or use a different cable.
6. Try to connect the camera to another computer, to see if the connection works with the other computer. If this does not work, chances are that there is something wrong with your camera. Contact the manufacturer's service desk. Look up this information on the manufacturer's website.
7. Try to transfer the photos to the computer by using the camera's memory card.

You can also transfer photos directly from the memory card, also called an SD card. You will need to have a card reader to do this.

Nowadays many computers are equipped with a built-in memory card reader that can read several types of cards.

The card readers can also be bought separately, and connected to one of the computer's USB ports. If you intend to buy a card reader, you need to make sure that your type of memory card is supported by the reader.

If necessary, you can check the camera's manual to find out where the memory card is located.

☞ **If necessary, connect the external card reader to your computer**

☞ **Insert the memory card into the card reader (in the card reader in your pc or the external card reader)**

In the next section you can read how you transfer photos from your camera to your computer.

8.9 Importing Photos From Your Digital Camera

You can start importing the photos:

👆 **Click**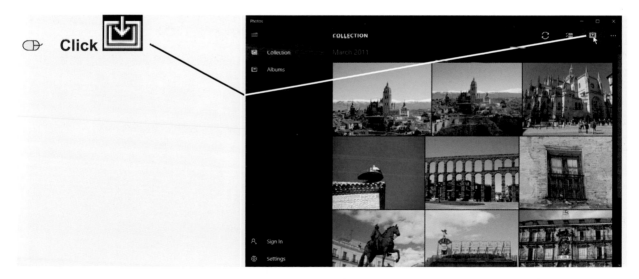

When multiple devices are connected to your computer, you will see this window:

☞ **Click the name of your camera**

☞ **Click** **Choose a device to imp**

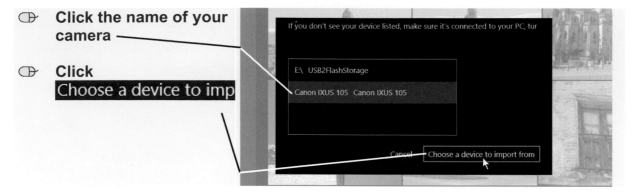

Windows will show how many new photos are found. In this example five photos are found. For now, you will import all photos:

☞ **Click** **Import**

After the import process has finished, you will see the *Photos* window again:

In order to view the new photos:

☞ **Drag the scroll box down**

Now all the photos have been copied from the camera to the computer. The computer will remember which photos have been copied. The next time you connect your camera, the computer will not recognize these photos as new, and will not copy them. Only the new photos you have taken after you have imported the previous photos, will be imported.

💡 **Tip**

Transferring photos through File Explorer
When we were writing this book, it was not possible to import just a few selected photos through the *Photos* app. But you can do this in *File Explorer*. In the *Tips* at the end of this chapter you can read how to do this.

Now you can close *Photos*:

☞ **Close** *Photos* 𝄞⁶

☞ **Disconnect the camera from the computer**

💡 **Tip**

Change the name of the folder
If you want to change the name of the folder, you can do that in *File Explorer*. You will find your photos in the *Pictures* folder:

☞ **Open** *File Explorer* 𝄞³²

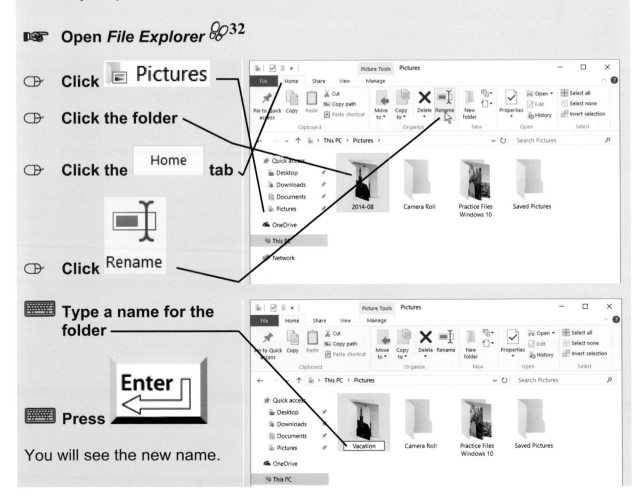

☞ Click 🖼 **Pictures**

☞ **Click the folder**

☞ **Click the** Home **tab**

☞ **Click** Rename

⌨ **Type a name for the folder**

⌨ **Press** **Enter** ⏎

You will see the new name.

💡 **Tip**

More about working with digital photos
Besides the options for working with digital photos in the *Photos* app, there are several other programs available for photo editing. If you are interested in editing and/or managing photos on your computer, you can take a look at the Visual Steps titles regarding digital photo editing. On the **www.visualsteps.com/show_serie.php** web page you will find an overview of all available books. All of these books have been written using the same step-by-step method as in this book. You will be presented with lots of examples and screen shots, and learn how to work with the program that is discussed.

8.10 Playing a Video File

You can use the *Movies & TV* app to play video files that are stored on your computer. The practice files also include a video. You can use this file to practice with in this section.

This is how you open *Movies & TV*:

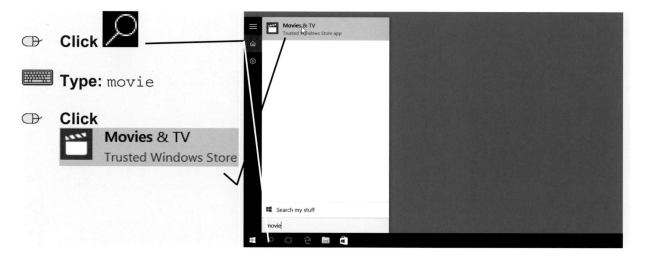

Click 🔍

⌨ **Type:** movie

Click
      Movies & TV
      Trusted Windows Store

Movies & TV will open. Apart from playing videos on your hard disk, this app can also play movies and TV shows that can be purchased or rented via the *Store*.

Click  Videos

You will see the practice files. You may see more video files on your own computer.

Play a practice file:

Click *Video1*

HELP! My window looks different.

If your window looks different, you can widen the window by dragging the window border. Then you will probably see a window similar to the one above.

The short video will be played:

If you do not move the mouse, the buttons and the progress bar

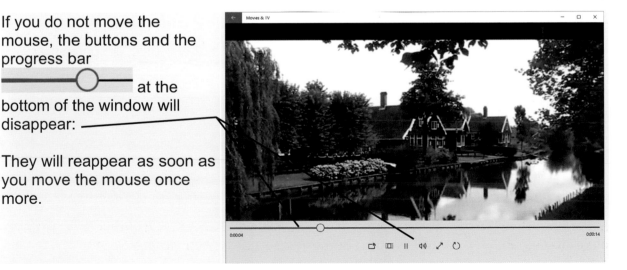 at the bottom of the window will disappear: ——

They will reappear as soon as you move the mouse once more.

Tip
Pause play

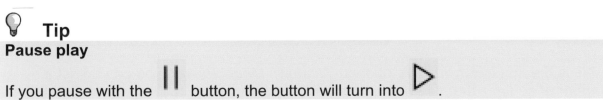

If you pause with the ▐▐ button, the button will turn into ▷.

When the video has finished playing, you can replay it by clicking the ▷ button:

For now this will not be necessary.

Close the window:

☞ **Click** ✕

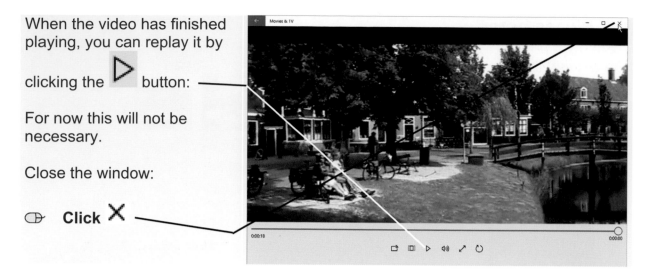

➥ **Please note:**

Unfortunately, you cannot play a DVD with the app. In *Windows 10* you will need to have a separate program in order to play a DVD. You can also download an app in the *Store*. On the website that is accompanied with this book, you can find a bonus chapter about downloading apps. See *Appendix D Opening the Bonus Online Chapters*. If necessary, ask an experienced computer user to help you.

8.11 Opening Windows Media Player

Windows Media Player is a program that you can use to play music, among other things. You open it like this:

☞ **Click** 🔍

⌨ **Type:** media

☞ **Click**

If this is the first time you have opened *Windows Media Player*, you can adjust a number of settings that determine how the program works. For now, you can use the default settings.

➥ **Please note:**

If you have previously opened *Windows Media Player* you will not see the next window. If that is the case, you can continue with the next step.

☞ **Click a radio button ⦿ by**
Recommended setting

☞ **Click** [Finish]

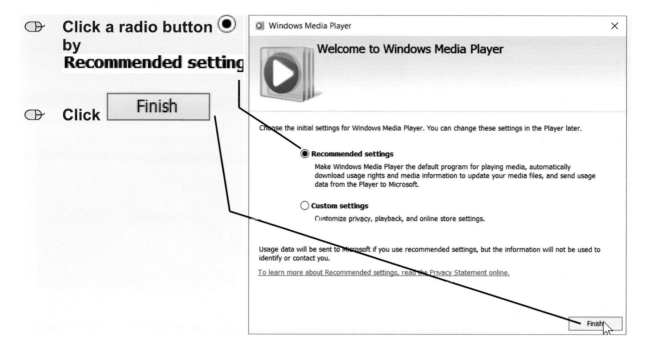

Once the settings have been adjusted, *Windows Media Player* will search your computer for music files.

In this example no music files are found:

But your own computer may contain some music files.

8.12 Playing a Music CD

On most computers, *Windows Media Player* is set as the default music player for most common audio files. When you insert a music CD into the CD/DVD player, *Windows* will immediately start to play it with *Media Player*.

➥ **Please note:**

In order to follow the examples in this section and the next few sections, you will need to have a music CD. Here is an example:

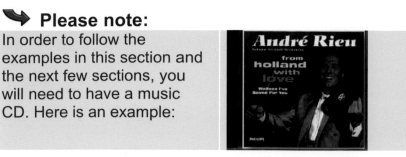

See what happens when you insert a music CD into the computer:

☞ **Insert a music CD from your own collection into your computer's CD/DVD drive**

☞ **Carefully close the tray**

✖ **HELP! I do not have a CD/DVD drive.**

Some computers do not have a CD/DVD drive. If this is the case, you can just read through this section.

✖ **HELP! Nothing happens after I have inserted a CD.**

If nothing happens after you have inserted the original CD, this CD might be protected against playback on computers. Try a different music CD instead.

☞ **Click** ▶

The first track is played:

If you are connected to the Internet, *Windows Media Player* will look for information on the CD, by default. When a CD is recognized, you will see the cover image and the track titles here:

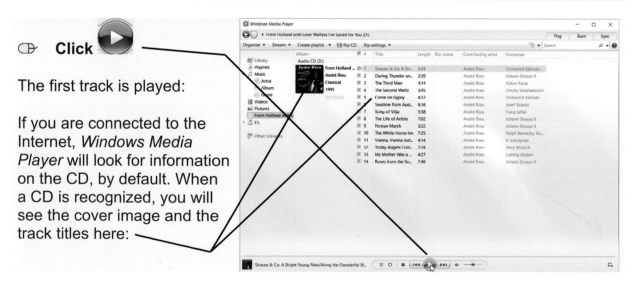

HELP! I see a much smaller window.

This means *Windows Media Player* is displayed in the *Play now* view. You can return to the larger window:

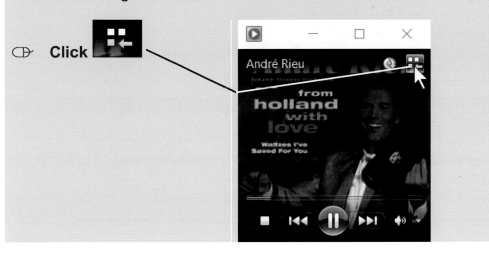

☞ **Click**

HELP! The volume is too loud or too soft.

If you want to turn the volume up or down, you can use the *Volume* slider —————.

To turn the volume down:

☞ **Drag the slider to the left**

To turn the volume up:

☞ **Drag the slider to the right**

If the volume is not yet right, then read *section 9.12 Setting the Sound*.

💡 Tip

Quickly turn off the volume
To mute the sound right away:

☞ **Click** 🔊

To turn the volume on again, click 🔇 once more.

Just like with your regular CD/DVD player you can skip to the next track by clicking just once. At the bottom of the window:

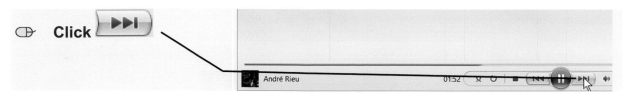

- **Click** 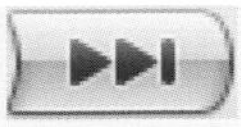

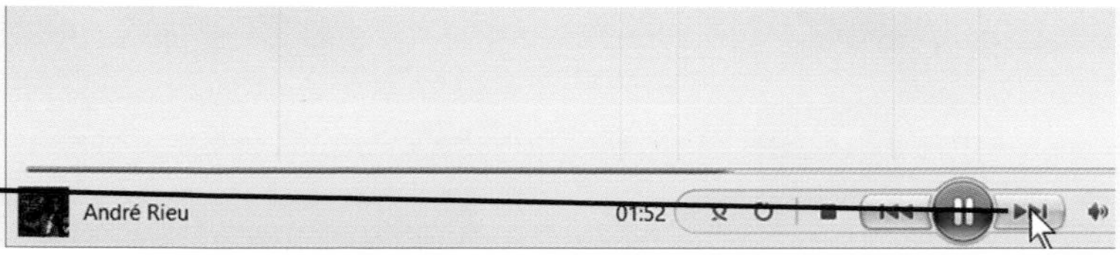

Tip

Quickly skip to your favorite song
If you know exactly which track you want to hear on this CD, you can play it right away:

- **Double-click the track or the track's title, for example** Track 6

The track will be played right away.

This is how you return to the previous track:

Track number 2 is played:

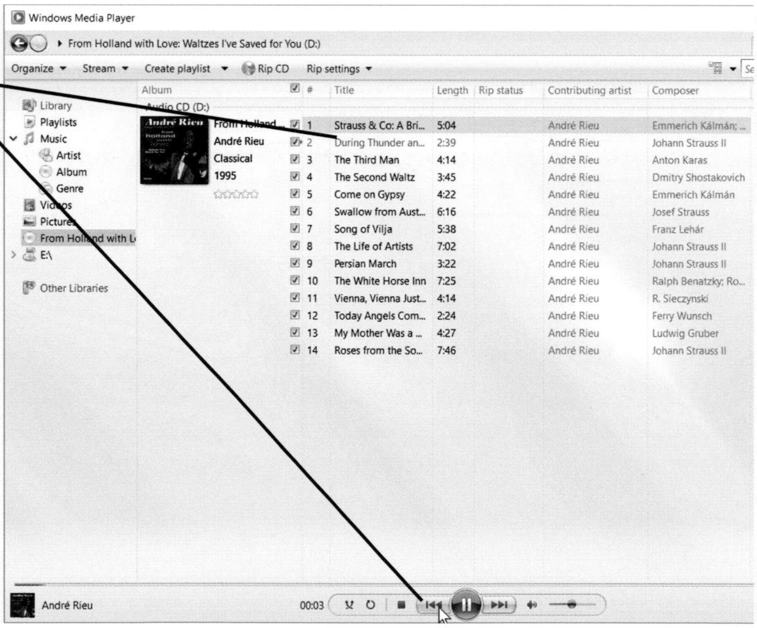

- **Click** 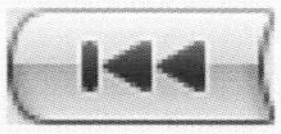

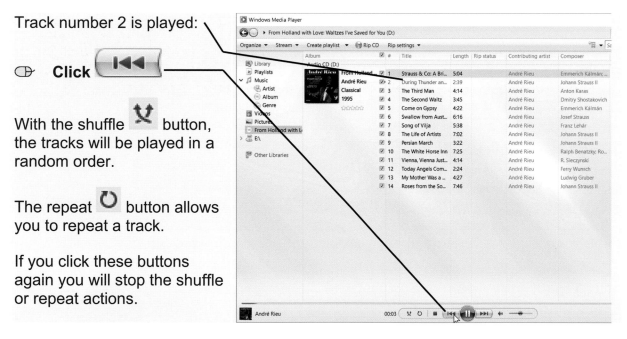

With the shuffle 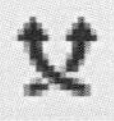 button, the tracks will be played in a random order.

The repeat  button allows you to repeat a track.

If you click these buttons again you will stop the shuffle or repeat actions.

You can also pause the music:

- **Click** 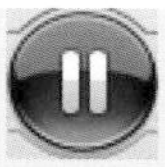

 turns into :

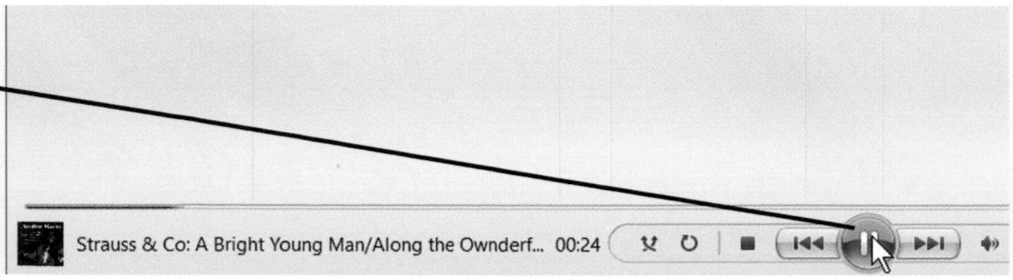

If you want to completely stop the music from playing:

⏏ **Click** ■

Now you can close *Windows Media Player*.

☞ **Close *Windows Media Player*** ⸹⸹⁶

☞ **Remove the CD from the CD/DVD player**

In this chapter you have learned what you can do with photos, music CDs, and video files in *Windows 10.* By doing the exercises in the next section you can repeat what you have learned.

💡 **Tip**

Learn more about music in Windows Media Player
You can do even more with *Windows Media Player*. For example, you can create playlists, and copy music from a CD to your computer. You can learn more on this subject in the sequel titles concerning *Windows 10.* You will find an overview of all the books on *Windows 10* at **www.visualsteps.com/show_serie.php**

8.13 Exercises

The following exercises will help you master what you have just learned. Have you forgotten how to do something? Use the number beside the footsteps to look it up in the appendix *How Do I Do That Again?*

Exercise 1: View a Photo and a Slideshow

In this exercise you can take a look at a photo and view a slideshow.

☞ Open *Photos*. $\mathscr{C}^2$

☞ Open a photo from one of the practice files. $\mathscr{C}54$

☞ Browse to the photo of the man on horseback. $\mathscr{C}55$

☞ Browse to the photo of the stork's nest. $\mathscr{C}55$

☞ View the slideshow of all the photos in the folder. $\mathscr{C}56$

☞ Stop the slideshow. $\mathscr{C}57$

☞ Go back to the home window of the *Photos* app. $\mathscr{C}58$

☞ Close *Photos*. $\mathscr{C}6$

Exercise 2: Play a Video

In this exercise you can practice playing a video.

☞ Open *Movies & TV*. $\mathscr{C}2$

☞ Play the video file called *Video2*. $\mathscr{C}59$

☞ Pause play. $\mathscr{C}60$

☞ Resume play. $\wp$**61**

☞ View the rest of the video.

☞ Close *Movies & TV*. $\wp$**6**

Exercise 3: Play a Music CD

In this exercise you can practice playing a music CD in *Windows Media Player*. You can also give the shuffle option a try.

☞ Open *Windows Media Player*. $\wp$**2**

☞ Insert a music CD into your CD/DVD player.

☞ Skip to the next track. $\wp$**62**

☞ Pause play. $\wp$**60**

☞ Resume play. $\wp$**61**

☞ Play the tracks in random order. $\wp$**63**

☞ Skip to the next track. $\wp$**62**

☞ Repeat one of the tracks. $\wp$**64**

☞ Disable the shuffle (random play) function. $\wp$**65**

☞ Disable the repeat function. $\wp$**66**

☞ Stop the CD from playing. $\wp$**67**

☞ Remove the music CD from your CD/DVD player.

☞ Close *Windows Media Player*. $\wp$**6**

8.14 Background Information

Dictionary

Driver	Software that ensures that a device (such as a digital camera or a printer) can communicate with *Windows*. Every device needs a driver in order to function.
Firewire	A fast cable connection between the computer and an external device, such as a photo camera.
Import	Transferring digital photos from your digital camera to your computer.
Memory card	Memory in the shape of a card on which you can permanently store data. There are several types of memory cards. Their capacity ranges from 4 GB to 512 GB or more.
Movies & TV	An app with which you can view video files on your computer. You can also rent or purchase movies through the Internet.
Mute	(Temporarily) turn off the sound.
Photos	An app with which you can view, share, rotate, and crop photos, among others.
Shuffle	Playing tracks in random order.
Slideshow	An automatic display of all your images on a full screen.
Track	A song or another individual audio fragment.
USB port	A rectangular communication port in the computer universally suited for many devices such as photo cameras.
Windows Media Player	A program for playing and managing music and videos.

Source: Windows Help, Wikipedia

8.15 Tips

♀ Tip

Import individual photos through File Explorer
With *Photos* you can only import all the (new) photos on your camera to your computer at once. If you want to select individual photos and transfer them to your computer, you need to use *File Explorer*. This is how you do it:

☞ **Connect your digital camera to the computer**

☞ **Open *File Explorer* 👣³²**

Open the window with the photos:

⊕ **Click [🖥 This PC]**

⊕ **Double-click your camera**

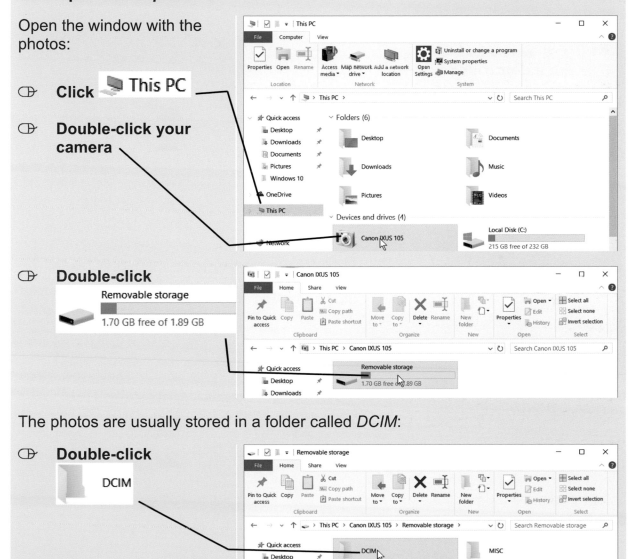

⊕ **Double-click**
Removable storage
1.70 GB free of 1.89 GB

The photos are usually stored in a folder called *DCIM*:

⊕ **Double-click**
DCIM

- Continue on the next page

☞ **Double-click the**
folder with the photos

Please note: sometimes you
may need to search for a
while to find the folder
containing the photos.

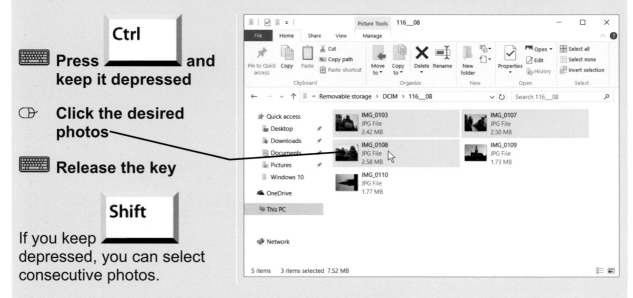

You will see the thumbnail images of the photos stored on your camera. This is how
you copy these photos to the *Pictures* folder on your computer, for example:

⌨ **Press Ctrl and**
keep it depressed

☞ **Click the desired**
photos

⌨ **Release the key**

Shift

If you keep **Shift**
depressed, you can select
consecutive photos.

In this example we will transfer the photos to the *Pictures* folder:

Copy
to ▾

☞ **Click Copy to ▾**

☞ **Click 🖿 Pictures**

In order to copy the photos,
you can use all the options
you have read about in
Chapter 5 Files and Folders.

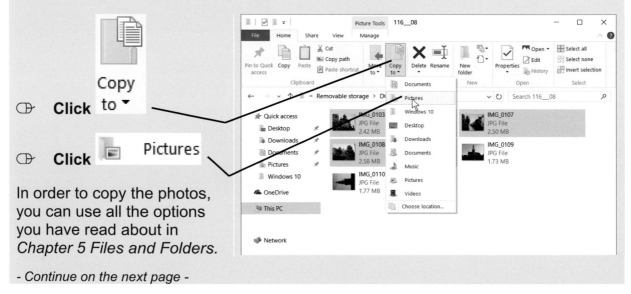

- Continue on the next page -

The photos will be copied. After they have been copied, you can disconnect the camera.

☞ **Disconnect the camera from the computer**

💡 Tip
Listen to music with Groove Music
You can also play and manage the music files on your computer with *Groove Music*. Besides this, you can use this app for downloading music from the *Store*.

☞ **Open *Groove Music*** ✌²

You will see the home screen of *Groove Music*:

Search for music on your computer: ―

Create a playlist: ―

Buy music online in the *Store*: ―

This is how you play music on your computer. You can search for an artist, for example:

☞ **Connect your speakers or headphone to your computer**

🖰 **Click 👤 Artists** ―

You will see all the artists of which you have songs saved on your computer:

🖰 **Click an artist**

- Continue on the next page -

An album by this artist
appears:

☞   **Click a track**

You will see several options:

☞   **Click** ▶

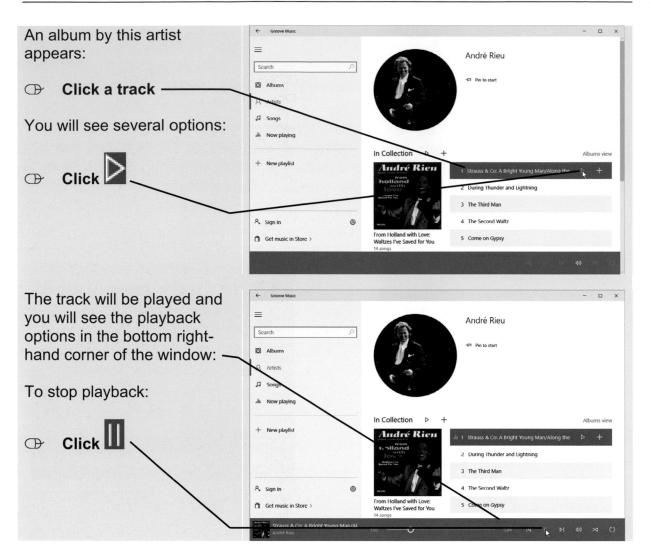

The track will be played and
you will see the playback
options in the bottom right-
hand corner of the window:

To stop playback:

☞   **Click** ❚❚

9. Useful Settings

Now that you have acquired the basic knowledge and skills necessary to work on a computer, it's time to take a look at some of the options to make it more comfortable, fun and easier to use. As it happens, there are lots of components on your computer that you can adjust or set up to suit your own needs and preferences.

Adjusting the settings on your computer can make difficult operations easier and also prevent harmful things from happening in the longer run. For instance, you can adjust your mouse so that it is easier and more comfortable to use. This will also help you from overburdening your hand or wrist.

In this chapter you will learn how to change the Start menu, the image on the lock screen, and the desktop background (or wallpaper) and adjust them to suit your own tastes. You will also read about other aspects important to seniors, such as declining motor skills, eyesight, and hearing and what can be done on a computer to accommodate these changes. Feel free to experiment and find out whether new settings can be an improvement for you. Any setting that you change or adjust can always be undone and restored to its original state.

In this chapter you will learn how to:

- add program and app tiles to the Start menu;
- change the size of the Start Menu
- move tiles and create groups in the Start menu;
- open the *Settings*;
- update *Windows* and update apps;
- change the image on the lock screen and the desktop background;
- set up the mouse;
- change the size of letters and icons;
- set the screen saver and adjust the sound;
- adjust the power options.

➥ Please note:

Some of the changes made to the settings require certain access rights to your computer. If you have a *Guest* account on the computer you are using, you will have limited authorization to make any changes. Sometimes *Windows* will ask you to enter a password when you want to change a setting that requires more extensive user rights. If you do not have this password, you can just read through the section in question, or ask the computer administrator to grant you access rights.

9.1 Adding Program or App Tiles to the Start Menu

You can use the tiles in the Start menu to open a program or app. It is very easy; you just need to click the desired tile. You can also change the order of the tiles in the Start menu to suit your own needs. As you work with your computer for a while longer, you may find that you use some programs and apps more frequently than others. You may have also installed a new program or app on your computer. These programs and apps are sometimes placed in the Start menu right away, but sometimes they do not appear in the Start menu.

You can easily add tiles for programs and apps that are not displayed in the Start menu. One example of such a program is *WordPad*. You can practice adding a new tile to the Start menu for that program. Here is how you do it:

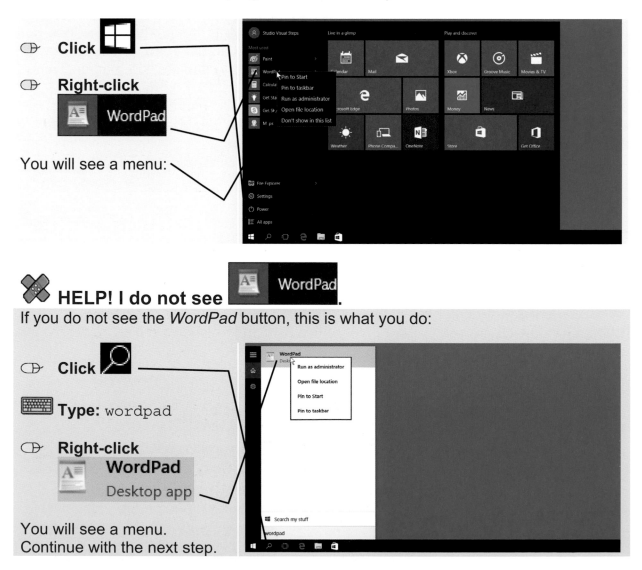

☞ **Click** [Windows icon]

☞ **Right-click** [WordPad]

You will see a menu:

🩹 **HELP! I do not see** [WordPad].

If you do not see the *WordPad* button, this is what you do:

☞ **Click** [search icon]

⌨ **Type:** wordpad

☞ **Right-click** [WordPad Desktop app]

You will see a menu.
Continue with the next step.

Add *WordPad* to the Start menu:

☞ **Click Pin to Start**

Notice that you can also attach the program or app to the taskbar.

This way, you can easily and quickly open frequently used programs and apps right from the taskbar.

WordPad has now been added to the Start menu as a new tile. From now on you can open this program right away, by clicking the tile:

9.2 Changing the Size of the Start Menu

If you have just started using *Windows 10*, the Start menu will not be very extensive. In due time, you will probably have more programs and apps. Some of these programs and apps will appear in the Start menu and the number of tiles will gradually increase. You can easily enlarge the Start menu to view more programs and apps at once. You do that like this:

☞ **Place the pointer on the top edge of the Start menu**

The pointer turns into ↕:

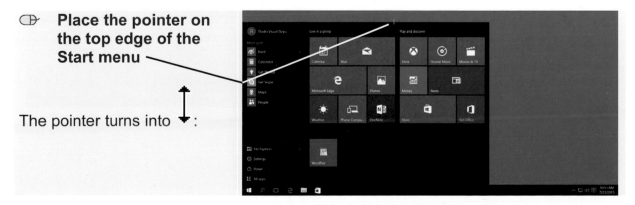

☞   **Drag the pointer
        upwards**

The Start menu will increase
in height:

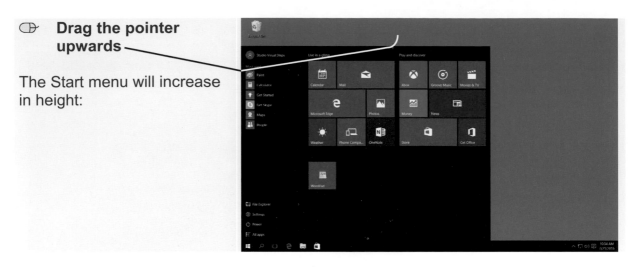

You can also make the Start menu wider or smaller, if you wish. To do that, place the
pointer on the right edge of the Start menu and then drag the pointer to the right or
left.

9.3 Moving Tiles and Creating Groups in the
Start Menu

You can change the order of the tiles, if you wish, or arrange the tiles in various
groups. In the following exercise you will be creating a new group for the *WordPad*
and *Mail* tiles:

☞   **Drag the *Mail* tile**

**to the right-hand side
of the *WordPad* tile**

Now these two tiles are joined in a group. You can name this group. In this example, we will call it *Exercise*. You can also choose another name for the group, if you wish. And you do not need to use the same tiles as in this example; you can also add other tiles to the group.

☞ **Click above the two tiles**

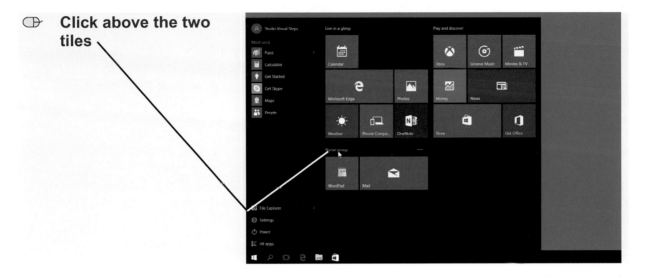

Name the new group, call it *Exercise*:

⌨ **Type:** Exercise

⌨ **Press** Enter

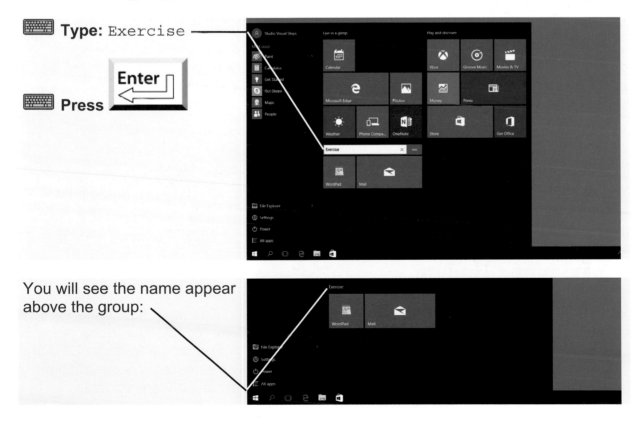

You will see the name appear above the group:

If you want to remove the tiles from the group, you can just drag them out of the group. When all the tiles have been removed from the group, the group name will automatically disappear.

9.4 Settings

If you would like to change any of the desktop or system settings in *Windows 10*, you need to use *Settings* app. You can open the *Settings* app from the Start menu:

☞ **Click**

The *Settings* window will be opened:

The window is filled with all sorts of subjects, arranged by category:

Each category is indicated by an icon:

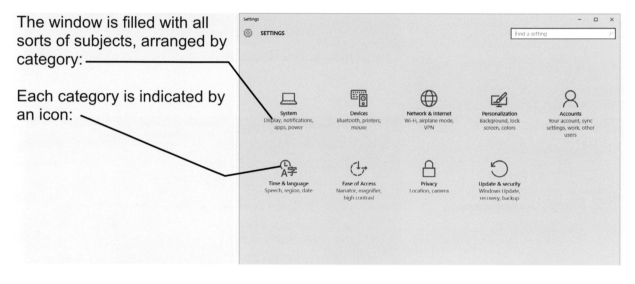

You can open the window for a particular category by clicking its icon. In the next section you will be taking a look at *Windows Update*.

9.5 Windows Update

Windows Update is an important component in *Windows*. The main function is to check if you are using the most recent version of *Windows 10*. *Windows 10* is constantly being updated, extended and enhanced. It is of particular importance that you have the latest updates and revisions to the security measures. These additions and improvements are distributed by Microsoft in the form of software updates.

➥ **Please note:**

Microsoft never sends software updates through email. If you receive an email with an attachment that claims to be Microsoft software, or a *Windows Update*, you should never open the attachment. Delete the email at once, and do not forget to delete this email from the *Deleted Items* folder as well. This type of email is sent by criminals who try to install harmful software on your computer.

If you want to be sure that you are using the most recent version of *Windows 10*, you need to check to see if *Automatic updates* is enabled. You do that as follows:

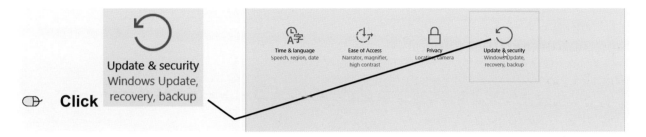

☞ **Click** Update & security Windows Update, recovery, backup

The *Update and Security* window will be opened on the *Windows Update* tab:

In this example, the system will automatically search for *Windows* updates:

You can also look for new updates yourself, by clicking

Check for updates:

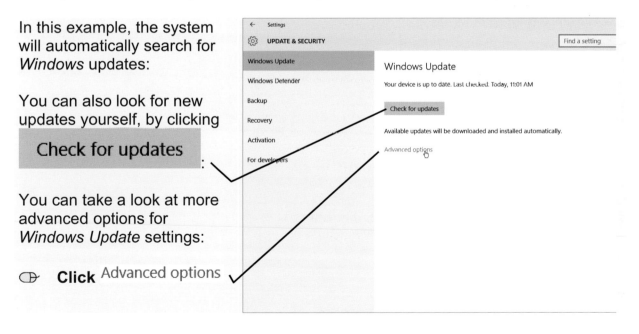

You can take a look at more advanced options for *Windows Update* settings:

☞ **Click** Advanced options

If you see
Automatic (recommended)
in the window, the automatic
update has been enabled:

If you do not see this:

☞ **By**
    Choose how updates are i
    click ⌄

☞ **Click**
    Automatic (recommen(

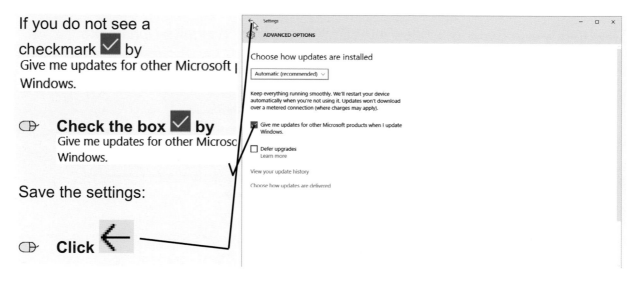

You can also enable the installation of updates for other Microsoft programs, if
desired:

If you do not see a

checkmark ☑ by
Give me updates for other Microsoft |
Windows.

☞ **Check the box ☑ by**
    Give me updates for other Microsc
    Windows.

Save the settings:

☞ **Click** ←

In the *Update and Security* window:

☞ **Click** ←

Now the *Windows Update* settings have been saved.

☞ **Close** *Settings* ∂∂⁶

9.6 Updating Apps

The default setting in *Windows 10* for updates made to apps is for them to be downloaded automatically. However, the updates are not always downloaded immediately. Your computer may also have a different setting for these updates. You can manually search to see if updates for apps are available. You do that like this:

☞ **Open the *Store*** ✍²

💡 **Tip**
Open the Store from the taskbar
You can also open the *Store* from the taskbar:

👆 **Click** 🏪 **on the taskbar**

Store will be opened. Here you can update apps, like this:

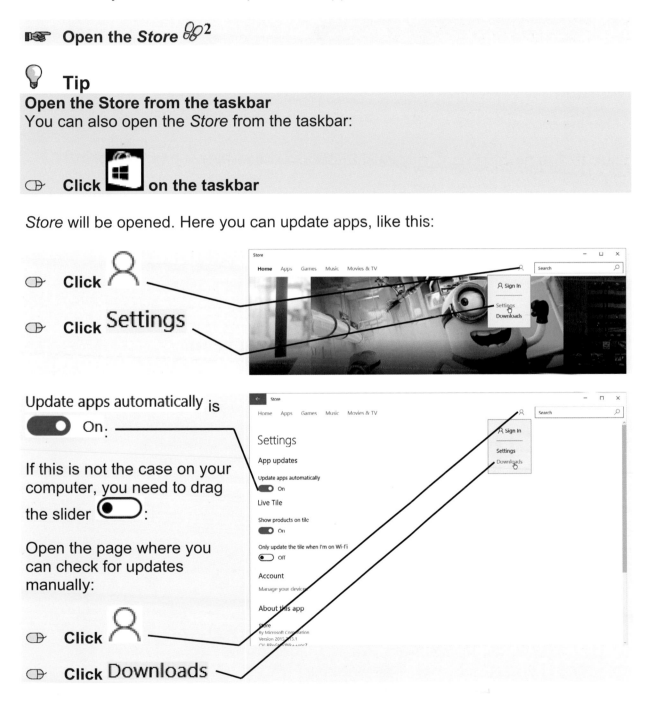

👆 **Click** 👤

👆 **Click Settings**

Update apps automatically is 🔘 **On.**

If this is not the case on your computer, you need to drag the slider 🔘:

Open the page where you can check for updates manually:

👆 **Click** 👤

👆 **Click Downloads**

Check for updates:

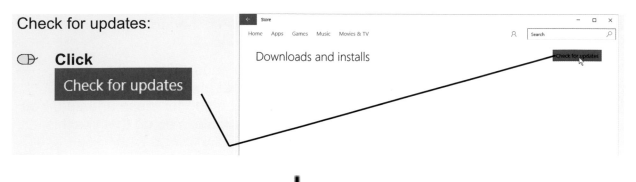

⊕ **Click**

    Check for updates

If any updates are found, you will see ⬇ to download the updates. Just click it and follow the instructions in the window, if necessary.

Close the window:

☞ **Close the *Store* window** 🐾⁶

🔖 **Please note:**

Windows programs will usually receive automatic updates. Programs manufactured by other companies, such as *Picasa* by *Google*, will often have an option in the Help, Extra, or Options menu with which you can check for updates. Some programs will tell you if there are any updates as soon as you open them.

9.7 Changing the Image of the Lock Screen

You can change the image of the lock screen as well. You do this from within the *Settings* window:

⊕ **Click** ⊞ , ⚙ **Settings**

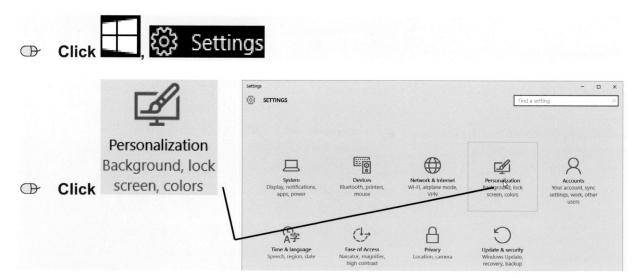

    Personalization
    Background, lock
⊕ **Click** screen, colors

You will see the *Personal Settings* window. Here you can change the image on the lock screen:

On the left-hand side of the window:

👉 **Click** Lock screen

You can select one of the standard images provided by *Windows*. Click the desired image: ——

Another option is to use one of your own images that you have saved on your computer:

👉 **Click** Browse

👉 **Select the desired photo** ——

👉 **Click** Choose picture

If you do not want to use one of your own photos, click Cancel.

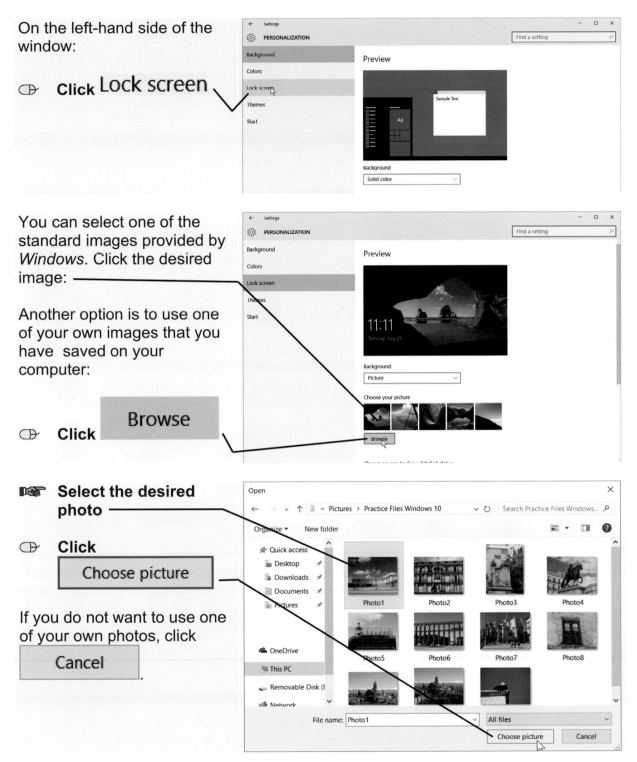

You will see the *Personal Settings* window with the new image of the lock screen:

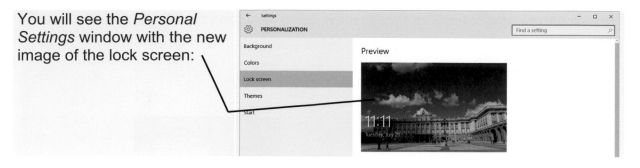

In the next section you will learn how to change the desktop background.

9.8 Changing the Desktop Background

Many people like to use a calm background (also called wallpaper) when they are working on their computer. But if you think your own background is rather dull and want to see something livelier, or you just want something else for a change, you can set a new background. Selecting a different background is very easy. You can change the desktop background by selecting an image or color yourself:

If you want to use an image that comes with the *Windows* system:

In the upper left corner of the window:

☞ **Click** Background

☞ **By** Background, **click** ⌄

☞ **Click** Picture

Note that you can also display a slideshow with multiple photos.

👆 **Click the desired image** ――――――――

If you want to use an image that is already stored on your computer, click

Browse. Then select the desired image, as explained in *section 9.7 Changing the Image of the Lock Screen*.

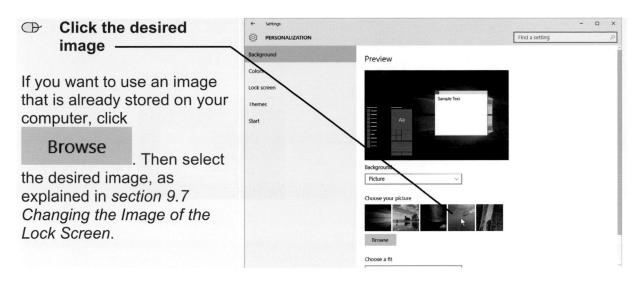

If you prefer not to use an image, but a specific color instead:

👆 **By** Background **, click**
∨

👆 **Click** Solid color

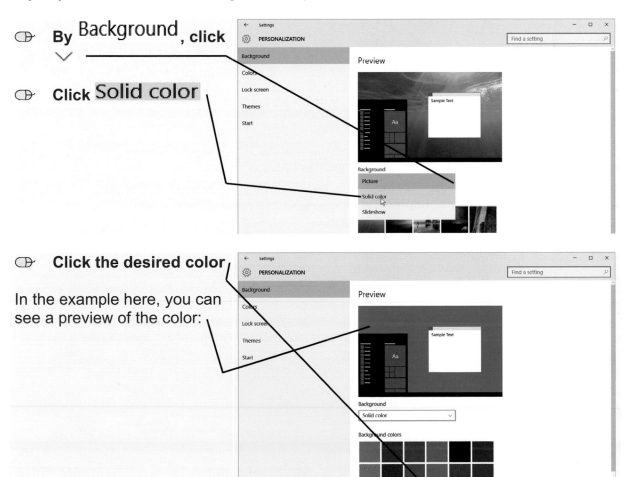

👆 **Click the desired color**

In the example here, you can see a preview of the color:

In order to save the desktop background and go back to the *Settings* home screen:

In the upper left corner of the window:

⊕   **Click** ⬅

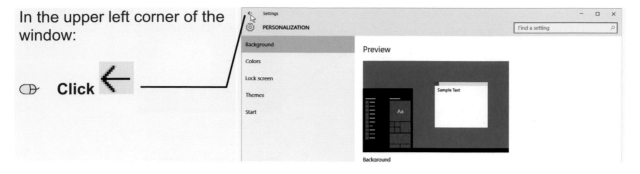

You will see the new desktop background you have chosen. If on second thought you are not satisfied with the background, you can repeat the actions in this section.

9.9 Setting Up the Mouse

Are you still having difficulty using the mouse even after sufficient practice? You may find the mouse easier to use if you adjust some of the settings for it. Here are the settings you can adjust:

- the speed of the pointer;
- he double-clicking speed;
- the button functions for left-handed users;
- the size and color of the pointer.

You can take a look at some of the options:

You open the options for the mouse by clicking the *Devices* category:

⊕   **Click**

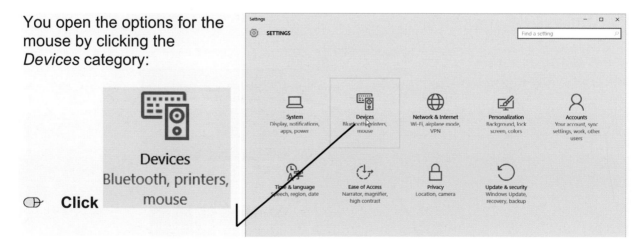

You will see the *Devices* window:

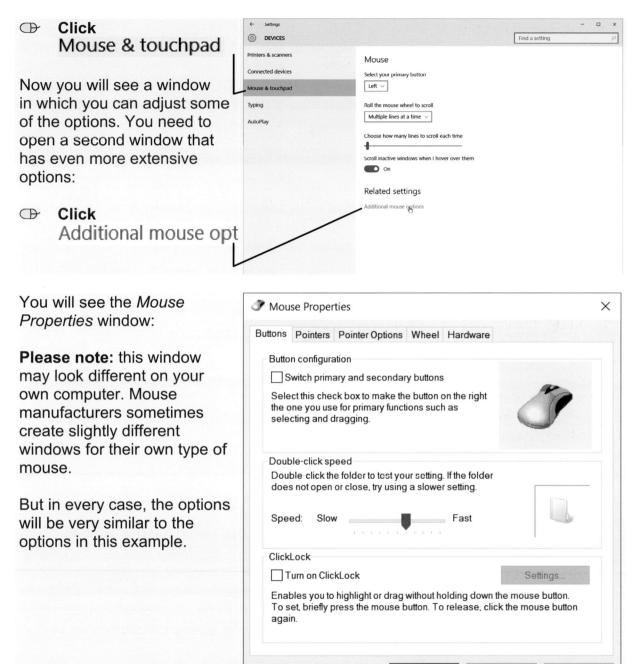

⊕ **Click**
   Mouse & touchpad

Now you will see a window
in which you can adjust some
of the options. You need to
open a second window that
has even more extensive
options:

⊕ **Click**
   Additional mouse opt

You will see the *Mouse
Properties* window:

Please note: this window
may look different on your
own computer. Mouse
manufacturers sometimes
create slightly different
windows for their own type of
mouse.

But in every case, the options
will be very similar to the
options in this example.

The speed of the mouse determines the connection between the movement of the
mouse on the table top and the movement of the pointer on the screen.

- If the pointer is set to *fast*, a very small movement of the mouse will move the pointer quickly across the screen.
- If the mouse is set to *slow*, you will need to move the mouse quite a lot more to move the pointer just a little bit across the screen.

The setting that satisfies most people is when the pointer speed is adjusted in such a way that when you move the mouse within an area as big as a CD case, the pointer on the screen moves along from one corner of the screen to the other.

If you feel that your pointer speed is too fast or too slow, you can try adjusting the speed. Here is how you do that:

☞ **Click the tab**

    Pointer Options

☞ **Drag the slider**
    towards Fast **or** Slow

You will not notice the effect right away, after you have moved the slider. You will need to apply the new setting first:

☞ **Click** Apply

Now you will notice the change once you move the mouse.

Mouse Properties   ✕

Buttons | Pointers | Pointer Options | Wheel | Hardware

Motion

Select a pointer speed:

Slow ———————▮——— Fast

☑ Enhance pointer precision

Snap To

☐ Automatically move pointer to the default button in a dialog box

Visibility

☐ Display pointer trails

Short ————————▮— Long

☑ Hide pointer while typing

☐ Show location of pointer when I press the CTRL key

OK | Cancel | Apply

You can keep moving the slider, until you have found the speed that suits you. Do not forget to click Apply , in order to apply the new setting.

💡 Tip

Visibility of the mouse pointer

Do you regularly lose sight of the mouse pointer after working a while? You can increase the pointer visibility in order to get a clear view of the position of the mouse by adding an extra effect to the pointer. You can add a so-called *tail* or *pointer trail*. In the *Mouse Properties* window:

☞ **Check the box** ☑ **by** Display pointer trails

Or:

☞ **Check the box** ☑ **by** Show location of pointer when I press the CTRL key

You can also make the pointer more visible by enlarging it. You do this by clicking a different tab:

☞ **Click the** Pointers **tab**

☞ **By** Scheme, **click** ✔

You will see a list with various options. These may differ on your own computer.

☞ **Click** Windows Standard (extra large) (system sch

Apply the effect:

☞ **Click** Apply

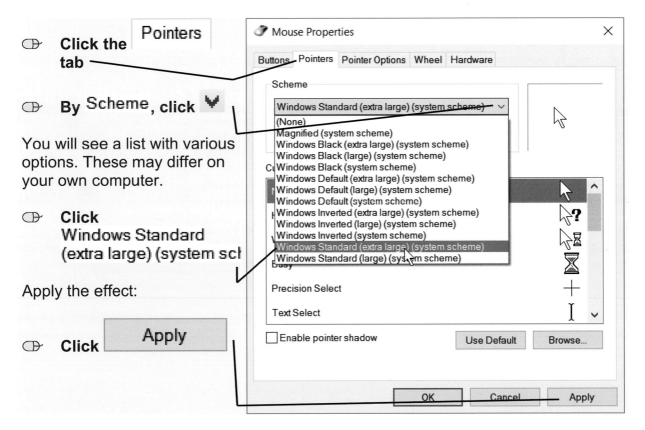

Now you will see that the pointer has become quite large: . If you like this, then just leave the setting this way. If you do not like this, you can revert back to the regular scheme Windows Standard (large) (system scheme), or you can select one of the other options.

In the list of pointers you will also see some with a black arrow: . This version is easier to see on the screen for some people.

You can also adjust the speed of double-clicking. If you are not fast enough when double-clicking, *Windows* will not recognize your two clicks as a double-click. A different setting may make it easier for you to double-click.

- *Slow down* the speed of the mouse if double-clicking is a problem.
- *Increase* the speed of double-clicking if you want to use rapid double-clicks (as an experienced user).

☞ **Click the** Buttons **tab**

☞ **Drag the slider to** Slow

In the window you will see a test box. There you can check whether your double-click is properly recognized by *Windows*:

☞ **Click** Apply

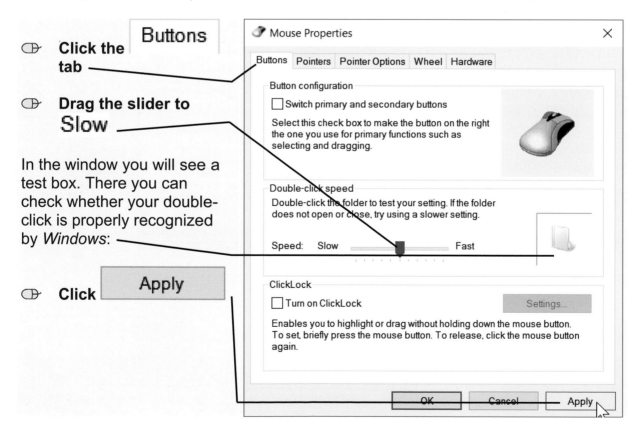

✖ HELP! I have a problem with double-clicking.

Here is another trick you can use:

☞ **Click the icon once**

The icon will turn blue, indicating that it is now selected.

 **Press** Enter ↵

The window will be opened.

If you are left-handed, you can place the mouse on the left side of the keyboard. You can also switch the functions of the buttons on the mouse so that you can click with your left hand's index finger:

➥ Please note:

If you are right-handed, you do not need to change anything.

☞ **Check the box ☑ by** Switch primary and secon

The functions of the mouse buttons have been swapped right away.

From now on, you need to use the *right mouse button* when you see the instruction *Click*:

☞ **Click** Apply

When you have finished adjusting all the mouse settings:

☞ **Click** OK

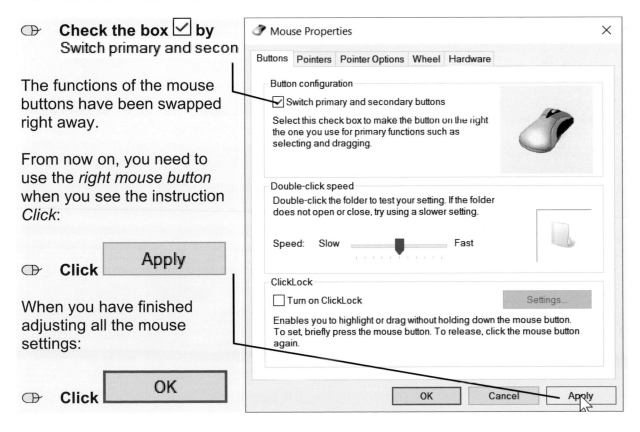

➥ Please note:

If you have just swapped the mouse functions, in future you will need to use the *left mouse button* when you see the instruction *Right-click*.

All the adjusted settings have been saved.

You will see the *Settings* window again. Note that you can switch the functions of the mouse buttons in this window too:

☞ **Click ←**

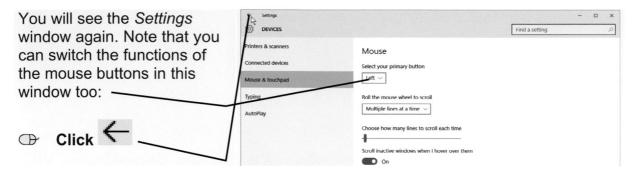

9.10 Changing the Size of Letters and Icons

If you find it difficult to read letters and icons, you can display them in a larger size. The *Settings* window is still open:

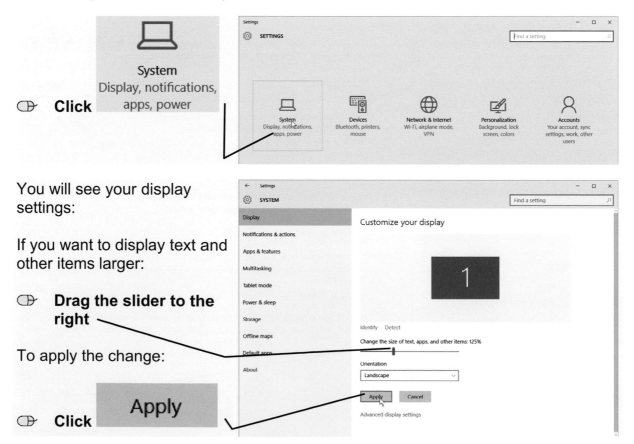

☞ **Click** System
Display, notifications, apps, power

You will see your display settings:

If you want to display text and other items larger:

☞ **Drag the slider to the right**

To apply the change:

☞ **Click** Apply

If you want to permanently change the font size, you need to sign off:

☞ **Click**

Sign out now

You will be logged off.

☞ **Sign on** 👣¹

Notice that the size of the text and other items on the desktop have been adjusted.

9.11 Setting Up a Screen Saver

If you have not used your computer for a while, you may see an animated image on your screen. This is known as a *screen saver*. You can set your own screen saver in *Windows*.

☞ **If necessary, open *Settings*** 👣²

If certain topics are not displayed in the *Settings* window, you can find them easily by using the search box in the *Settings* window. Search for a screen saver:

In the upper right corner of the window:

☞ **Click the search box**

⌨ **Type:** screen saver

You will see the search results:

☞ **Click** Turn screen saver on or off

A new window is opened. In order to set up a screen saver:

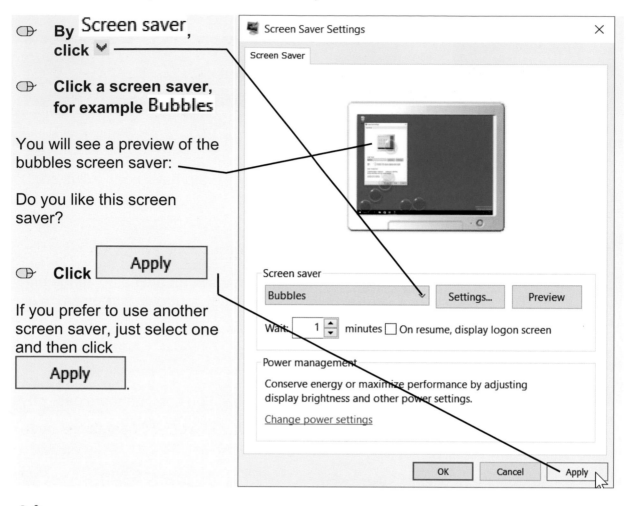

☞ **By** Screen saver,
click ❯

☞ **Click a screen saver,
for example** Bubbles

You will see a preview of the
bubbles screen saver:

Do you like this screen
saver?

☞ **Click** [Apply]

If you prefer to use another
screen saver, just select one
and then click
[Apply].

🩹 HELP! I do not see a new window

If you do not see the window with the screen saver setup right away, it may have
opened in the background. Use the taskbar to open the window:

☞ **Click**  **in the taskbar**

When you are completely finished:

☞ **Click** [OK]

Tip

Screen saver with photos

If you have some nice pictures on your computer, you can use them as a screen saver. By Screen saver , select the Photos option. Next, you click Settings... . Now you can choose the desired settings in the window that appears. In this case, you are actually using the screen saver as a slideshow. The slideshow will start after a period of time of inactivity.

 Tip

Set a waiting period

If you have selected a screen saver, you can also set the inactivity period: Wait: 1 minutes . Change the inactivity period by clicking the arrow buttons .

☞ **Close** *Settings* ⁶

9.12 Setting the Sound

If you use a program or app in which sound files are played, you will sometimes need to adjust the sound level. These are the options you have:

• set the sound level in *Windows* itself;
• set the sound level in the program or app that is used;
• set the sound level with the volume button on the computer, on the speakers, or on the monitor.

These three options have a connection with each other. If the sound in *Windows* is very low, or turned off completely, you will not hear anything even if you turn the volume knob on your computer way up high.
If this is the case, you need to adjust the sound level in *Windows* first.

The best way of setting the sound level is by playing music on your computer. In *section 8.12 Playing a Music CD*, you learned how to play music.

The speaker icon 🔊 is located on the far, right-hand side of the taskbar. With this icon you can set the sound level for *Windows*.

☞ **Click** 🔊 ————

You will see a little window with a slider. You can use this slider to turn the sound level up or down:

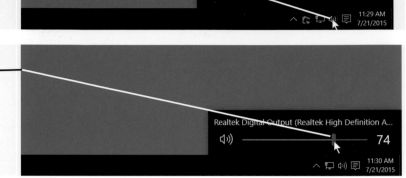

☞ **Drag the slider to the right** ————

Now the sound has become louder.

Most computers have a button somewhere, with which you can turn the sound higher or lower, or turn it off.

On some computers, such as a laptop, the buttons are located on the computer itself. On other computers, these buttons or knobs are placed on the speakers. If the speakers are built in to the monitor, the buttons will be placed on the monitor.

☞ **Adjust the volume with these buttons**

Now you should clearly hear the sound.

❌ HELP! I still do not hear any sound.

Do you still not hear any sound?
☞ **Check if the speakers are connected correctly and press the buttons once again**

Still no sound?
☞ **Read the manual**

You may be able to find some clues there that will help you.

Still no sound?
☞ **Contact your computer supplier**

9.13 Adjusting the Power Scheme

The *Windows* power scheme is a collection of settings that manage the energy usage of your computer. Sometimes it can be useful to take a closer look at the power scheme. For example, if you think your screen turns dark too soon or if you have a laptop that goes into sleep mode when left idle for just a few seconds.

Take a brief look at the power scheme of your computer.

☞ **Open** *Settings* 𝒪𝒪²

Click

System
Display, notifications,
apps, power

You will see the *System* window:

☞ **Click** Power & sleep

You can view more
extensive energy settings:

☞ **Click**
Additional power settings

Windows contains the following default power schemes that will help you manage the energy usage of your computer:

- **Balanced (recommended)** : This scheme ensures full performance when necessary, and saves energy when the computer is not used for a while.
- Power saver : This scheme saves more energy, compared to the option above. The computer and the monitor can be disabled or switched to sleep mode earlier.
- High performance: This scheme ensures optimum performance. Laptop users will notice that their battery depletes faster if they use this scheme.

Your own computer may have other schemes available that have been given by the computer manufacturer.

⟐ **By**
   Balanced (recommended
   click
   Change plan settings

If the performance of your desktop computer or laptop is satisfactory, you do not need to change these settings. In that case, you can just read through this section. But if you are not satisfied, for instance, because your screen turns dark too soon, or your laptop goes into sleep mode too quickly, you can adjust the settings. Desktop computer users will see the following settings:
You can change the settings by selecting a different period of time by

🕐 **Turn off the display:** and ⚫ **Put the computer to sleep:**.

When you have finished
changing the settings:

⟐ **Click** | Save changes |

If you do not want to change
anything, click | Cancel |.

Laptop users will also see settings for 🔋 **On battery** and 🔌 **Plugged in** . You can change these too, if you wish.

🩹 HELP! I cannot change the power scheme.

If your computer is part of a company or organizational network, such as a school or a business, the systems administrator may have disabled or even removed some components. In that case, you may not be able to adjust the power scheme.

☞ **Close the *Power Options* window** 👣⁶

☞ **Close *Settings*** 👣⁶

Tip

How do I wake up my computer from sleep mode?
The sleep mode saves energy. Before the computer goes into sleep mode, all the open documents, programs and apps are saved. The computer can be taken out of sleep mode very quickly (usually within a few seconds) and you can resume working. Enabling the sleep mode can be compared to the pause play function on a DVD player. The computer immediately stops all operations and starts them up again so you can continue working where you left off.

Most computers can be woken up from sleep mode by pressing the power switch of the device. However, computers may differ in this respect. You might also need to press a key, click the mouse, or open the cover of a laptop or notebook, in order to disable the sleep mode.

☞ **Read the documentation or manual that came with your computer**

There you will find more information on this subject.

In this section you have learned how to adjust the power settings of your computer. If you are not satisfied with a specific setting you have changed, you can always restore the original settings. If you want to do this, just go back through this section once more and click the option to apply the default or standard setting as needed. By now you have almost reached the end of this chapter, and you have seen how to change various settings in order to make it more comfortable and easier to use your computer. This chapter does not include any additional exercises. If you wish, you can experiment a bit further with the settings you have learned to adjust in this chapter.

On the website accompanying this book you can find bonus chapters, such as a chapter about downloading apps. You can read more about this in *Appendix C Opening the Bonus Online Chapters*.

9.14 Visual Steps Website, Newsletter and Follow-Up Books

By now we hope you have noticed that the Visual Steps method is an excellent method for quickly and efficiently learning more about computers, tablets, other devices and software applications. All books published by Visual Steps use this same method.
In various series, we have published a large number of books on a wide variety of topics including *Windows*, *Mac OS X*, the iPad, iPhone, Samsung Galaxy Tab, Kindle, photo editing and many other topics.

On the **www.visualsteps.com** website you will find a full product summary by clicking the blue *Catalog* button. For each book there is an extensive description, the full table of contents and a sample chapter (PDF file). In this way, you can quickly determine if a specific title will meet your expectations. You can order a book directly online from this website or other online book retailers. All titles are also available in bookstores in the USA, Canada, United Kingdom, Australia and New Zealand.

Furthermore, the website offers many extras, among other things:
- free computer guides and booklets (PDF files) covering all sorts of subjects;
- frequently asked questions and their answers;
- information on the free Computer Certificate that you can acquire at the certificate's website **www.ccforseniors.com**;
- a free email notification service: let's you know when a new book is published.

There is always more to learn. Visual Steps offers many other books on computer-related subjects. Each Visual Steps book has been written using the same step-by-step method with short, concise instructions and screenshots illustrating every step.

Would you like to be informed when a new Visual Steps title becomes available? Subscribe to the free Visual Steps newsletter (no strings attached) and you will receive this information in your inbox.
The Newsletter is sent approximately each month and includes information about
- the latest titles;
- supplemental information concerning titles previously released;
- new free computer booklets and guides;
When you subscribe to our Newsletter you will have direct access to the free booklets on the **www.visualsteps.com/info_downloads.php** web page.

Photo Editing on the iPad for SENIORS
ISBN 978 90 5905 731 9

Topics covered in this title:

crop, rotate and straighten photos - adjust exposure and contrast - add effects, text and other objects - create a collage and slideshow - share your photos

Digital Photo Editing with Picasa for Seniors
ISBN 978 90 5905 368 7

Topics covered in this title:

sort and organize photos into albums - enhance and retouch photos - create collages and make gift CDs - create movies and slideshows - print and share photos online - import photos

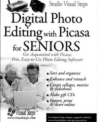

For more information on these books and many others, click **www.visualsteps.com**

9.15 Background Information

Dictionary

Desktop background	The desktop background is the area you work in on your computer. You can select one of the backgrounds that come with *Windows*, use a digital photo from you own collection, or set a plain, single-color background.
Notifications window	The *Notifications* window is used for displaying important messaged regarding the status of your computer. This window may contain messages regarding computer security, among other things.
Power scheme	A power scheme or plan is a group of hardware and system settings that are used to manage the power usage of your computer. Power plans can help you save energy, enhance system performance or maintain a balance between these two functions.
Screen saver	An animated image or pattern that is displayed on the screen when the mouse or keyboard have not been used for a certain period of time. *Windows 10* offers a number of different screen savers.
Security and maintenance	In the *Security and Maintenance* window you can check whether any computer problems need solving.
Settings	The *Settings* app is the window in which you can adjust the settings for *Windows* components and devices. The components are arranged by category.
Sleep mode	The sleep mode is intended to save energy. Before the sleep mode is enabled, all open documents, programs and apps are saved in the computer's memory. The computer can restore itself quickly (waking out of sleep mode usually within a few seconds) so you can resume working.

Source: Windows Help

9.16 Tips

💡 Tip

Security and maintenance
In the *Security and Maintenance* window you can check whether there are any problems with your computer that need solving. This is how you open the window:

☞ **Open** *Settings* 🦶²

👉 **Click the search box**

⌨ **Type:** security

👉 **Click**
Security and Maintenanc

You will see the *Security and Maintenance* window:

👉 **If necessary, by**
Security **, click** ⌃

You will see the status of the main components regarding your computer security, such as:
- *Firewall*
- *Virus protection*
- *Spyware and unwanted software protection*
- *Other security settings*

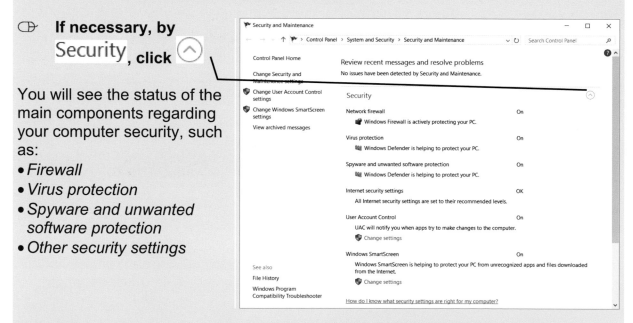

You will be able to see at a glance if there are any current problems on your computer. In the window displayed above all the items are turned on. The window on your own screen may look different. If necessary, ask an experienced computer user to help you.

💡 Tip

Notification window

If you are using *Windows 10*, you will regularly see notifications displayed in the bottom right-hand corner of the screen. These are messages sent by *Windows* and other programs, for example, concerning updates or any problems.

In this example you see a notification regarding the installation of an update for *Acrobat Reader*.

If you want to find out more about a notification:

☞ **Click the notification**

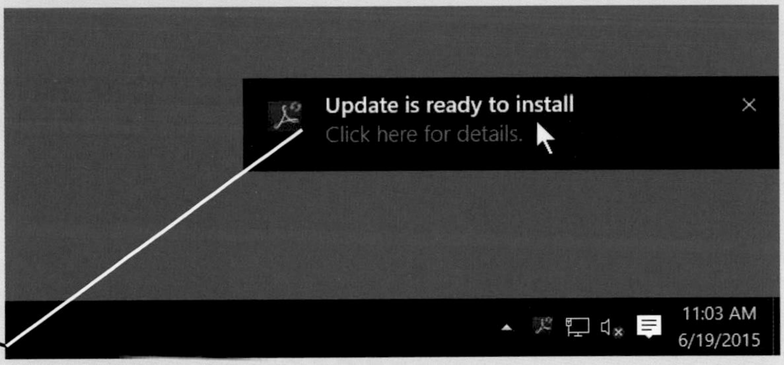

Now you will see the update window of *Acrobat Reader*:

If you want to update the program:

☞ **Click**

Install

☞ **Follow the instructions in the next few windows**

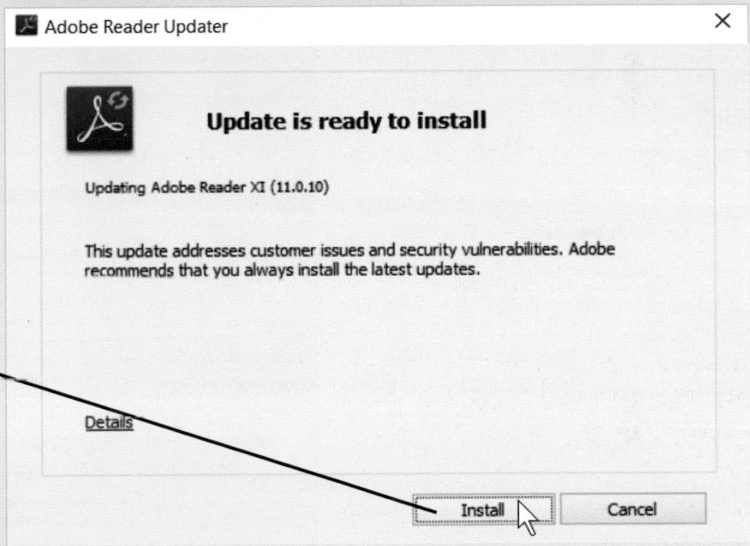

- Continue on the next page -

The notification will disappear by itself, after a few seconds:

You can also close the message yourself:

☞ **Place the pointer on the notification**

☞ **Click**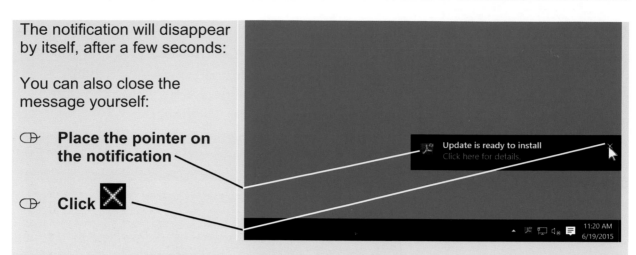

Besides separate notifications on the screen, you can also view a summary of all the notifications in the *Notification center*:

You can open the *Notification center* using the system tray on the right-hand side of the taskbar:

☞ **Click**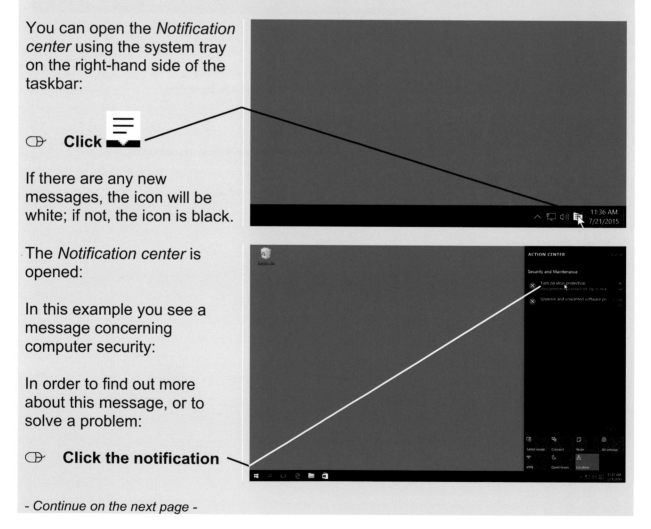

If there are any new messages, the icon will be white; if not, the icon is black.

The *Notification center* is opened:

In this example you see a message concerning computer security:

In order to find out more about this message, or to solve a problem:

☞ **Click the notification**

- Continue on the next page -

In this example there was no active antivirus program. *Windows* has immediately solved this problem and activated the antivirus program:

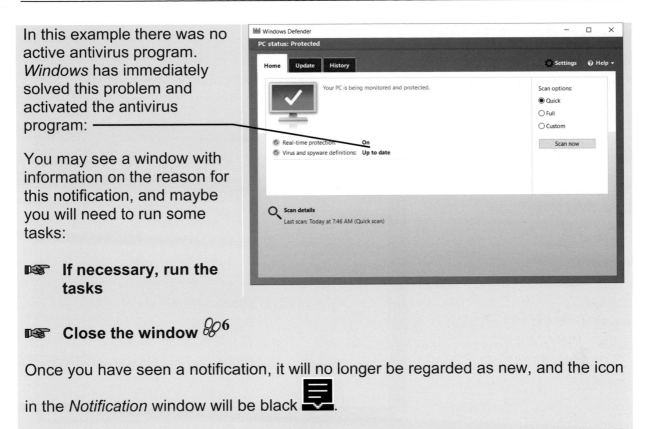

You may see a window with information on the reason for this notification, and maybe you will need to run some tasks:

☞ **If necessary, run the tasks**

☞ **Close the window** ✂️**6**

Once you have seen a notification, it will no longer be regarded as new, and the icon in the *Notification* window will be black 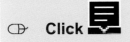.

You will open the *Notification* window again:

👉 **Click**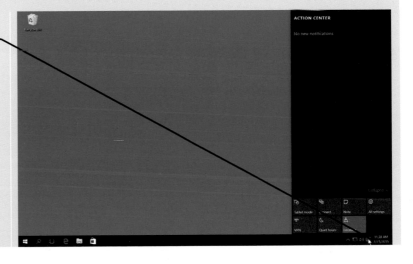

The previous notification has been removed:

There are some more buttons at the bottom, and among them is a button that directly opens *Settings*. You will probably not use this button very soon.

💡 Tip

Search for settings using the search function on the taskbar
You can very easily find settings by using the search function on the taskbar. You do that like this:

☞ **Click** 🔍

⌨ **Type one or more keywords, for example:** `mouse`

☞ **Click the desired search result**

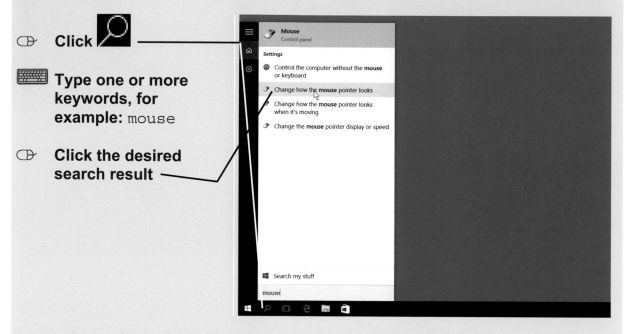

The corresponding window will be opened.

💡 Tip

Set up the search function
The search function may be set up as a button, or as a search box on your computer. This is how you change it:

☞ **Right-click the taskbar**

☞ **Place the pointer on** Search

☞ **Click the desired option**

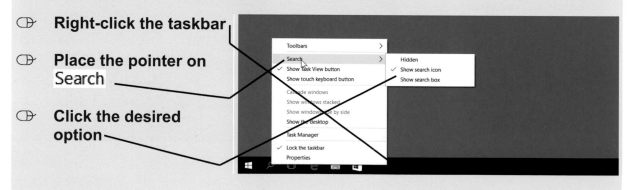

- Continue on the next page -

It is also possible to search the Internet through the search function. If this option has not yet been enabled, you can enable it like this:

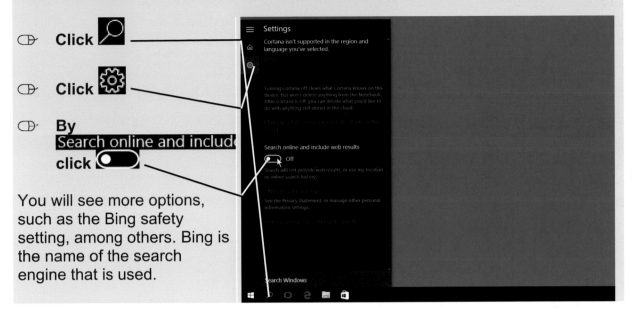

Click 🔍 ───

Click ⚙ ───

By
Search online and include
click ⬭ ───

You will see more options, such as the Bing safety setting, among others. Bing is the name of the search engine that is used.

💡 **Tip**

Turn live tiles on or off
In the Start menu you will see some tiles with an image that keeps changing all the time. These are Live tiles that display current information, for example, the weather, or news items. You can turn the information on these Live tiles on and off.
This is how you turn on a Live tile:

Right-click a tile ───

Click Turn live tile on

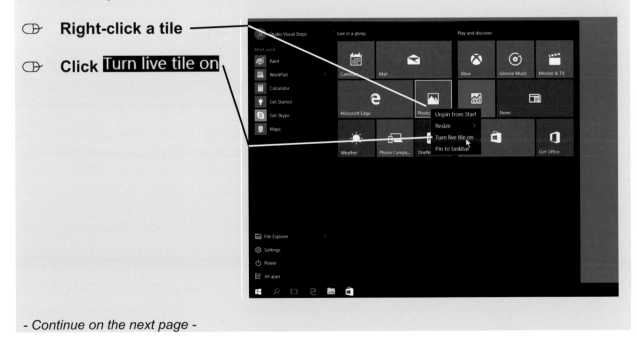

- Continue on the next page -

You can turn off a Live tile in the same way:

 Right-click the tile

 Click
Turn live tile off

Note that you will also see an option for changing the size of the tiles: ————

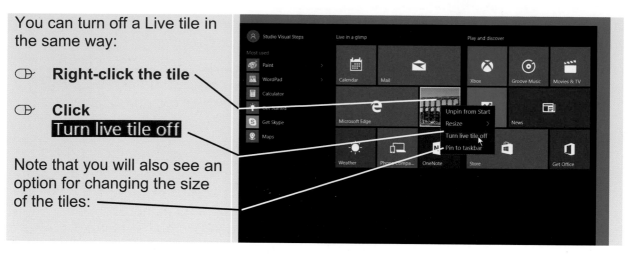

💡 Tip

RSI Prevention
If you use the mouse for an extended period of time, you may suffer from a condition known as mouse fatigue or RSI (Repetitive Strain Injury). RSI can be prevented by assuming the correct posture when working with the computer. Make sure your lower arm, wrist, and hand are in a horizontal position. Your wrist and hand should lightly rest on the table or desk. Apart from this, regular breaks and variation of your posture are important. See the *Background Information* at the end of *Chapter 3 Working with Text* for more information.

💡 Tip

Ergonomic mice?
A good computer mouse is shaped to fit ergonomically into the hand. However, these are often only suitable for users who are right-handed. Other mice are universal and can be used in either hand.

ergonomic   *universal*
right-handed

The mouse is the part of the computer that gets the most intensive use. Make sure you use a suitable mouse. Some manufacturers also make an ergonomically-shaped mouse that is for left-handed use.

💡 Tip

The position of the monitor
According to various safety regulations, your monitor should be placed in front of you at a distance of 23 to 28 inches from your face. The top of the monitor has to be at the same height as your eyes. If you have half-sized reading glasses or multifocal glasses, the monitor can be placed a bit lower.

Tip

Your reading glasses and the monitor

The distance between your face and the monitor is somewhat larger (23-28 inches) than your glasses can handle. Reading glasses are made for a reading distance of about 16-20 inches. Theoretically, you should be able to read the letters on the monitor well enough, using the 'long-sighted' part of your multifocal glasses.

If this is not the case and you can only read well by using the short-sighted part of your glasses, you can move the monitor a bit closer. And you can position the monitor as low as possible, so you will not need to force your head upwards, in order to use the reading part of your glasses. This will quickly result in neck fatigue.
If you cannot read the letters on the monitor well enough with the 'far-sighted' part of your glasses, you should ask your optician for advice. There exits special 'monitor' glasses that are attuned to a reading distance of 23-28 inches.

 Tip

Adjusting the monitor

A monitor has controls for adjusting the brightness and contrast of the screen, among others, just like a television set:

On some monitors, these control buttons may be hidden behind a cover or flap:

Often, there are also several options for changing the position of the image on the screen. This can be important if part of the *Windows* window is not displayed correctly (falls off the screen).

Take your time to adjust your monitor in the best possible way. You can also read your monitor's manual for extra information.

 Tip

Connect extra speakers

If you are not satisfied with the quality of the sound, you can connect different speakers to your computer.

Computer speakers

- Continue on the next page -

On the front and/or back of the computer case you will find three connectors for devices that have to do with sound: a microphone, a head phone, and extra speakers.

Sometimes, the word OUT is written next to the connectors.

Three connectors

With a plug you can easily connect the speakers. Computer speakers come in all sorts of types and sizes. They are available at computer, electronic stores and other retail outlets.

Tip

Connect a head phone
The very best sound is undoubtedly the sound you hear through a head phone. You can choose any volume level you want, without disturbing others. Almost every type of head phone can be connected to the computer. You do not need any specific computer model.

Of course, the plug has to fit. Some computers have a separate head phone connection, indicated by a small sign. Often you can just connect the head phone directly to the speaker.

If your computer does not have a specific head phone connection, you can connect the head phone to one of the three connectors mentioned in the previous *Tip*.

Appendix A. Clicking and Dragging in Solitaire

The card game *Solitaire* is not only very popular among computer users, but also an extremely pleasant way to practice working with the mouse. The game requires a lot of clicking and dragging. This section describes how to play the game.

The Rules for Solitaire

The card game *Solitaire* is a default game on your computer. You are going to play this card game later on. First we will explain the rules for this card game.

You now see this window with eight piles of cards:

At the top left there is a pile of cards that are face down, called the *deck*. You can turn over the cards in this pile by clicking the deck.

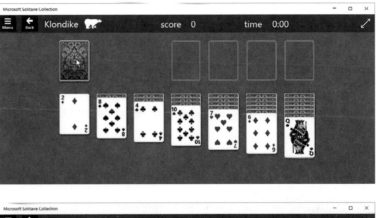

The top three cards are turned over when you have clicked the top left pile:

You can place a card in the correct spot by dragging it with the mouse.

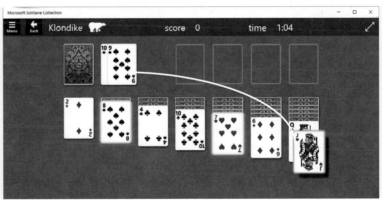

You can move the card to one of the seven lower piles, called 'row stacks'. There you release the mouse button.

- If the card can be played here, it will remain there.
- If the card cannot be played here, it will remain face up and returns automatically to the pile.

Do you already know how to play this version of the card game *Solitaire*?
Then you really already know how to play: try to play all of the cards and get them all up to the suit stacks.

Do you not know how to play this version of the card game *Solitaire*?
Then you can read the objective of the game and the rules below.

The Objective

- The objective of this game is to play all of the cards in proper order from aces to kings on the suit stacks at the top right. Next to the deck, you see the empty

   spaces for the four suit stacks:
- The first card that you can play on these piles is the ace; then you must play the two, three, four, and so on, up to the king.
- Spades, clubs, diamonds and hearts each have their own pile.

Some of the cards are divided over seven stacks:

The rest of the cards are in the deck at the top left:

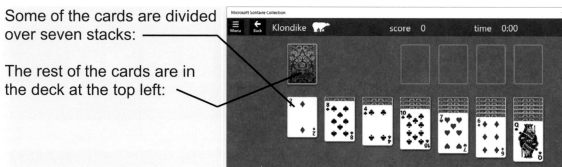

The Beginning

You must try first to play cards on the seven playing stacks.

You can take a card from these stacks by *dragging* it with your mouse:

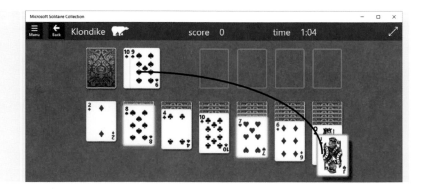

Please note:

A card can only be played on these seven stacks if it is the next descending card of the opposite color: red eight on black nine, black jack on red queen, and so on.
In *Solitaire*, the **king** is the **highest** card and the **ace** is the **lowest**.

The Seven Stacks

You can play a card from one of the playing stacks to a different playing stack:

This can only be done if the card fits.

In this way you must try to turn over all of the cards and play them on one of the row or suit stacks.

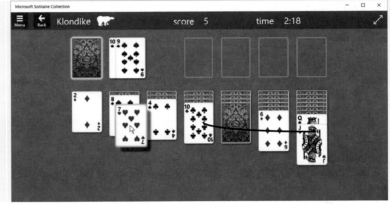

But there are a few more things you need to know:

If there is a stack of cards that fits onto a different stack, you can move the entire stack by dragging the first card in the stack:

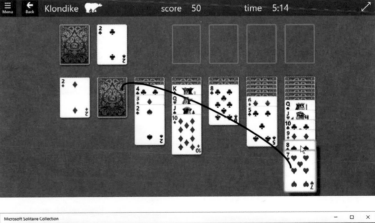

If one of the seven playing stacks at the bottom is emptied, you can only start it again by placing a **king** there:

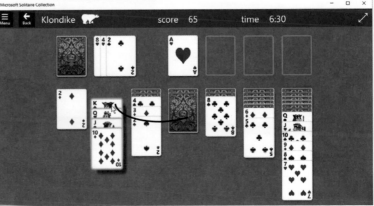

Once your entire deck has been turned over, you will see a circle in the empty space. You can turn back the pile of cards from the deck that could not yet be played by clicking the circle:

Playing Suits

You can also play cards by suit. There is a space for each of the four suits at the top right of the window.

If an ace has turned up, you should start the suit stacks by moving it to one of the four spaces, as illustrated here with the ace of hearts.

You can move cards to a suit stack not only by dragging them, but also by double-clicking with the left mouse button:

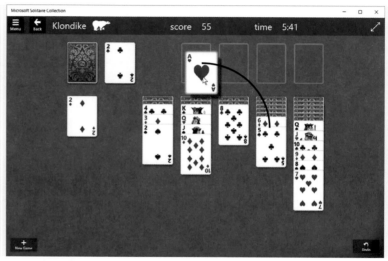

If a two of spades turns up later, you can play it on top of the ace of spades:

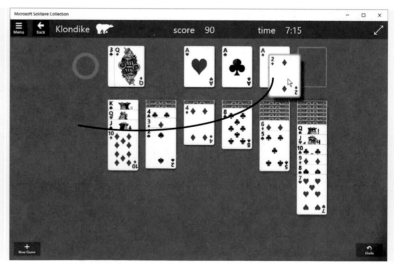

End of the Game

You have won the game if you succeed in completing all of the four suit stacks, one for clubs, one for diamonds, one for hearts and one for spades.

You are 'stuck' if you can no longer turn over cards from the deck or move any of the cards in the stacks. The best thing to do when this happens is to start a *new game*. This is explained later on.

💡 Tip

Paying attention and a bit of luck!
Solitaire is a game in which you must pay attention. You have to continually look carefully to see if a card can be played somewhere. But you also need a bit of luck. Even the very best players can not win every game.

💡 Tip

Always pay attention to the following:
- Look to see if a card can be played on one of the seven row stacks.
- Check to see if you can play a card on one of the four suit stacks.
- Do not turn cards over from the deck until you have played all of the cards that you can.

Starting Solitaire

You can open the *Solitaire* game using the search function:

Click 🔍

⌨️ **Type:** solitaire

Click
Microsoft **Solitaire**
Windows app

You will see the window *Choose an account*. If desired you can combine an account to the *Solitaire* game. You do not have to do this right now. You can close this window:

At the bottom of the window:

☞ **Click**

> Close

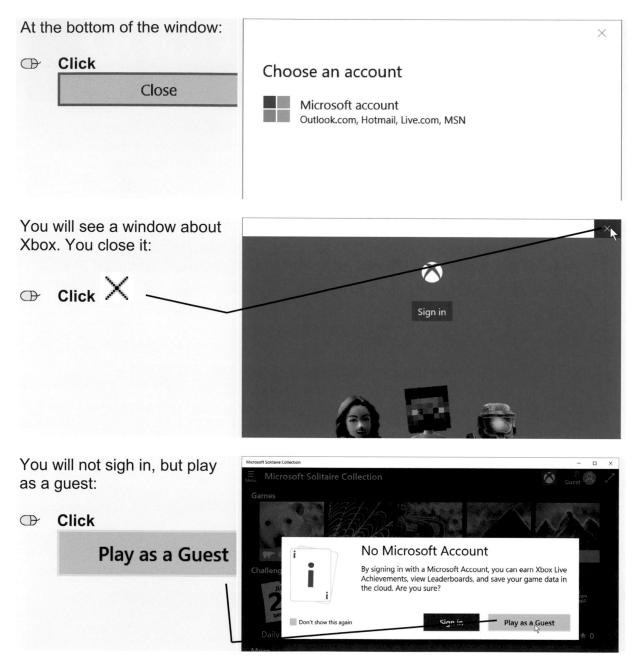

Choose an account

Microsoft account
Outlook.com, Hotmail, Live.com, MSN

You will see a window about Xbox. You close it:

☞ **Click** ✕

Sign in

You will not sigh in, but play as a guest:

☞ **Click**

> **Play as a Guest**

Microsoft Solitaire Collection

Microsoft Solitaire Collection

Games

Challeng

No Microsoft Account

By signing in with a Microsoft Account, you can earn Xbox Live Achievements, view Leaderboards, and save your game data in the cloud. Are you sure?

Don't show this again   Sign in   Play as a Guest

Daily

You will see a window with multiple games:

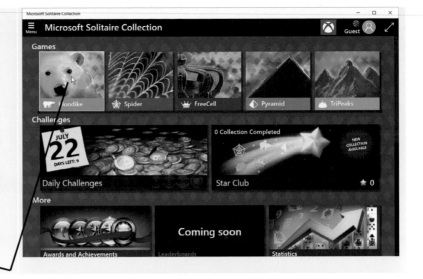

The *Solitaire* game is called *Klondike*. You open it:

☞ **Click**

First you will see some information about the game. You close this:

☞ **Click**

Close

You now see this window with eight piles of cards:

At the top left there is a pile of cards that are face down, called the *deck*. You can turn over the cards in this pile by clicking the deck.

☞ **Click the pile**

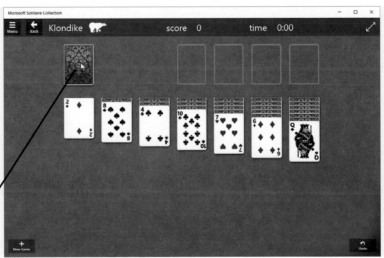

The top three cards are turned over when you have clicked the top left pile:

You can place a card in the correct spot by dragging it with the mouse.

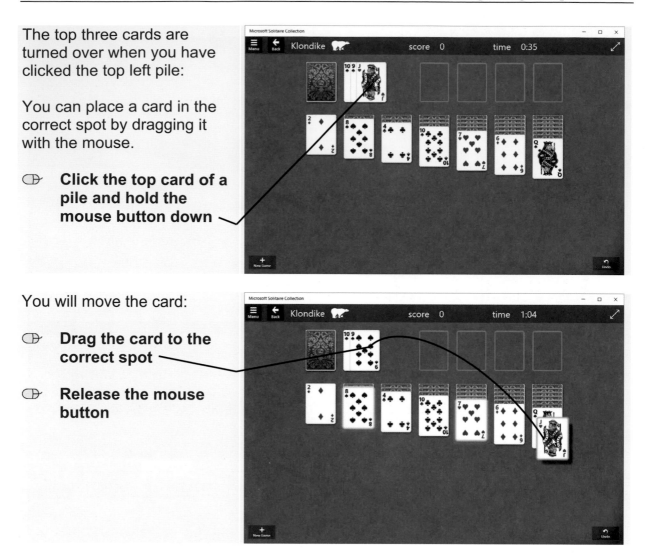

☞ **Click the top card of a pile and hold the mouse button down**

You will move the card:

☞ **Drag the card to the correct spot**

☞ **Release the mouse button**

You can continue the game by dragging the cards to the right spot. Follow the rules at the beginning of this appendix.

☞ **Play all of the cards and get them all up to the suit stacks**

A New Game

You are 'stuck' if you can no longer turn over cards from the deck or move any of the cards in the stacks. The best thing to do when this happens is to start a *new game*.

This is how to start a new game:

At the bottom left side of the window:

Click

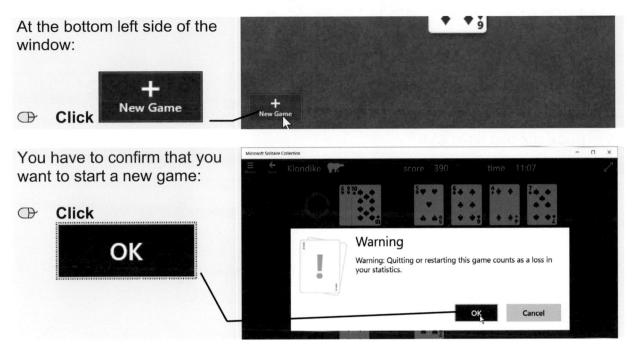

You have to confirm that you want to start a new game:

Click

OK

Now the cards will be shuffled and redealt. You can start playing the game again.

To end a game:

At the top right-hand corner of the window:

Click ✕

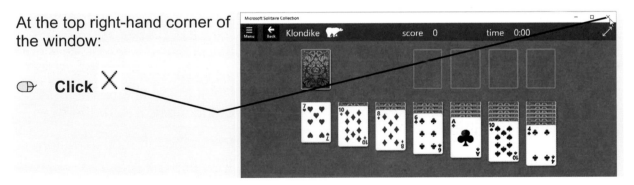

Appendix B. How Do I Do That Again?

In this book you will find many exercises that are marked with footsteps. 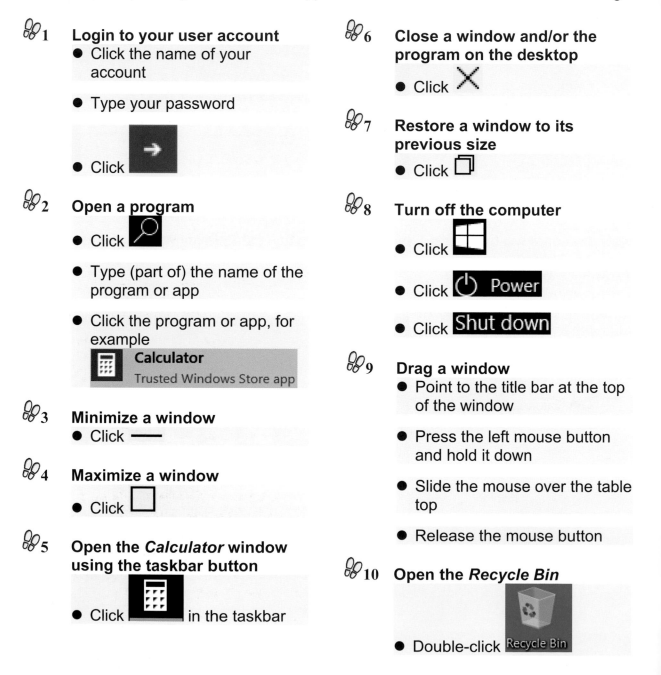x
Find the corresponding number in the appendix below and see how to do something.

1 Login to your user account
- Click the name of your account
- Type your password
- Click →

2 Open a program
- Click 🔍
- Type (part of) the name of the program or app
- Click the program or app, for example
  Calculator Trusted Windows Store app

3 Minimize a window
- Click —

4 Maximize a window
- Click ☐

5 Open the *Calculator* window using the taskbar button
- Click ▦ in the taskbar

6 Close a window and/or the program on the desktop
- Click ✕

7 Restore a window to its previous size
- Click ❐

8 Turn off the computer
- Click ⊞
- Click ⏻ Power
- Click **Shut down**

9 Drag a window
- Point to the title bar at the top of the window
- Press the left mouse button and hold it down
- Slide the mouse over the table top
- Release the mouse button

10 Open the *Recycle Bin*
- Double-click 🗑 Recycle Bin

❦11 Drag the scroll box
- Point to the scroll box
- Press the left mouse button and hold it down
- Slide the mouse slowly - upwards or downwards
- Release the mouse button

❦12 Return to the start page of News
- Click ←

❦13 Open a file
- Click [File]
- Click 📂 Open
- If necessary, click 📄 Documents on the left side of the navigation pane
- Click the name of the file
- Click [Open]

❦14 Start a new paragraph / line
- Press [Enter ↵]

❦15 Delete a letter, or a selected text fragment (could be a word, sentence, or paragraph)
If the cursor/pointer appears on the right side of the word:
- Press [Backspace ←]

If the cursor/pointer appears on the left side of the word:
- Press [Delete]

If the text is already selected:
- Press [Delete] or [Backspace ←]

❦16 Move cursor to the beginning of the line
- Press [←]

❦17 Move cursor to the end of the line
- Press [→]

❦18 Open a new text
- Click [File]
- Click [New]

Do not save changes:
- Click [Don't Save]

❦19 Save document
- Click [File]
- Click 💾 Save
- At File name:, type the name of your file
- Click [Save]

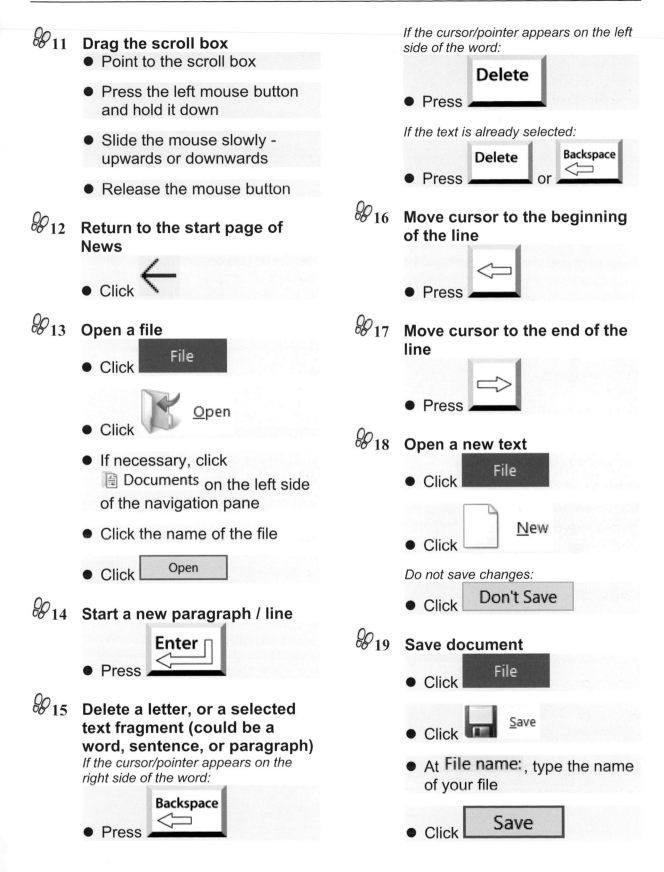

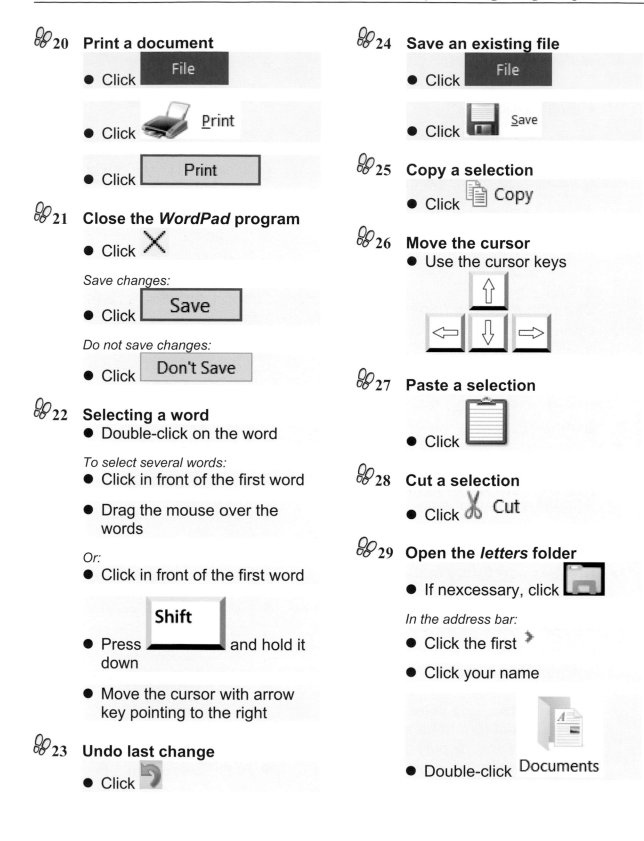

20 Print a document

- Click **File**

- Click 🖨 **Print**

- Click **Print**

21 Close the *WordPad* program

- Click ✕

Save changes:

- Click **Save**

Do not save changes:

- Click **Don't Save**

22 Selecting a word

- Double-click on the word

To select several words:

- Click in front of the first word

- Drag the mouse over the words

Or:

- Click in front of the first word

- Press **Shift** and hold it down

- Move the cursor with arrow key pointing to the right

23 Undo last change

- Click ↩

24 Save an existing file

- Click **File**

- Click 💾 **Save**

25 Copy a selection

- Click 📋 **Copy**

26 Move the cursor

- Use the cursor keys

⬆ ⬅ ⬇ ➡

27 Paste a selection

- Click 📋

28 Cut a selection

- Click ✂ **Cut**

29 Open the *letters* folder

- If nexcessary, click 📁

In the address bar:

- Click the first ❯

- Click your name

- Double-click **Documents**

- Double-click letters

30 Open a folder from the taskbar

- Click [icon] on the taskbar

31 Opening a folder
In a folder window that is already open and displaying the folder:
- Double-click the folder

32 Open the *Personal folder*

- Click [icon]

In the address bar:

- Click >

- Click your name

33 Return to a previously visited folder or return to a folder visited after the current one

- Click ← or →

34 Create a new folder in the folder window

- Click the Home tab

- Click New folder

- Type the name of the folder

- Click **Enter**

35 Copy a file to a folder
- Select a file by clicking it

- Click Copy

- Double-click the correct folder

- Click Paste

36 Change the name of a file or folder
- Click the file or folder

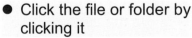

- Click Rename

- Type the new name

- Press **Enter**

37 Delete a file or folder
- Click the file or folder by clicking it

- Click ✕

Or:
- Click the file or folder by clicking it

- Press **Delete**

38 Go to the top of the web page
- Drag the scroll box upwards

Or:
- Roll the mouse wheel away from you with your index finger

39   Open a web page
- Click the address bar
- Type the web address
- Press **Enter**

40   View a previously visited website
- Click ←

41   Add a website to favorites
- Click ☆
- Click ☆ Favorites
- Click **Add**

42   Open a favorite
- Click ≡
- Click ☆
- Click the favorite website

43   View a website visited after the current one
- Click →

44   Zoom on a web page
- Click ▪ ▪ ▪
- By **Zoom**, click ＋ or —

45   Searching the Internet
- Click the address bar
- Type a keyword
- Press **Enter**

46   Open a search result
- Click a search result

47   Create an email message
- Click ＋

To add the email address of the recipient:
- By **To**, type the email address

To add a subject:
- Click Subject
- Type a subject
- Click the white area below the subject
- Type a message

48   Send an email message
- Click ▷ Send

49   Open the *Inbox*
- Click ⬜
- Wait a few more minutes, and click Inbox

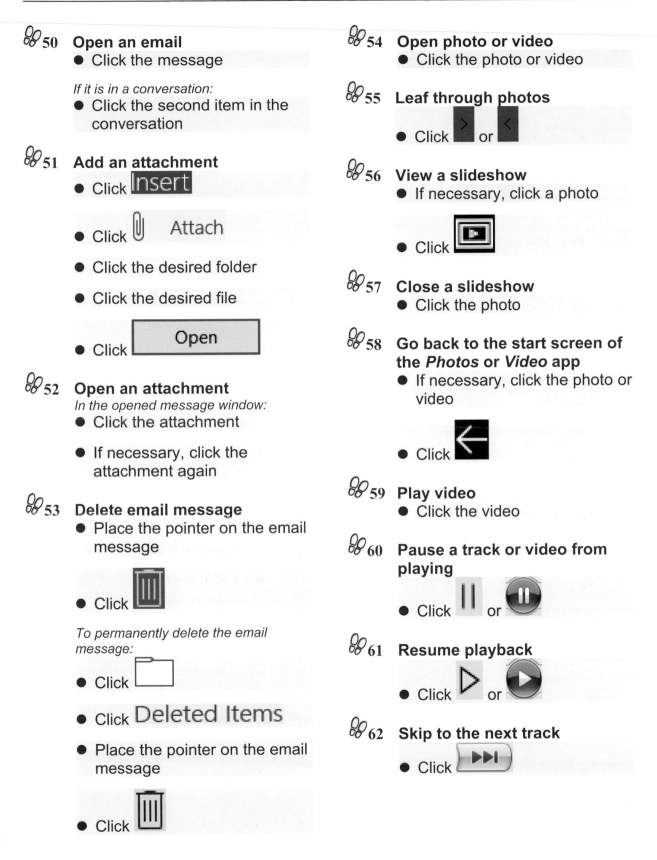

50 Open an email
- Click the message

If it is in a conversation:
- Click the second item in the conversation

51 Add an attachment
- Click **Insert**
- Click 📎 Attach
- Click the desired folder
- Click the desired file
- Click Open

52 Open an attachment
In the opened message window:
- Click the attachment
- If necessary, click the attachment again

53 Delete email message
- Place the pointer on the email message
- Click 🗑

To permanently delete the email message:
- Click 📁
- Click Deleted Items
- Place the pointer on the email message
- Click 🗑

54 Open photo or video
- Click the photo or video

55 Leaf through photos
- Click > or <

56 View a slideshow
- If necessary, click a photo
- Click ▶

57 Close a slideshow
- Click the photo

58 Go back to the start screen of the *Photos* or *Video* app
- If necessary, click the photo or video
- Click ←

59 Play video
- Click the video

60 Pause a track or video from playing
- Click ❚❚ or ⏸

61 Resume playback
- Click ▷ or ▶

62 Skip to the next track
- Click ⏭

63 Play tracks in random order
- Click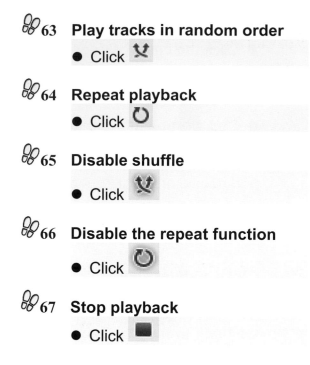

64 Repeat playback
- Click

65 Disable shuffle
- Click

66 Disable the repeat function
- Click

67 Stop playback
- Click

Appendix C. Downloading the Practice Files

In some chapters you will need to use several practice files. You can download these from the website accompanying this book.

☞ **Open** *Edge* $\mathscr{QP}^2$

☞ **Open the web page www.visualsteps.com/windows10senior** $\mathscr{QP}^{39}$

👆 **Click**
Practice files

You will see the folder with the practice files:

You are going to copy this folder to the *Pictures* folder.

👆 **Click**
Windows 10 Practice Files

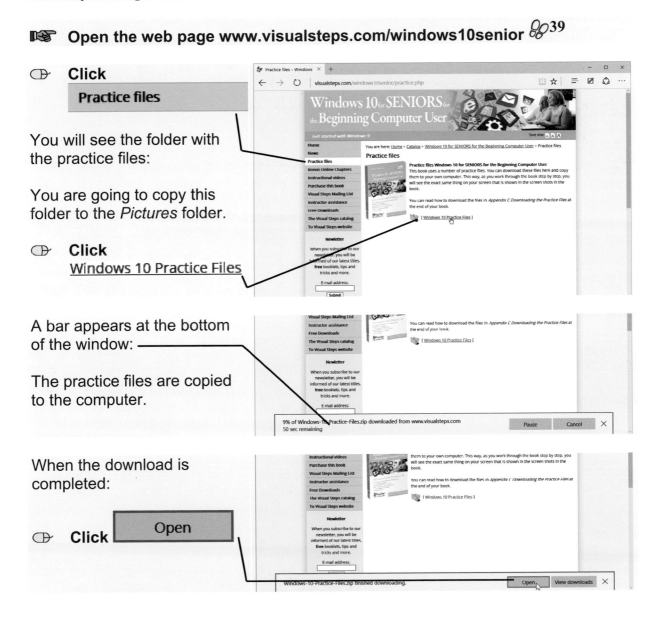

A bar appears at the bottom of the window:

The practice files are copied to the computer.

When the download is completed:

👆 **Click** Open

The *Windows 10 Practice files* folder is stored in the *Downloads* folder on the computer and this folder is now opened. This folder is a compressed folder. This means that the files in the folder are compressed so that the file size is smaller. If you want to use the files in a compressed folder, you need to unzip (or extract) the folder first:

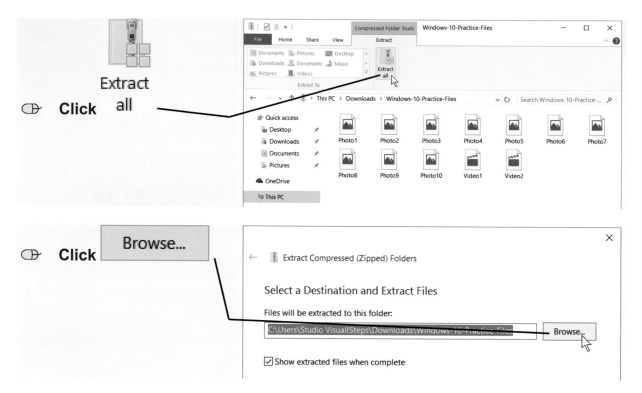

You are going to create a new folder with the name *Practice files Windows 10*:

☞ **Click**

Select Folder

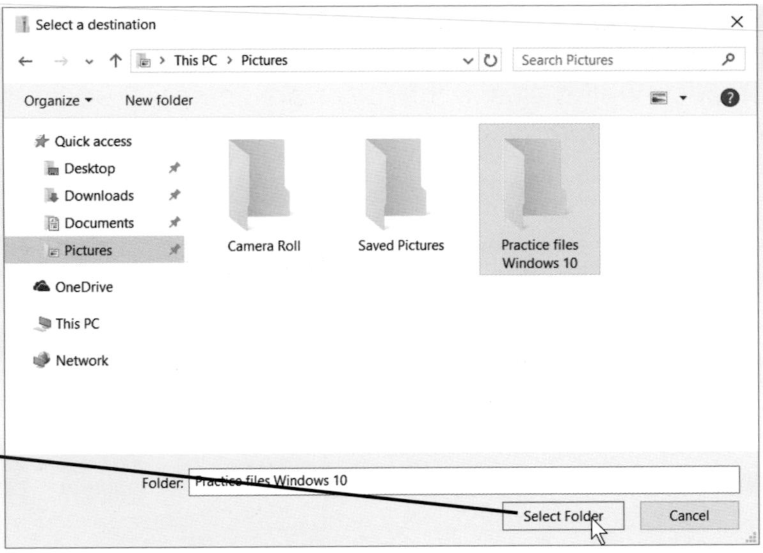

Now you are going to extract the files in this new folder:

☞ **Click** **Extract**

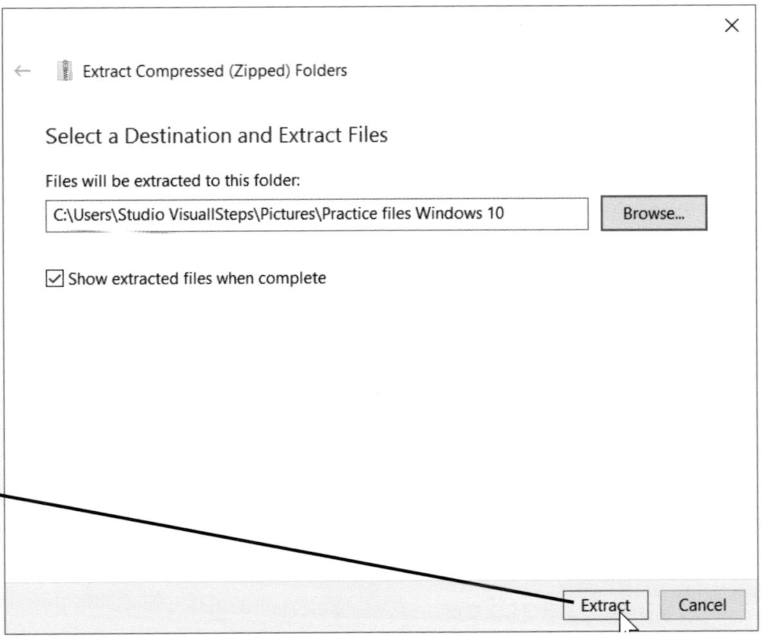

While the files are being extracted, you see this window:

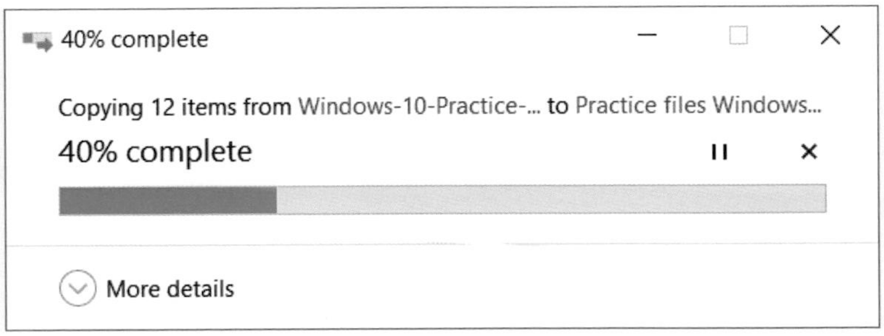

You will see the practice files that go with this book. There are a couple of photos and two videos. You are going to move the videos to the *Videos* folder:

☞ **If necessary, by** 🖥 **This PC** **, click** ⟩

☞ **Click** **Video1** **and keep the mouse button pressed**

☞ **Drag the file to** ▣ **Videos**

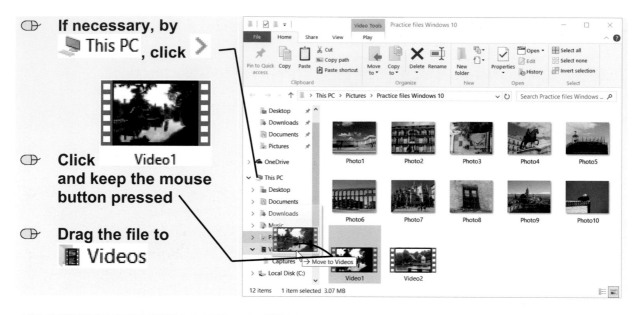

☞ **Do the same thing with the file called Video2**

☞ **Close the window** 👣⁶

The compressed folder *Windows-10-Practice-Files* has been saved in the *Downloads* folder. This window is still opened. You can delete the compressed folder:

☞ **Click** ⬇ **Downloads**

☞ **If necesary, click the folder**

☞ **Click the** Home **tab**

☞ **Click** ✕

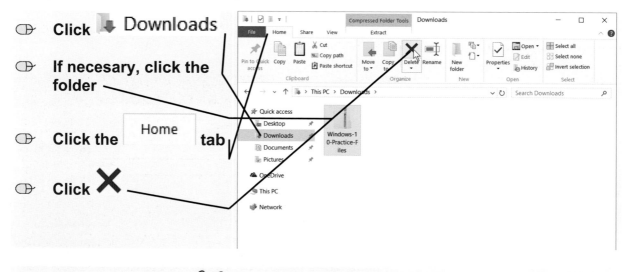

☞ **Close all windows** 👣⁶

Now you can continue with the chapter.

Appendix D. Opening the Bonus Online Chapters

This is how you open the bonus online chapters on this book's website:

☞ **Open *Edge*** 👣²

☞ **Open the web page www.visualsteps.com/windows10senior** 👣³⁹

You will see the website that goes with this book:

🖰 **Click**

Bonus Online Chapters

Now you will see this web page:

To open the bonus chapter:

🖰 **Click**
Start downloading »»

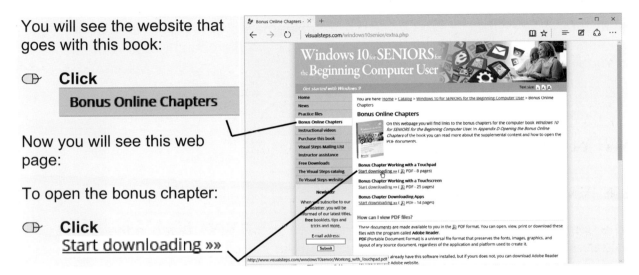

You will see a new tab in *Edge*. The PDF files are secured by a password. You need to enter the password to open the PDF file:

⌨ **Type:** 97415

🖰 **Click** **OK**

Please enter a password.

OK   Cancel

Now you will see the Bonus Chapter:

You can see the rest of the chapter by dragging the scroll box:

The blue progress bar at the top indicates the progress of the download. When this bar is gone, the whole document is opened:

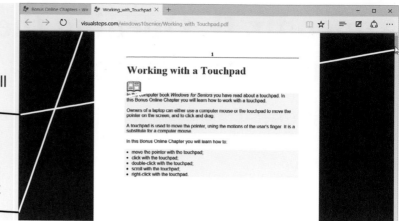

In *section 6.14 Printing a Web Page* you have learned how to print a web page. You can print a PDF file the same way. You can also save the document to your computer. This way you can open it later on.

⊕   **Right-click the document**

⊕   **Click**   Save as

The *Documents* folder is opened by default:

To save the document:

⊕   **Click**   Save

The document will be saved in the *Documents* folder.

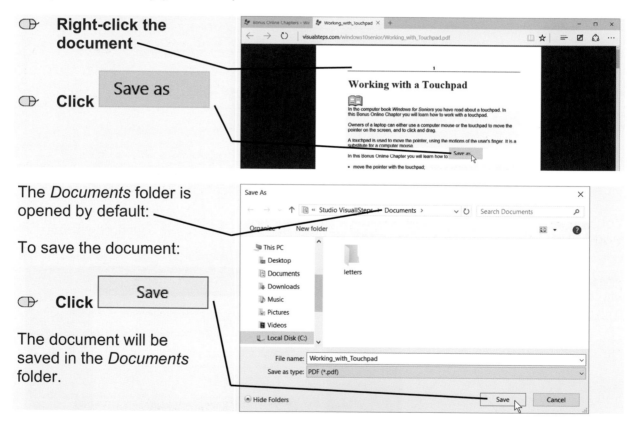

You can work through this bonus chapter in the same ways as you worked through the chapters in the book. After you have finished reading, printing or saving the file, you can close *Edge*.

☞ **Close** *Edge* ℘℘6

Appendix E. Opening the Instructional Videos

There are a number of instructional videos available on the website that accompanies this book. In this appendix you can read how to open and view these videos.

☞ **Open *Edge*** ✌️²

☞ **Open the www.visualsteps.nl/windows10senior web page** ✌️³⁹

You will see the website that goes with this book:

⊕ **Click**

  Instructional videos

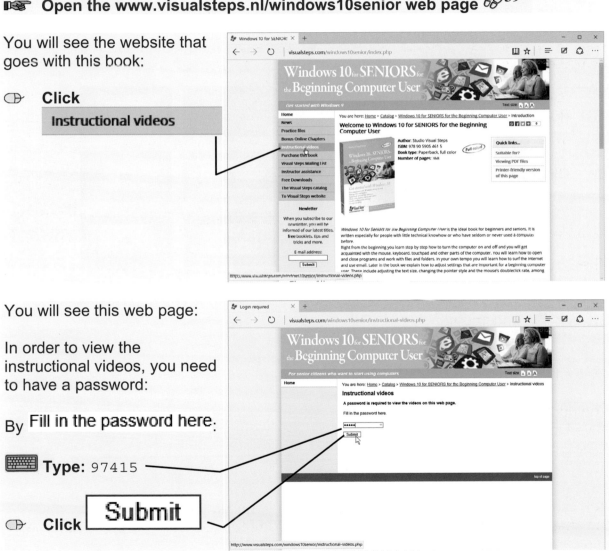

You will see this web page:

In order to view the instructional videos, you need to have a password:

By **Fill in the password here**:

⌨️ **Type:** 97415

⊕ **Click** | **Submit** |

You will see several instructional videos:

This is what you do if you want to watch a video:

- **If necessary, drag the scroll box downwards a bit**

- **By the desired video, click**

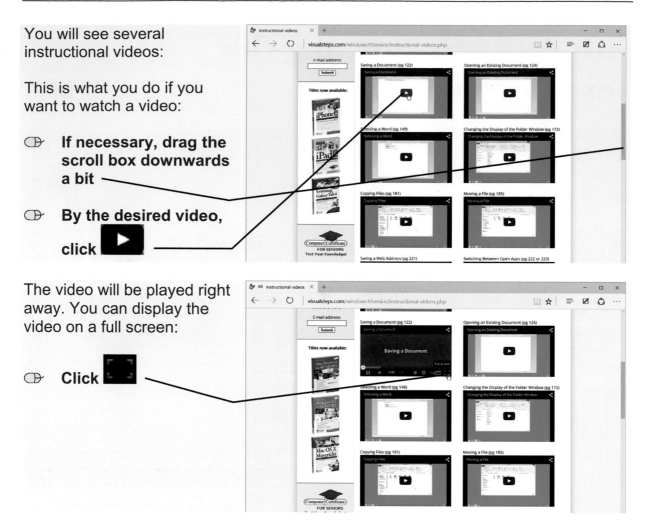

The video will be played right away. You can display the video on a full screen:

- **Click**

You may see an additional bar at the bottom of the screen. You can close this bar:

- **Click ✕**

The video quality may not be optimized. You can adjust the quality or resolution as follows:

In the bottom right corner of the screen:

⏏ **Click** [⚙]

⏏ **If necessary, click** [▼] **by** [Quality]

⏏ **If necessary, click** [720p ᴴᴰ]

You will see the video on a full screen. To pause the video:

⏏ **Click** [❚❚]

To continue playing the video:

⏏ **Click** [▶]

Here you see how much time has elapsed, and the length of the full video:

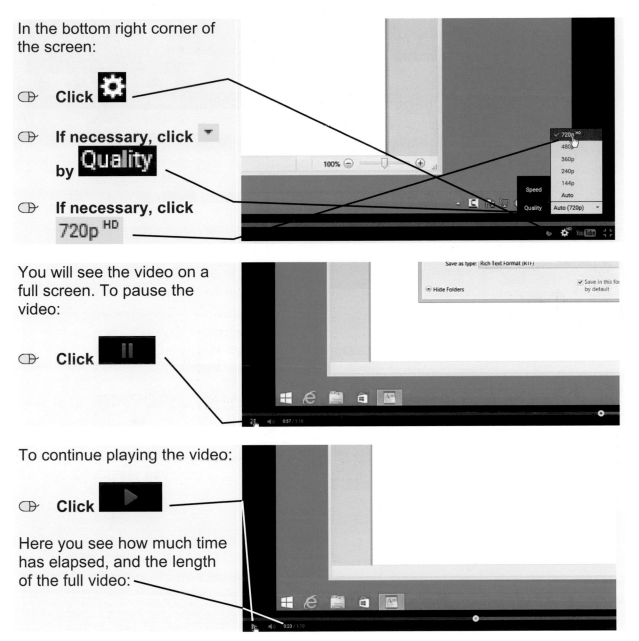

If you want to jump forward:

☞ **Drag**  **to the right**

To go backward, you do the opposite. Drag  to the left.

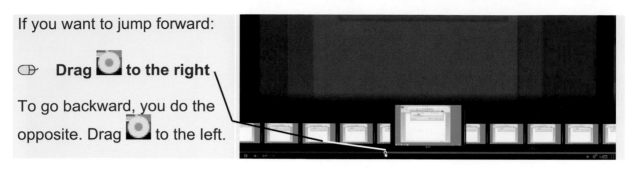

💡 Tip
Replay the video

Once the video has ended, you can view it again by clicking ⟳.

When the video has finished playing, you can close the full screen display:

⌨ **Press Esc**

You can open the other instructional videos in the same way.

☞ **Close** *Edge* ∂∂⁶

Appendix F. Index

Photo Editing on the iPad for SENIORS

There is so much you can do with an iPad. But one of the best applications is surely working with photos! There are many apps available that come with a variety of tools for enhancing your photos. You can spruce up the photos you took from a memorable event or vacation for example, and share them with others. And what about making a collage, slideshow or photo album?

HAVE FUN AND BECOME A PHOTO EDITING EXPERT ON YOUR IPAD

This user-friendly book shows you in a jiffy how to create and edit all of these types of projects. A number of photo editing apps are easy to use and free to download. They offer lots of preset filters, plus useful tools to crop, repair, lighten, darken or sharpen your photos. And if you want additional editing capability, you can purchase an app for a small amount with even more great features. You will learn how to use these apps with clear step-by-step instructions. You can get started right away with exercise pictures that can be downloaded from our website.

With the knowledge and experience you gain, you will soon be able to edit your own photos and turn them into works of art. It will surprise you how much is possible with photos on the iPad!

Author: Studio Visual Steps
ISBN 978 90 5905 731 9
Book type: Paperback, full color
Nr of pages: 312 pages
Accompanying website:
www.visualsteps.com/photoipad

Full color!

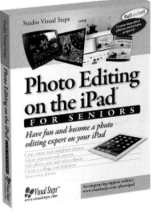

Learn how to:

- Crop, rotate and straighten photos
- Adjust exposure and contrast
- Add effects, text and other objects
- Create a collage and slideshow
- Share your photos

Suitable for:
iPad 2, iPad 3rd generation, iPad 4th generation, iPad Air, iPad Air 2, iPad mini, iPad mini 2 and iPad mini 3. If you have a new type of iPad, you can also use this book.